NUMERICAL ENIGMA

CLEVER FOX PUBLISHING
Chennai, India

Published by CLEVER FOX PUBLISHING 2023
Copyright © Ankit Parashar 2023

All Rights Reserved.
ISBN: 978-04-73519-07-0

This book has been published with all reasonable efforts taken to make the material error-free after the consent of the author. No part of this book shall be used, reproduced in any manner whatsoever without written permission from the author, except in the case of brief quotations embodied in critical articles and reviews.

The Author of this book is solely responsible and liable for its content including but not limited to the views, representations, descriptions, statements, information, opinions and references ["Content"]. The Content of this book shall not constitute or be construed or deemed to reflect the opinion or expression of the Publisher or Editor. Neither the Publisher nor Editor endorse or approve the Content of this book or guarantee the reliability, accuracy or completeness of the Content published herein and do not make any representations or warranties of any kind, express or implied, including but not limited to the implied warranties of merchantability, fitness for a particular purpose. The Publisher and Editor shall not be liable whatsoever for any errors, omissions, whether such errors or omissions result from negligence, accident, or any other cause or claims for loss or damages of any kind, including without limitation, indirect or consequential loss or damage arising out of use, inability to use, or about the reliability, accuracy or sufficiency of the information contained in this book.\

This is a work of fiction. Any references to historical events, real people or real places are used fictitiously. Other names, characters, companies and events are products of the authors imagination and any resemblance to actual persons, living or dead, is entirely coincidental. Any information in the story that has been presented as fact is public and has been sourced and researched from public records. The timing of certain events has been modified for the story.

NUMERICAL ENIGMA

ANKIT PARASHAR

For My Father,
Col (Retd.) Rajendra Kumar Sharma

Prologue

12.12.2007, Pasadena, California

10:22 PM.

Within the dark night, the sound of soft raindrops falling on Professor Gable seemed innocent. Beyond the alley laid his residence.

Walking through the empty alley, dodging the potholes in the dark quite skillfully with the help of his old, yet trusted walking stick which rested on his right hand, the seventy-year-old man paused for a moment.

Opening the umbrella he held in his other hand, the Professor looked up deeply towards the night whose darkness was occasionally perturbed by flashes of lightning, making the dense mass of clouds visible to him.

It's been raining cats and dogs for twenty-four hours straight, he thought.

"Damn, those buggers," he murmured to himself as he took a glimpse at the inner left pocket of his black, leather coat before hugging it tight against his body. Suddenly the Professor made his footsteps quicker.

I have to hurry… I must see the contents….

"Dad, where have you been?" a curious and worried voice interrupted the Professor's thought process as he came closer to the outskirts of his house.

Laura, his daughter in her late twenties, half soaked and gasping for breath had come running towards him. She was worried about him. It was unlike her father to leave home in weather such as this, that too without a message.

"Oh, nothing dear, I just had to make an urgent call to the university," he answered with surprise holding her hand as he moved her into the shade of the umbrella.

Call? He walked all this while in the night to make a call? She thought and asked, "Was it so urgent, Dad?"

"Let's talk when we get inside," he said, as they started to make their way towards a duplex bungalow with a historical stature, made of hard and moist-looking bricks a few meters away.

The shadow of the duplex in the lightning often fell all over and beyond the small fence surrounding it.

As they made their entrance by the kinder garden gate of the fence walking up to the door of their more than 40-year-old residence, Laura smiled innocently noticing how the wetness of water had made the windowpanes crystal clean.

Professor, however, had his mind on a totally different issue and hence was too self-conducted in his mind to comprehend the smile he saw. *I hope the search ends here…*

PROLOGUE

As they entered the hall, Laura noticed the strange silence of her father.

"Is something wrong, Dad? You look very distant," Laura asked softly offering to hang the umbrella and his black, leather coat on the hook beside the door.

"Nothing, darling, just the load of the work, that's all," he said, giving her only the umbrella and moving away from her without taking off the coat.

"Why didn't you call from the phone here?" she asked curiously, looking towards the landline placed on the side table a few steps away from her.

"It is out of service, it's been a week now," Professor responded with a weak voice. "I must say, seeing you were a bit of a surprise. When did you come back from New York?"

"I came…" before she could answer the question, she saw her father take an unusual pause.

Thinking something deeply he walked up to her. Before she could ask any more questions, the Professor said, "You should get some rest, it's late." He gave her a kiss on her forehead.

"Goodnight," he said and walked upstairs to the corridor and towards his room while he still had the coat on him.

She saw the urgency in his footsteps. Laura felt a sense of confusion in her heart and mind at the same time. As she saw him leave, an ocean of questions was running through her head. *Perhaps, waiting until morning would be the right thing to do.*

One thing was clear to her. Something had happened; she had never seen her father like this, never in her life.

As the Professor made his way to his room, his quick footsteps turned into a slow jog. He could hear his own heartbeat. It was getting louder with every passing second. He knew he had to hurry before it was too late.

Moving into his room, he shut the door tight behind him, his hand trembling. He took out a file from the inner left pocket of his coat.

He staggered towards the study table with a glint of enigma and joy in his eyes.

10:45 PM.

As he opened the file and moved his eyes over the papers and its contents, in an instant, they became wider. In a few moments, tears came floating down his face.

With determination and hope glowing in his eyes, delving into his memories, with a faded smile, he whispered to himself, *"It's evident. After 48 years… David, I wish you were here. Finally, the quest of all mankind…"*

CHAPTER 1

Around half a century back,

1958

California Institute of Technology (Caltech)

It seems the influence of time then over even the smallest of things was inevitable except over a certain man. His name was David. The Professor remembered the beginning.

I was seventeen. We both were young, perhaps the only thing that we shared then until we became friends.

I still remember that morning. A lush, green garden thinning out the smell of fresh air, located near one of the borders of the Caltech Institute. It was a time when things seemed a lot quieter within the establishment. The humming of birds and the buzzing of the cool breeze was the only thing that could be heard around.

From a distance, a faded figure came walking down a slope towards the garden—a guy in his late teens. He seemed like one of the scholars of the university. He looked thin and worn out, his features quite sharp, narrow face, brown eyes and golden hair. He held a register close to his chest, pressing it against his maroon coat which corresponded to one of the famous student houses, *The Ricketts House*. It had something written over its left pocket—*Truth shall make you free*. He was wearing white pants and the shoes were shining black.

He sat on one of the benches next to the garden and took out a pen from the right pocket of his pants. He opened the register and started writing something down profoundly, like nature was mesmerizing him.

Raising his head briefly now and then, lost in his own thoughts, he would again return to his figures and notes.

It was about two hours, and he decided to leave.

A few meters away, two students were on a morning walk.

"Hey, John, you see that guy? He comes down here every day," one of them said with confidence.

"What's his name?" I asked, gazing at him.

"His name is David," he said, as they watched him walk back. "Let's go, John."

That was the first time I saw him. I came from an average Californian family. My mother was a housewife and my father was an owner of a general store and an engineer living in Pasadena. Being their only son, they had high expectations of me.

The California Institute of Technology was one of the pioneer institutions of this era. Every corner of scientific study known to mankind sprouted in this place. The major strength and depth of this institution lay in the fact that it held the finest of the intellectual minds this world had ever seen.

CHAPTER 1

This was my first year in the academy in the undergraduate program, when the affiliation of the J. P.L [Jet Propulsion Laboratory], went into the hands of NASA. J.P.L dates back to the 1930s, it was later co-founded in 1944. There was a huge uproar for this achievement within the university, I too was profoundly proud of myself for making it to the academy. There was a lot of excitement within me, I knew I was about to meet a lot of interesting people down here.

I always held an idea close to my heart. I believed that there were always two kinds of people a man comes across in his life, people who were forgotten by him and the people he remembers all his life.

I seldom knew life had carved a strange future for me.

In the beginning, I thought it was the facilities and the completeness of this institution that made it special. But it was not until I realized that the commitment and discipline made Caltech what it really was. Sometimes I wonder if things could have been different. *Man! I so wished that there were girls to hit on.*

Guess I wasn't the only one thinking that. The feeling was kind of obvious when I started speaking with people around me. Especially Jack. H. Wilson. Jack had a thing going for girls and he used to talk a lot about high school in Denver where he came from. Always showing off his cowboy hat his Australian Uncle gave him, he once told me, "Girls dig for the charm."

"Well, I sure hope they do, 'cause you aren't going to see a beautiful ass in a long time, not until college," I told him.

I used to notice graduate students. I soon knew if I had to pursue my graduation in Caltech, I didn't have the liberty to follow my prejudices. I was no longer the part of a society who couldn't care less about the things happening around them. I was here to make things happen, I was here to change the world and for that, certain sacrifices had to be made.

The ones who came before me had made this clear; the standards were set and now it was time for me to raise the bar. This made me realize how the former students who later became graduates of the academy came to achieve success. Not all of them did so and the ones who did only had a single difference, they were different with respect to the magnitude of their success. The interesting part is that there were only a few who were to be remembered forever.

To me, everything in my life seemed clear when I look back now; I think that was the best part of my life. I saw a lot of wholesomeness within the establishment. It gave every individual freedom of mind and matter. It was quite late, to be honest. It's now that I really understand its essence. Just thinking about it brings up a smile to my face.

Yes, things were truly magnificent, I can remember there were still talks of Einstein's photoelectric effect around and how he and other scientists had gone off to win the Nobel. It was a time when every single one of the graduate students wanted to win a Nobel. For me, this thought was amusing, as there was only one Nobel to win and too many candidates. The idea didn't infatuate me much, although being in an institution such as Caltech inspired one to think the opposite. Nevertheless, as I said, there were too many ducks in the pond.

It was my belief that destiny had brought me here. A man, no matter how strong he is, will eventually come to question the forces of nature. In the process of doing so, he will realize how weak he is. This is one of the fundamental laws of nature maintained by the creator. Caltech was a place where this fundamental aspect of nature was manipulated for the sole reason to understand it better. Caltech made one realize that a man is neither weak nor strong;

CHAPTER 1

it is only in the process of questioning the forces of nature on a scientific level that he would come to know of this fact.

For instance, if one has a good grip on reality on a scientific level, he will be able to predict certain notions of this reality accurately. This will give one a sense of control over things simultaneously, it will also tell one about limitations letting one know about his place and value respective to nature. There is no stream in the field of science that does this better than physics, so, I chose to concentrate and work more in that direction.

There were a lot of complex developments taking place in the field of physics; this inspired a lot of young minds to lead themselves to something new. Not to mention a couple of years ago, Linus Pauling had made an interesting development in chemistry by introducing ideas of quantum mechanics in the molecular structure of chemical bonds. He was awarded the Nobel for the same in 1954 and went on to achieve one more in 1962 for peace. The landmarks laid down by such people inspired the spirit of Caltech.

I was now sure that physics is the ultimate culmination of all scientific knowledge as it touched all realms of science, in one way, or another. To me, this was clear from the beginning of my pursuit of knowledge. However, as it turned out, I wasn't the only one.

There were few others who shared the same opinions as mine. One of them was Jack. I only found out later that he is crazy about physics. I would often spend my time with him discussing ideas and possibilities of natural physics. But while doing so I would soon realize he would be more engrossed in his vintage porn. In the process, I would find myself greatly at a loss as there was so much to know, with so little time.

This was the time I questioned reality for the way it was, however stupid it seemed. I bet a little bit of insanity in us is one of the reasons this world goes on. There were questions. Alright! But the answers would come in time.

Meanwhile, I used to spend time thinking about the subject of my research or otherwise watching American football. Playing it was never my cup of tea, but I really loved watching the game.

Physics, of course, had its own charm. In my case, it was quite similar to the attraction I had toward the opposite sex. There were always doubts, a little bit of contradictions and, of course, the stubbornness of matters. Oh…. and how can I forget there was always something new to look forward to? Physics was surely innovating…. The rest of the attractions were just fun, we didn't have much time for them though. We were there to study.

We had a day off once in a while. It usually used to happen on a weekend or sometimes twice a week. Some were too busy or for that matter in love that they chose to spend more time with their girlfriends, even on weekends. I can't blame them, I did it too, but my girlfriends were fat-ass books and physics assignments.

As I said, Caltech was all about discipline; it helped us to be on our toes. I still remember those painful assignments and those difficult nights of my life then. When I come to think of it now, I wouldn't have been here if it wasn't for those nights. My friend was right, it does take love and commitment to make things happen. I understood commitment but love was really never on my list. Today again, I realize they were one and the same thing. Love requires commitment, so does physics and only a physicist can understand this.

Physicists such as Newton and Galileo are my favorites, their pioneer personality and original thinking were their profound assets. I dreamt of being like them someday. I knew it was not going to be easy, but I had made my decision.

CHAPTER 1

The only thing left for me to do now was to work and have patience. This was going to be one hell of a ride!

I knew it would take me a lifetime to find something extraordinary. Thus, I started to interact with people of my interest. Just as the old man said, "A bird in the hand is better than two in the bush." I used to interact with a lot of graduate students. I tried to grasp something new and unique in their ideas. Unfortunately, there was nothing that I could find to be of my interest.

From my experience, I knew all the greatest physicists of all eras had been great seekers. They only achieved what they did after rummaging around for it in the right direction. That made them create landmarks which the common man came to define as laws of nature. So, they went on to become legends just like Newton and Galileo.

The destiny of this world is written by remarkable people. Caltech was recognized as one of the institutions where such legends rested. Maybe I was one of them, or maybe I wasn't, but I knew one thing. Some of them were among me, here in Caltech.

What I didn't know was the fact that.... one of them would turn out to be my best friend!

CHAPTER 2

1963

A year after I entered the Caltech graduate program in 1960, Jack made it to the next year though being a batch younger. I was still happy to know that he would be around.

I didn't know then that there was going to be someone else I was going to meet, someone unexpected, someone who would change my future and the future of a lot of things to come.

Three years after I got my degree in particle physics I started working on my research paper in Caltech itself. That was when we met. Strangely, it was not *in* Caltech that we convene.

"Is this seat vacant?" a voice startled me just as I made myself comfortable on one of the seats in the Rose Bowl stadium. The guy was wearing a brown jacket. He had a stubborn accent and somehow his face seemed familiar to me.

It was New Year's Day where the Rose Bowl Game was being viewed by a crowd of more than 98,000 fans. Wisconsin was taking against USC (University of Southern California) and everybody had huge expectations from this match.

CHAPTER 2

Before I could reply to him, he sat next to me. I was amused. He didn't even wait for me to answer. I sat quietly in resilience waiting for my silence to do the talking.

The stadium was full of joy filled with faces of laughter and enthusiasm. The anticipation was killing, and the crowd could not stop shouting the names of their favorite teams. He looked at me briefly.

"I hate waiting," he said, guessing I got offended. I believe he figured it out by the look on my face.

I was quite taken aback by that statement and it fueled my impatience. I took a short glimpse at his flashy face, as the sunlight was strong in the region of the stadium where we were sitting. "I am sorry, do I know you?"

I made sure that there was an objective tone in my speech as I spoke to him. It would piss him off and make him leave. At least that was what I thought then.

"I don't think so," he said carelessly engrossed in the crowd looking towards the field.

What a stubborn ass! My impatience was getting the best of me as I was trying to hold on to my horses.

After a few minutes of silence, he spoke.

"But I think we should," he said with an inexplicable look in his brown eyes shadowed behind the golden hair falling over his forehead.

"What?" I said in confusion and apprehension.

"Well, you asked me if you knew me. I don't think we do but, I'm just implying we should," he said, still looking towards the field with a consistent smile on his face.

"I don't understand. What do you mean?" I said, still confused about where this conversation was going.

"I think we can be friends," he said with a shrug and looked at me briefly.

"Ha- ha- ha…," I laughed sarcastically. "I wonder from where you drew that conclusion from."

"Come on, I know you have been trying to make me leave for quite some time now," he said confidently.

"So, you noticed. I guess I made it obvious, didn't I?" I said, in confirmation.

"Of course, you did, even a jackass could make it out from the look on your face," he said, taking out two chewing gums from the left pocket of his jacket and offering me one.

"You are one stubborn piece of ass," I said, taking the gum.

"I know! So are you," he said smiling, looking back towards the field.

"What makes you think *I'm* stubborn?" I said, with a faded smile coming back to the point.

"That smile of yours, not to mention you still want me out of here," he said looking at me with dry humor.

"I assume you have me all figured out," I said, with a sense of modesty. Not that I was trying to become friends with him but

CHAPTER 2

talking to him was kind of interesting. It is not every day that you get to interact with witty people. At least not in a football stadium.

"Careful there, this is the first time we have met. Although I know, it won't be the last time," he said, sharply looking straight at me.

"What? Are we becoming friends now?" I said, thinking this is fun.

"If you're enjoying this conversation just as much as I am, I don't think there would be a need for me to answer that question," he said, beaming with unfathomable thoughts.

"Ha ha…" I gave a light laugh before replying, "You sure have your way with people."

"I'm born with a distinctive modus operandi," he said, putting his hand inside his other coat pocket. He took out what seemed like cylindrical glasses with a titanium frames. Wearing them he gave me a friendly grin.

"Good to hear that," I said, with a smile.

"What time the game begins?" I asked eagerly, looking at my watch. It was almost time for the game to begin.

"I assume they are going to delay the game today for a few minutes," he said, glancing at the crowd.

The stadium was crammed with people of all ages. I couldn't believe my eyes. Young or old, everybody in this Rose Bowl stadium wanted a glimpse of their favorite teams.

After what seemed like ages the teams came on the field and the crowd busted in applause. It wasn't every day that they got to see their favorite teams fighting out for the national title.

"Which team are you supporting?" he asked as we both raised ourselves to give a standing ovation to the teams.

"I don't know. I think I like both. What about you? Who is your favorite?" I said and asked as we made ourselves comfortable back in our seats.

"I think the USC would take this title," he said with a nod. "They have a strong lineup of players, you see," he said, looking concomitantly at the teams and me.

"You may be right, but I think Wisconsin has also come a long way. I don't think they should be underestimated, and I have heard they have a really good quarterback," I said, giving a brief thought.

"Yes, I assume that they won't give in so easily. After all, they didn't come this far just to lose, did they?" he said with a mocking smile.

"Of course not," I said with a nod. "But I believe you'll still go with the University of Southern California, won't you?"

"As a matter of fact, I will and if I'm not wrong, you are supporting Wisconsin," he said with assurance.

"I must say you can really read people well," he accomplished.

"So can you, this is going to be a good game," I said with a thoughtful smile.

"I'm sure it will be," he said with a glimmer of instinct in his voice, looking towards the field.

A flying dove caught our attention as we anticipated the beginning of the game.

CHAPTER 2

"Let's have a bet," he said, trying to sound humorous. I could make out that he was bad at it.

"What are you trying to say?" I replied.

"If my team wins we would be friends. If not, this would be the first and the last time we would meet each other," he said sternly.

"That is one weird way of becoming friends," I said laughing at myself wondering how this meeting would end.

"Well, if you ask me, it is the best way to come to a decision in an argument between two obstinate people," he said, giving a fair smile. He knew I was up for it.

Logically we didn't even know each other's names, therefore the whole idea sounded kind of reasonable. It would be hard for me to say what really made things simple but, I guess it was the obduracy in both of us that did the work. There was something common in us after all.

"Rational enough. I presume we should say goodbye to each other just in case we don't get to say it after the game," I said with a challenging look on my face.

"It was nice meeting you," we said, looking at each other with exigent poise, and shook hands.

Funny, when I think about it now. A goodbye before hi! That was how our friendship began. That was the first time I felt there was something different about him, something different about his personality.

He never told me his name then and he never asked me mine, that was his way of doing things. By no means would he ever let anyone know what was going on in his head. I bet his instincts knew how that game was about to end but he never uttered a word.

I like to think he always waited for the right moment to say things or to enact them and he always knew when the time was right to make things happen. That was the distinctive modus operandi he told me about.

All of a sudden, the crowd started to roar in delight as they heard the whistle for the game to begin.

"Enough of the chess talk," I said as the game grabbed my attention.

"And so it begins…" he whispered.

Things seemed exciting right from the beginning of the game. I believe he was quite settled by the way things went in the first half of the game. In the beginning, the first touchdown by Wisconsin was enough to enhance my enthusiasm.

"Are you still going to support the University of Southern California?" looking towards him, I asked in doubt. The look on his face was unperturbed as he watched the game closely.

"There is something about me you should know," he said, in a very calm and composed manner, watching the game.

"What is it?" I asked, trying to sound curious.

"I don't go back on my words or for that matter, my decisions," he said instantly, turning his face towards me with sharp arrogance. "Besides the game has just begun. There is a lot more to come."

I could see what he meant during the next few minutes, the USC made its position clear by scoring three consecutive touchdowns.

CHAPTER 2

The fans of the University of Southern California celebrated as the score by the end of the first half was 21-7. The USC had taken the lead all right and I found him relaxing and giving me kick-in-the-ass expressions after the first half.

"You can hold your horses, the game isn't finished yet. There is still a second half left of the game," I said, in a hard voice.

"I guess you're right, but I don't see any hope left in the game anymore," he said, in a slapdash fashion and started yawning.

Son of a bitch!

After the beginning of the second half, the University of Southern California made another touchdown making the lead almost impossible to catch up to.

"Best of luck," he told me. I don't know if he was trying to criticize me or to buck me up.

The next few minutes of the game made it one of the greatest college football games in the history of American football. A 17-yard scramble by Wisconsin made the margin reduce to 28-14. This was just the start of Wisconsin's powerful second-half scoring drive. However, the University of Southern California was not about to take this lightly and they elevated their lead from 28-14 to 42-14 with the help of two touchdowns. This gave them a comfortable edge in the game.

It was only fifteen minutes left in the last quarter of the game when Wisconsin proved their worth by making three incredible touchdowns. This made them to come almost at par with the USC.

The climax of the game was nail-biting, people were yelling with all that they had as were we.

He told me that he found himself in need for a cola during the last few minutes of the game.

Wisconsin's three straight passes after the free kick, including a 19-yard touchdown pass and a foul by USC narrowed the score to 42-37.

Time expired shortly after that; USC won the title, but Wisconsin's efforts did not go unnoticed. The 1962 Badgers proved to be a team that never gave up, a characteristic that is rare in the world of sports.

"This game is going to be history," I said, wondering about how the events of the game turned out, noticing faces of despair and listening to the sound of cheers around me.

"You bet it is," he replied in a style that seemed rather virtuous.

Gazing at the crowd passing by we looked at each other with composure.

"Hi, name's David," he said, going in for a handclasp.

"My name is John. So, David, huh? I think I have heard that name somewhere before," I said, accepting his gesture. "So, you really think two adamant strangers can be friends?" I said, sounding a bit reluctant about the situation.

"I think persistence can be fruitful, we wouldn't be sitting here and still be talking otherwise," he said with self-confidence.

"Does this ever occur to you that may be this meeting was destined to be?" I spoke.

A wide smile appeared on his face before he replied, "For people who believe, there are no coincidences, my friend."

CHAPTER 2

The buoyancy in his eyes still makes me wonder what force was behind them. However, in the first meeting, I did think his nature was a bit arrogant, but it was not until I grasped it is just the way some people are meant to be.

It has been a long time but, those words still flutter in my mind now and then.

For people who believe, there are no coincidences…

CHAPTER 3

As soon as the crowd flowed out of the stadium and the rush decreased, we started to walk towards the exit comfortably. Soon we saw ourselves facing broad daylight again. *Refreshing*, I thought to myself.

"So, David. You never told me what you are doing here in California," I asked.

He was still wearing the glasses. I could see now that he had an athletic build. His shoulders were quite broad, and although he had a narrow face, he had a good height of about close to six feet. Somehow, I felt I knew him.

"Well! I am here to revive some memories."

"What kind of memories? I mean memories related to your personal life or those to your profession?" I tried to sound as casual as I could.

"Kind of both," he said. "My personal and professional life has not been so very different," he said looking down towards his footsteps.

"Why is that?" I felt a sense of compatibility which after his reply became quite obvious to me.

CHAPTER 3

"I was in Caltech. I studied there, I left for MIT about three years back for graduation after meeting a colleague of mine regarding a research paper meanwhile working on my own ideas. Now I'm back at Caltech to complete my master's majoring in physics. You tell me what your story is like?"

I should have known after all. His face did seem very familiar to start with for an outsider. As it turned out we were not so much strangers after all.

"Not very different from yours, except that I never left anywhere," I replied before giving a light smile.

"What do you mean?" he questioned with confusion, staring at me.

"I mean I am in Caltech doing first year of my master's in particle physics."

"You got to be kidding me! So, we are not strangers and not so different from each other after all, huh? What do you think?"

"I think I can go with the stranger part of that statement," I said, walking along. I always knew that we were not so different but I never showed or accepted it in our friendship. Alas! I guess he always knew.

"Ha-ha... fair enough, but this is our first meeting and I tell you, John. We do have a lot in common irrespective of the fact that we have a long way to go. Not that you will agree with me, will you?"

"Yeah, right..." I was very unfussy about the way things were going. I had no clue then that what he said was going to happen, for real.

"Hey man, I'm just kidding. I'm never going to see you again," he said, testing the endurance of the situation.

"Is that so?" I asked with a relieved expression.

"Ouch! Did I just use the right statement on the wrong guy? I like the way you bounced it back on me though."

"Bet you did," I said with a smile.

"Can't help it, man, like I said I don't go back on my words," he said.

"So, what is it that you really go back on? I mean you don't think everything that you've done up till this point in your life has been perfect or, are you going to tell me that your ego is too big to adjust itself into a petite definition that a word like perfect implies?"

"Well, I don't know much about perfection or imperfection, John. All I can say is that I don't have any regrets in life," he said with a carefree note, looking around and noticing the shops in the corner and a few people walking close to us.

"I didn't mean to get you all serious, you know," I said, just in case. I was getting to understand why he was so casual about things and in between, I was also starting to like his laid-back attitude.

However, I do realize the more things are calm and relaxed on the outside, the more they are anxious and unsettled on the inside. I don't know how much of that was true in the case of David.

"Hell! I don't give a damn about anything, at least till a point when it doesn't start to bother me much. I have never been serious about anything, John."

CHAPTER 3

His obstinacy had become obvious to me by now, but I always thought that it was for a good reason. Well, not always for a good reason but I guess I can count the odds out because in the end, everything just turned out to be fine.

I wonder if things could have been different, I wonder if things could have happened in a different way. If that were to be true, I wouldn't have been here remembering all those times we shared.

We both got busy soon after we reached Caltech and only after two days got a chance to interact quite unpredictably. In the past 5 years, it had become a habit of mine to go out for an early morning walk. That's when I saw David sitting on one of the benches. It reminded me of how I had seen him the first time, years back. An astonishing fact came to my mind when I saw David. We must have been in the same undergraduate program only in a different batch. *Wow*, I thought as I gazed at him from a distance. Unlike the first time, he looked more unoccupied.

"Hey there, what's up with you?" I said coming closer to him.

"I thought we were not seeing each other again," he replied with a smile.

"I think it's destiny," I said mockingly.

"You know I don't believe in destiny, John."

"Yeah, I know we were batch mates," I said, casually sitting next to him.

"What! Are you kidding me? Wait a minute, are you the geek kind of guy who used to be seen carrying heavy books all the time? Damn, John, look at you. You turned out to be just fine," he said patting my shoulder.

"Yeah, you don't look like a junkie either," I said, shrugging.

We laughed and I shifted the topic to academics about what happened in the last two days and we started talking physics. This was where the interesting part of our lives began.

"The quest of physics is foremost the most interesting and challenging aspects of human understanding of this nature," David started to explain. "It began with Sir Isaac Newton who formed the notions of rest and motion of bodies. Newton's contribution to physics is known through his theory of gravitation. Newton wrote a book called ***Principia Mathematica*** which was published in 1687. It is known to be the most influential book in the history of science. Newton's views of rest and motion were described by his three laws and dominated the realms of physics for almost three centuries. Newton's three laws of motion are, in principle, the foundations of modern mechanics. In Caltech, when studying physics, this is considered to be the first phase in the evolution of the subject."

Thinking deeply, he continued, "In the second phase which came in 1905, Newton's laws had to be manipulated because reality no longer had a static picture. Times were different then. This was the phase of Albert Einstein who came up with the theory of relativity. It was because of relativity that rest and motion had to be given a different definition which was in accordance with the perspective an individual had in a three-dimensional space.

"Relativity itself came to be in two parts, first (in 1905) was known as the Special Theory of Relativity. As the physicist, it was essential to know that it was special because time was not absolute. It was not the same for everyone. In this sense, in Special Relativity, time for two entities will change when the distance between them in this universe would be massive or such in magnitude that it would be measured with the respect to the speed of light.

CHAPTER 3

"If we fast forward, almost eleven years from this time, in 1916, Einstein came up with a theory of General Relativity which showed gravity as the carved curvature of space-time. (Universe)," David said, showing me a picture [See picture 1.0] from one of his books.

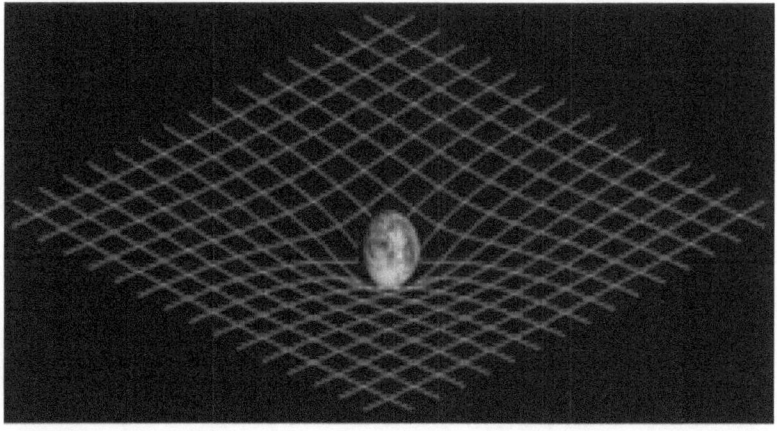

(1.0)

He went on to say, "Einstein, by his theory of General Relativity, established the fact that motion of planets and other heavenly bodies is elliptical (Just as that of a boat or a ship getting sucked in a whirlpool) due to the curvature of space-time. This elliptical motion otherwise is known to us as gravity.

"Relativity helped physicists to understand the universe and its nature on a massive scenario whereby predicting the motions of planets and other heavenly bodies with great accuracy. However little this understanding may have been, it has served to be of great value to humans. Today, we can precisely predict the next lunar eclipse. After the laurels of Special and General Relativity that helped in the understanding of the universe on the massive level, it was time for physicists to look and observe the reality and this universe on its smallest of levels."

David cleared his throat before saying, "This gave birth to the third phase of physics which came into effect through the study of quantum mechanics. After dealing with the massive nature of this universe it was time to look at the diminutive. Apart from many other things, quantum mechanics is a study of rest and motion on sub-atomic levels. The third phase of physics still influences our study of nature and of this universe. Before I came to Caltech, quantum mechanics had already led to many inventions and ideas. It was still a major phase of our study."

I was listening to him carefully as he came to a conclusion, "The fourth phase of physics is its end, in form of the fusion between the two major scientific theories of all time—the fusion of the theory of relativity and quantum mechanics. It would be the ultimate and the highest benchmark for physics to achieve. It is known as Unified Field Theory (U.F.T.). Such a dream was yet to be realized or as a matter of fact, still is. It will be the end of physics and so every physicist in Caltech is striving to achieve this goal."

I assume most people working in the field of physics around the globe were thinking the same. It would not be wrong for me to say that when I was doing my masters in Caltech it was a period of the third and fourth phases of physics. Thus, David helped me realize how physics had evolved from being static to relative and from explaining the big to slowly describing the small.

There were other notions of physics too which had their beginning much earlier. They inclined more towards metaphysics, so I thought of them as of no importance. The scientific profoundness of physics felt more challenging to me unless, of course, digging the grave of some old Greek philosopher I could find a lost treasure map. That would be something.

Now again, I had a fundamental track which was laid down by the most important physicists of all time.

First, there was Newton and his laws of rest and motion, and then there was Einstein with his theory of relativity. Next came the

CHAPTER 3

monumental theory of quantum mechanics which constituted ideas of physicists and mathematicians alike. Some of them were Werner Heisenberg, Max Planck, Louis de Broglie, Albert Einstein, Niels Bohr, Erwin Schrödinger, Max Born, John von Neumann, Paul Dirac and Wolfgang Pauli. Finally, the puzzle of reality was to be solved by the fusion of two basic theories, the theory of relativity and quantum mechanics.

The assumption that this fusion was close was nothing but a mere illusion then. As of now, nothing can be said but there are still possibilities. I could not precisely tell if such a theory existed although science has always been a field where developments were made before their time.

"To me, if I had to make such a fusion a reality, I had to observe nature on a greater note to understand its specific constituents," I said looking at David.

David answered, "In Caltech, this is not difficult as an individual is provided with the right facilities and is equipped with the suitable environment."

However, such a thing is not simple. The observation of things on a microscopic level is a very difficult thing to do. This was approved by Werner Heisenberg in 1927. His understanding is known famously by his uncertainty principle. It stated that on the atomic level one could not measure the position and the velocity of the particle simultaneously.

"His uncertainty principle did make life certainly miserable for some in Caltech, years after he founded it," David said mockingly.

This made me think how the uncertainty principle governs the architecture of quantum theory.

NUMERICAL ENIGMA

Although when the uncertainty principle was founded, it was well acknowledged there were many whose belief in quantum mechanics became unstable. One such person was Einstein. His idea for the quantum theory is laid down by his famous saying, "God does not play dice." Einstein's judgment was based on the fact that nature did not have any place for a chance to exist. There was a reason or logic behind everything.

At first, I too was profoundly impressed by his thoughts but as I worked on the parameters and findings of the quantum theory, I was disappointed. The theory has inevitability in the form of its probabilistic nature. One could not deny that in practice.

I mean I could not find any way to resolve the implications of quantum theory.

There was always the probability to know either the position or the velocity of a given particle and never at once one could know both. It was like the principal was hardwired into the system of quantum mechanics.

There were many like me working on the same issue, but it hardly ever made a difference. It was not like we couldn't, but the thing was just too complicated.

The curiosity to know more about quantum during my master's in particle physics engrossed me. Unfortunately, it is the most complicated theory known to the human race. Certain accolades too have been given to the theory by the following extraordinary individuals.

"Anyone who is not shocked by quantum theory has not understood it." – Niels Bohr, its principal architect

"I think I can safely say that nobody understands quantum mechanics." – Richard Feynman;

CHAPTER 3

"Quantum theory provides us with a striking illustration of the fact that we can fully understand the connection though we can only speak of it in images and parables." – Werner Heisenberg

"This (quantum) theory reminds me a little of the system of delusions of an exceedingly intelligent paranoiac, concocted of incoherent elements of thoughts." – Albert Einstein

And,

"The theory of quanta is similar to the other victories in science; for some months you smile at it, and then for years you weep." – Hendrick Kramer's

Despite the fact that the theory was inevitably time-consuming and complicated during my second year when I was completing my master's in physics, I decided to concentrate my all on it.

Three years back, Donald Arthur Glaser, a graduate of Caltech, was awarded the 1960 Nobel Prize in physics for his invention of the bubble chamber. This boosted my self-confidence and my grasp of something new. Caltech was always a happening place. There was always one or the other development coming to the surface.

Coming back to our conversation, David started to talk again, "I was always compelled by the ever-touching ideas of physics which were so close to reality. I mean, at one point, it does seem obvious but to me, it was always miraculous. The reason is, it confirmed the underlying order of this reality. It gave us the fabrics and the tiny connections that are not at once visible to the naked eye, but which constitute the events of our daily lives," he continued.

David was right, for people who do not believe in miracles, I would advise them to study a little of this subject as they would come to know that reality is nothing less than a shot of wonder. Every spectrum of physics has a miracle to offer.

"From the ideologies of Newton to the formation of quantum mechanics, the journey of human curiosity indeed is miraculous," he said looking at me.

Listening to him I realized that the attention of many physicists differentiated on quantum realms. So, the field itself disintegrated in different aspects of reality. This made my interests shift more toward particle physics.

There were different contexts to reality quantum touched into, apart from particle physics. Some of them being condensed matter physics, solid-state physics, atomic physics, molecular physics, computational chemistry, quantum chemistry, and nuclear physics.

I was not very impressed with all this because the understanding of this shot would make the life of physicists even more complicated. Nevertheless, I could not help myself but think this was the right thing to do as it would finally give us the ultimate mechanics of this nature.

I had a hard time evolving the background of my research. Every spectrum of quantum was a detailed and complex understanding of its respective field of research. It was not different from particle physics. I didn't know how long my quest was going to take, or for that matter, how I would come to understand it.

There was only one answer to all the questions everyone was coming up with. It was the Unified Field Theory (U.F.T). It was this answer that everyone thought would bring a new era in physics or for that matter, would complete it.

CHAPTER 3

Coming back, I remember David excitedly saying, "Quantum has its influence on all kinds of existing scientific knowledge, the only place it could not come in accordance was with gravity. It is this gravity that forms the core of relativity theory in physics. Hence, the idea is to incorporate gravity and its properties on atomic and subatomic levels.

"When it comes down to predictability, relativity plays its role in a massive scenario whereas quantum depicts it on a minute picture of atomic and sub-atomic levels with the pinch of chance. So, this makes it clear that only after the U.F.T. we would be able to understand our place in this universe in a better way.

"Another reason why the U.F.T is considered to be of such uttermost importance is because it could lead one to the Theory Of Everything, (T.O.E.) which in turn could enable one to predict things in reality. That is to say, if one knew what constitutes this reality, one could defy reality. Yes, it is possible for one to know the future events and maybe alter those if one would come to understand the T.O.E; it basically signifies the understanding of the whole universe," he said.

There were rumors that U.F.T. itself was the T.O.E. as it was the fusion of the whole reality.

For all I could know they could be the right questions. This always perturbed me in solitude. The conditions of nature had made it clear it is only when you try you will succeed.

The findings of physics up to this point were superb, however, from this point, it slowed down.

Every notion has its limitations. It was the same with quantum and relativity. Both had become highly specialized fields of research and both of them had seen a maximum number of predicaments.

I found a lot of individuals shifting their interest of study as they believed physics was almost nearing its end. I couldn't have disagreed unless I realized knowledge and creativity were two endless notions.

From Newtonian mechanics to quantum mechanics, science had revolutionized to an extent that was unrealistic. Scientists and inventors such as Werner Heisenberg, Max Planck, Albert Einstein, Niels Bohr, Erwin Schrödinger, Max Born, Paul Dirac and Wolfgang Pauli had given an unimaginable closer and better picture of this world to its people.

We were working with applications and instruments with far more precision deriving most from their study. If I think of Caltech it gave a lot of revolutionaries in different fields and spectrums of science. Out of which most were to be accounted for physics.

I also came to realize, of all the people that were to achieve phenomenal success time was to play an important role. Remembering the day we had this conversation, I am sure it is this 'time' that haunted David as he pursued his quest for the truth.

So as to say, the men who made history were to be forgotten by it someday, sometime.... The answer rested somewhere in the future and to my horror, it did happen, but it seems nature has a balance of its own.

Time is a strange thing....

CHAPTER 4

1965

"An equation inscribed without creativity means nothing to me," he said with the uttermost confidence in his voice.

For as long as I had known him, David had a very strong instinct. Now, this had become evident to me.

My reasons were empty closures to him. They meant absolutely nothing. I would say that it was a time when we had our share of differences. Not that I would question his friendly attitude but sometimes his arguments and his reviews on my research subjects used to bug me.

It is within these arguments I would often see how most of the time his intuition would get the best of him. I didn't know then how right that was, but those arguments would often shake my belief in my way of doing things.

Once, we had a close encounter with a football player. I don't remember his name but I do remember the meeting quite precisely.

While he was giving his autograph David willingly handed over a piece of paper to him. He gave a confused look to David before looking at it.

"How did you know?" he asked David with a blank look handing over the piece of paper to me.

I looked at the paper and saw how David had predicted most of the strategy of the team. He had a neat lay-out of the formation of the team and the players on the paper.

"How did you know, tell me?" he asked David one more time.

"Well, I don't have a precise answer to that question of yours, sir. I believe it was more of a lucky guess," he said trying to go about things. I don't think he ever wanted anyone to know about his instincts although he couldn't hide such a fact from me now that we had been hanging out all this while.

That had more to do with proportions, it wasn't a lucky guess. David understood proportions/patterns very well. Almost all of reality, even the most unlikely of things has one, even in sports, for example, team formations on the field in football. I bet he knew about it.

I, on the other hand, was quite busy with my own things. The pressure was mounting on us day by day as we came closer to achieving our masters. Later during our last year, we both made a decision on joining Caltech as professors after completing our PhDs. We still had to devise the theories. I knew David had something on his mind, but he would never say anything.

Most of the time, he would tell me that it is not the right thing to do for now, but I was stubborn about it. It was how things had gone in the last few years between us. I never gave him a choice.

By the end of the last semester, we were together brawling and slogging our way to completing our master's. Yeah, we did it alright, and then came the PhDs.

CHAPTER 4

While working on our thesis, I would often tell him to be stern with his students, but he would pass it with a shrug saying, "Don't you have anything else to tell me because I'm tired of listening to your same old stuff again and again."

"Would you stop mocking me for once and listen to me? I am serious," I said a bit harshly.

"Come on, John. Don't you remember our good old days of nagging and being spoilsport?"

"I was never a spoilsport, David. *You* were and I did warn you a lot of times and god knows you never listen to me."

"Yeah, right…"

"You know what the worst part is, David?" I asked.

"What?"

"In all of these years, you haven't changed one bit."

"Ha-ha-ha-ha…"

"Yeah, right. Laugh your heart out but someday you will realize what I'm trying to tell you," I said confidently.

"That's not what I meant," he said looking at me.

"What I'm laughing at is the fact that if by chance I would have changed in the last few years we both would have not been friends."

The irony of that statement made me laugh. *Man, why do you have to always turn things around?*

"Jesus, John, you realized it now. Now isn't that something that we have been doing all this while," he said sarcastically.

I still remember the time that I would sit in one of those empty classrooms and boast of my achievements, not that it mattered now but it was fun talking about it then. Sitting on hard wooden benches, hearing the echoes of voices being bounced back from the large right walls and the smell of polished furniture swirling around us; those were some days of our lives. We did have a lot of space and there would be times when our professors would find us sleeping during lectures and would throw us out.

David told me he nearly had a suspension for over a week and the idiot was too lazy to even care about it.

"Why are we even here?" he would question childishly.

I wonder if the blurriness of his simplistic attitude did catch on to me or not in the first year of our Ph.D. I would hate it when he would talk about things in a very nonchalant manner.

Whenever I would taunt him, he would reply saying something like, "Go mind your own business."

I would be left eating my own words by then. That was how it all went in the first year that we got to know each other. I still wonder if it was due to pity or something interesting he saw in me that he was friends with me.

Whatever it was I was sure of one thing, nobody could stand him except me. His ego was too big for people to handle. Sometimes even for me, but I kind of learned to sustain it. Quite an achievement, I thought.

CHAPTER 4

On the other hand, he would always be really cool and relaxed about things in life like it was meant for him to bug people and go beyond the regulations breaking the rules.

The kind of free soul he was that it couldn't be helped with and even if anyone dared to deal with him the person would not last long. "Nobody could beat you in arguments, David. Not even me."

That was one of the good reasons for being friends with him. It is like they say, the good thing about being associated with people who have a high opinion of themselves is that the only person that they can really converse about is themselves. That's the way I used to mock him.

I told him that once. I still remember how furious he got with me and only after we went to watch a football game together that he said, "I forgive you but, that's just because your team won."

We always used to have bets on the football games we used to go and watch. It was interesting to see how the people in the stadium sitting close to us used to react when we both used to go overboard in our enthusiasm. Sometimes we used to end up spilling mustard sauce or coffee on someone and if I remember well, David did that intentionally quite a few times. He even tried to encourage me once to do the same unsuccessfully.

Apart from us, there were two other mates too who joined Caltech as assistants after achieving their master's.

Yes, there was Jack who became my assistant. He was always talking about girls. It's like they say, "Some people in this world never change." Then there was Rudolph, always amused and complaining about things after he started assisting David. I would say it was a time when we guys had fun.

Finally, we were there on the other side of the table teaching people instead of being taught. I never felt better but David and Rudolph felt otherwise.

Rudolph would keep complaining about how he would never get the respect and the courtesy he deserved around his colleagues.

David would be thinking about his past, about the days when he used to bug his teachers. Now he has become one, all thanks to me.

Jack would keep saying how he would never get time to spend with his girlfriend because he would always end up with some assignment or the other given to the students every day. In Caltech, as doctorates, we had to be really on our toes to get the best out of ourselves and the people around us.

I remember when I was a student how difficult it used to be for our teachers to cope with us and I can imagine David as a student with just about my eyes closed. I'm sure he would have been a pain in the ass. Thank god, he wasn't here.

I wish I was his classmate. That way I would have ended up witnessing all the fun. He was such a brat that the things he did then were still spoken of by the students coming from MIT for their masters. Most of them chose Caltech because of the equipment and devices needed for their masters.

I didn't know about them in the beginning, but later David told me about all the memorable times he had while he was a student.

"Why does he get to have all the fun and I don't?" I would ask myself stupidly, not realizing it was good to be a person who has a third perspective on things.

Surprising as it may seem, David had impressed a lot of people in the institution. He was noted as one of the best in Caltech. I

CHAPTER 4

still don't understand what he was working on. I believe it was his creative aspect of looking at things that made him the best and so many who knew him were inspired to be like him including me.

I would often try to be carefree and careless as he was, but I could never make it. It was like I was never made for it.

The perceptivity of the matter became clear when David told me, "You have a sense of discipline, John and most importantly you have the elegance that makes you different and unique from others."

He told me to concentrate on those skills and see if I could notice some changes happening around me.

Soon I started to explain Jack things more carefully and more precisely and saw that he was gaining more and more interest in my research.

Later, I smiled at him arrogantly. My way of thanking him for giving me that piece of advice. To which he boasted of being the best like he always did.

"Come on, David. Can't you try to be modest for once in your life?" I said, taunting. I knew what he was about to say.

"Look who's talking," he said with a smile.

"Forget it, there's no point arguing with you."

Meanwhile, Jack and Rudolph were doing quite good, now that I was also getting the grove of this thing called creativity.

Soon we all started to spend more time together. However, it was not new to Jack as he had already seen me spending a lot of time with David during the time of my masters.

He would often complain, "Hey, John. How come you don't come to see a bowl with me anymore?"

I told him about David and that I have been busy with some papers. I guess he understood. He didn't ask me about David much again but I saw that now all of us were spending more time together, he and David were becoming friends.

Meanwhile, Rudolph was always eating David's brain, complaining about something or other all the time. I never really liked him much. Jack didn't like his attitude either although they were like good friends.

"You talk a lot, you know," Jack said to Rudolph.

"Well, if it isn't for you I wouldn't have been talking so much," he replied to Jack and moved away from him.

"What do you mean?" Jack asked in amusement.

"At least I talk sense. All you do is blabber about some shit night you spent with your girlfriend," Rudolph replied in irritation.

"Hey, is that your frustration talking? I really don't think so because if you ask me, you're jealous. Besides I prefer talking about girls rather than hearing your sad lecture endeavors," he said giving a tedious expression.

"They're not endeavors. My colleagues don't respect me and I don't think that is something a friend should make fun of," Rudolph said giving a serious look.

"Relax man, Rudolph, you know he's kidding," David interrupted their conversation with the sudden arrival.

CHAPTER 4

"That's my brother," Jack said with a smile, getting up and giving him a handclasp.

"Don't think I'm taking his side, Rudy. It is just that I think it is a better option to talk about females after draining your brains out on at least a dozen papers," David said, looking at Rudolph.

"Damn right you are!" Jack said in a plundering voice. He looked towards David and gave him a quick wink. David knew what he was trying to say but he didn't want to be harsh on Rudolph. He knew Rudolph had been having some hard days in the past few weeks.

Every time David would try to speak to Rudolph, he would turn his back towards him. After a while he stopped speaking much with Rudy because he knew every time he would try, Rudy would make an excuse and in some way or the other try to ignore him.

This had become quite awkward but none of us could help it. It was Rudolph who had to realize this, but he was really cocky. So we didn't want to interrupt the flow of things and lead time to make the important changes.

In between, I and David both spoke for a long time about this, about why Rudolph would act so weird in between our conversations while we would be together. I mean all four of us—David, me, Jack and Rudolph.

David would often just talk about him in a casual way telling me that Rudolph is going through a tough time and once he was done with it, he would be just fine and things would be back to normal again. It was not that they were not friends but they always had a kind of uncomfortable gap between them when they were seen together.

Being an optimist, David always believed in the positive view of things, be it his professional life or his personal life.

"I don't think that things will always be the way they are, John. Today he may not appreciate me as his colleague, but the biting wit is in the fact that he will have to respect me for who I am, his professor and a member of this faculty. That, it seems, is more than enough for me," David said, thinking deeply and gave a smile looking at me.

"I guess you are right," I replied with a smile. *I rather hope you are right...*

"Things would be normal again soon. We have to finish a lot of assignments," David said, standing up. So that's how everything went for almost 5 years. *Almost...*

All was fine for the next 5 years. *I wish he could see this coming, but he didn't.*

A research paper went missing.

Soon things were about to become drastic.

CHAPTER 5

1971

By now all four of us had become great friends, David, Rudolph, I and Jack. But I and David were more like brothers. It happens when you tend to spend a decade with a friend who is more like a genius jackass. Anyway, Rudolph still had his share of arguments with all of us, but he did come around the past few years. Jack too now had started understanding Rudolph a bit more carefully. Things had become subtle between the four of us. We had come to realize each other's pros and cons and had learned to accept each other.

However, the experience did come forcefully but the beers made it simple. Not to mention we had our share of funny arguments and pressure in the last five years. All of it was coming to an end as we approached our final thesis, and so was my journey with David in Caltech.

It was like any other day in Caltech. He would have never thought it would turn out to be his last within the establishment.

A man gasping for breath moved his footsteps even quicker glancing at the names written over the offices. It was the college faculty building. Suddenly his body jerked and stopped. Without even knocking he threw himself through the closed doors.

The Principal, Mr. Richard Moll was astonished to see someone rushing into his office at odd hours like this.

"Mr. Moll, sir," the man said struggling for air to fill his lungs.

"Oh, for Christ's sake, what is it?" he said lifting his face up, pushing the papers aside on his desk with a strong look in his old eyes visible through his dense glasses.

"The papers… papers… they are gone," he said with uttermost urgency.

"What are you talking about?" Mr. Moll responded in anguish.

"They disappeared this morning, sir. I opened my locker in the physics lab and they were gone," the Ph.D. student replied fumbling, the words barely coming out of his mouth.

"You must be out of your mind. This is impossible," he continued. "How could you have let this happen, Cody? These were important papers related to future developments in quantum mechanics, I was counting on these. You know you had a breakthrough. Anyway, this cannot go well with my reputation and neither with yours. I want a complete search of the rooms of all doctorial pupils within the institution. The moment you find something suspicious let me know."

"Very well, sir, I am sure I'll find them before the day comes to an end," Cody said nervously. There was no way he thought such a thing would happen.

The news of the incident reached others, including me and David. At first, we thought it was a joke but soon the seriousness of the

CHAPTER 5

situation crawled upon us. Our rooms were checked rigorously without any decency and by the time it was over it was like a tornado had swiftly passed our rooms without any warning.

This was very amusing for both David and me, "Why are they suspecting us? The culprit can be someone from outside." David said.

"Maybe, but their primary suspects, for now, are the people within Caltech," said Rudy walking towards us from the opposite side of the corridor where my room was. David and Rudolph put up together while I and Jack shared a room.

"Did they check yours too?"

"Yeah, they are checking everyone's, even the worker section."

"Man! Mr. Moll is taking the matter strongly," I said.

"He is going to suspend the person if it turns out to be someone within the establishment," said Rudy powerfully as if he really meant it.

However, that was not David's main concern. "Whose papers were they and what were they all about?" he asked looking towards Rudy.

"Well, I don't know much but from what I have heard they belonged to Cody Canyon and they were related to quantum theory, something related to many worlds interpretation of quantum mechanics," he said casually. From his face, he was not looking much bothered about the whole thing.

Many worlds interpretation is a postulate of quantum mechanics that asserts there exists other worlds or universes parallel to ours, which in turn implies that there can be multiple universes, each having a past and future of its own. However, it does not mean that one can move from one universe to another. It just questions our reality to be the only reality as a whole.

David had told me a few days back that he is working on a similar thesis. The revelation by Rudy shocked David a bit. I could see his face turning a bit serious which, in his case, was rare.

"It's ok. I don't think they are going to find anything anywhere near us. Whatever it is they are looking for, they are looking at the wrong place," I said before giving David a smile. He responded with a weak smile.

There was something going on in his mind for sure.

"Hey, guys. I think you both should carry on. I got something important I need to catch on to, I'll see you both later," David said, walking backward and moving away.

"What's up with him?" Rudy asked confusingly.

"I don't know. But he'll be alright, I know him," I said putting my hand over Rudy's shoulder as we both walked towards his side of the corridor.

As David was making his way back to the physics lab a lot of questions filled his mind, at first he couldn't remember who Cody was. Then he suddenly remembered having a casual conversation with Cody a few months back. It was a brief conversation and Cody knew that David was working on a similar thesis as his. Now that somebody had stolen Cody's hard work, David was worried that the same might not have happened to his thesis too.

"Why would somebody do something like that?" and the answer immediately crossed his mind as a retrospective question, "Has it something to do with the UFT?"

CHAPTER 5

He was sure something was happening behind his back for quite some time now. He had often seen his room all messed up during his absence quite a lot of time. It was like somebody was searching for something but couldn't find it.

He never spoke to me about all these things until later. He knew that this would get me unnecessarily upset. On the other hand, he was quite sure during those moments that he wouldn't be able to hide all of this from me and the others anymore.

What was the idea behind all this chaos that suddenly induced his life? As he reached the lab he realized that he had forgotten the physics lab locker keys back in his room. So, he rushed back quickly, grabbed the keys which he remembered he kept in his pants the other day and was about to move out of the room when he saw a bottle of ink spilled over a few papers on the desk.

This is not the way he remembered the room was when he left a few minutes back.

"Had somebody been here while I was away?" he looked over his other belongings and saw that a few of them were a bit shuffled and out of place.

None of this made any sense to him it was only a few hours ago that their room was inspected by the faculty and there was nothing that they found to be of their interest.

"Why then somebody would do the same all over again?"

The strange situation made David forget about his entire research thesis but then he remembered and decided to rush back to the lab. This time as David was making his way back to the lab he thought, *I hope there are no more surprises*.

As soon as he reached the lab, he reluctantly moved toward his locker. He paused for a moment as if praying to himself before he opened his locker. The papers were there. Nothing had happened to them. He was relieved.

His hands reached out to take a look at them. That's when he noticed there was something wrong. There were too many. His papers were there but there were some additional papers about the same subject.

"These papers…these papers, they are not mine."

That's when it hit him. These papers belonged to Cody. *I need to get these back to him before it's too late.*

His mind was rushing through a million thoughts and that's when his eyes got a glimpse of another piece of paper. Unlike others, this was isolated like a letter or something.

Taking it out, he quickly opened it.

Meet me at 4:00 am inside Throop Hall – J.C.

"Who is J.C?" David questioned himself. He knew he had to meet him to know what was going on but before that, he had to get rid of the papers.

The best way he could do it was to give these papers to John. He was trying to think of a solution to get this done while simultaneously looking at the papers in his hand. Yet again, something in Cody's paper got his interest.

He looked at it again, this time more carefully.

"Oh my god! That's it… I found it, I found the answer. The theory is complete," he screamed to himself inside his mind.

CHAPTER 5

"What are you doing here?"

A voice from nowhere startled David. It was Jack. He had been looking for David for quite some time now. Coming over to him he said, "John has been looking for you, where have you been?"

"Listen, Jack. You need to get these papers to John, it's really important. They belong to Cody. Tell him that I found them in the lab under the table," David said pausing for a second before pointing him towards a table.

"Tell him that I'll see him in two hours back in my room, alright?" he continued stressing his words making sure that Jack understands each word.

"Hey, but… what's happening, why are you in such a hurry and where did you get these papers from? I don't understand?" Jack said in confusion.

"You have to trust me, Jack. These papers are very important if they don't reach good hands at the right time a lot of people will be in trouble. Now can you do this for me?" David responded strongly.

"Ok, I'll do it," Jack said, nodding his head.

"Good! That's what I expected. You are my friend Jack and I can trust you. Now go." David said with a smile knowing Jack was up for it, after all, that's what friends are for. He gave Jack a hug as he left.

David now was looking at his watch. He had fifteen minutes lead to get to Throop Hall.

At the same time, he didn't want anyone to know what he was up to. So, he had to do it smoothly and carefully. He took a few

Ph.D. books out of his locker before closing it, so that he might look like any other doctorate guy and made a move.

He knew Jack would get to me sometime soon so he had to reach the Hall before Jack reaches me or else everybody would be searching for him.

A few minutes later David was making his way to the hall.

He kept looking back now and then. The thought of somebody stalking him had been on his mind for a while. Now looking back, he noticed how strangely his room was always messed up when he returned from his outings. His things used to always look like they have had some foreign influence on them in his absence. Back then he thought it might be Rudy, but now he knew somebody had been sneaking in on him.

David was thinking about a lot of things, his mind was trying to connect pieces. Soon the thoughts about the papers overtook all his other thoughts.

"Many worlds…many worlds," that's all he was muttering to himself as he was quickly walking towards his destination.

David knew if his calculations were correct, he was on to something. He wanted to talk about this to me so badly, but he knew he didn't have time for all of this. He had to meet the mystery guy, Mr. J.C. "Whoever he was, he knew about my research extensively," David thought to himself.

Another thing crossed his mind. Whoever had kept Cody's paper in his locker was trying to set him up. "Who could it be? I never did anything wrong to anyone," there were so many questions pounding on his mind. "Perhaps I could get a few answers when I see Mr. J.C.," thinking about it, he started walking ever more quickly.

CHAPTER 5

Soon he reached the Hall.

While climbing the footsteps, a lady student with bright eyes and golden hair came to him and handed him a note.

Basement – Last corridor

During this moment I was having a word with Jack. Jack explained the whole situation.

"These are the papers that belong to Cody," Jack said, handing over the papers to me. I in turn rushed to give Cody back his papers.

"Have you seen Cody?" I asked one of my colleagues running across the corridor.

"Yeah… he and Mr. Moll are inspecting David's room," he replied.

This in turn led me back to David's room.

"Cody, here is your paper," I said as I dashed into the room.

"Oh thank goodness…I thought I was never going to find them. Where did you find them?" Cody responded and bounced towards John in enthusiasm. Mr. Moll was watching the scene from a distance.

"Ah, I found them under the table in the physics lab," I said simultaneously looking at Cody and turning my face toward Mr. Moll.

"Thank you, John," Cody said shaking his hand. "Mr. Moll, I think our work here is done. I knew David could never do something of this sort," he said again looking at Mr. Moll.

As they were about to move out of the room, I stopped them.

"Excuse me! What do you mean by that, something of what sort? I mean, I thought David's room had been inspected already. I am just curious," I asked looking at Cody in particular and Mr. Moll halfheartedly.

"Well, you are David's good friend as far as I know. Therefore I must tell you we received a note a few minutes back that David had stolen Cody's papers," Mr. Moll said occasionally looking at everyone.

"Who gave you the note?" I asked as my heart almost skipped a beat thinking David was about to be expelled and it would be his last day in Caltech.

"We don't know and I think it doesn't matter anymore as everyone can see now that you have resolved the matter quite nicely. Good day, son, and I would be looking forward to hear from you about your thesis," Mr. Moll said, leaving the room.

David had reached the basement and as he came to the last corridor, he could see a faint figure standing on the opposite end. When David started to walk towards the faint figure the floor beneath his feet started shaking.

At the same time, John noticed something strange. The walls around him had started trembling.

A shiver ran through mine and David's spines. In a second I knew what it was. *Earthquake!*

David saw as uneven vibes went through his body and extended to the walls around him. Within a quick second, all the questions running in his mind disappeared and a more prominent feeling

CHAPTER 5

took its place—fear. Before he knew what was happening, the pieces of the side walls started to collapse as he glanced toward the faint figure exiting from the far end. At that very moment, he realized he was standing in the middle of the corridor. His body could no longer sustain the balance and in a split second, it fell to the ground. He started to feel dizzy, and breathing uncomfortably he struggled to stand up but soon found his feet disagreeing to bear the command of the brain signals sent through his nerve impulses which by now were unsystematic. The fracturing sound of a segment of a weighty ceiling right above him and the breaking up sidewalls surrounding it grabbed his attention.

He felt as if the time had stretched beyond his grasp for his life to come to an end.

Meanwhile, somewhere else, Jack told me to open my eyes slowly which I had kept pressed forcefully for the last couple of seconds. As I opened my eyes I was praying for David to be in good shape. The earthquake had ended, I looked at Jack and we both took a deep breath before acknowledging a sign of relief. I told Jack to find Rudy.

Soon I reached Throop Hall. All I found was his jacket, his books and a note. *Meet me at 4:00 am inside Throop Hall – J.C.*

Jack and Rudy were looking for David all over the place. I had told Jack to keep the events of the last few hours between us.

I didn't tell Jack about the note. There was no sign of David anywhere.

The next day they found a crack in the Throop Hall building. A small quantity of furniture and walls had fallen over within certain parts of the building including the sidewalls of the basement. It was here that they thought he had crumbled and died.

I had kept the note I found earlier. Again, we searched all around the campus. David was nowhere to be found.

This was indeed David's last day in Caltech…

It was later found that there were spots of blood on the floor of the last corridor in the basement and maybe it was worst…

It wasn't just his last day in Caltech… it was the last day of his life.

CHAPTER 6

A week had passed and there was still no sign of David, I was mystified by the whole episode.

The authorities had given up hope. The forensic tests revealed that the spots of blood on the floor of the last corridor in the basement near the collapsed ceiling belonged to David. Although his body had not been found, from the looks of it most had assumed him dead.

Rudy was convinced by the events. However, I and Jack found it hard to believe that David was no more.

The Throop Hall building was one of the most prestigious constructions within the Caltech campus and the crack left by the earthquake had stained its existence.

Following the course of actions, there was something that had been bothering me for a couple of days. It was the note that was handed over to Mr. Moll. I had started to think that somebody was trying to set David up.

I decided to take a look at David's room one more time but without telling this to Rudy or Jack. Whoever was behind this was very clever and for all I knew it could be anyone.

As I was quickly going through the drawers, cupboards and David's personal belongings, I found the missing piece of paper from Cody's research subject.

I was sure now that there was someone behind all these wicked happenings. I was now more careful about who I was speaking to and about what. An uneasy feeling had latched itself on me. What if somebody had killed David and made it look like an accident? Yes, taking the advantage of the earthquake to make it look like he died in a natural disaster.

It was up to me then to find his killer or killers if there were others who plotted his death. But why would somebody do something like that?

I decided to talk to Rudy about what David was researching. That was the only way to know the reason behind his death. There was definitely someone who had been eyeing him for a long time now. Maybe Rudy knew something about it. I told Rudy that I wanted to have a conversation with him in private and called him to my room.

"What are you talking about, John? Have you gone nuts? Why would somebody try to murder David? You have lost your mind," he barked in enragement.

"I can't answer all your questions, Rudy. But you have to tell me if you know anything about this, anything at all," I calmly responded.

"No, I don't and you have lost it, John," he said again in frustration moving away from me, trying to ignore my question.

At this moment Jack came walking in. "What's going on in here?"

CHAPTER 6

"John thinks somebody has murdered David," said Rudy looking towards Jack.

"Okay, John, you need to get a grip on yourself. We all know that you were a very good friend of David, but you have to understand that he is not alive anymore. He was a friend to all of us, it's a hard time. But we need to hold on to our lives and you have to understand he was not murdered. Are you listening to me, man?" Jack said walking towards me.

"No, you don't understand. It is not over, somebody is behind this, somebody killed him and it's the same person who was trying to set him up," I said showing the piece of Cody's paper to them.

"Where did you find this?" asked Jack curiously looking at the piece of paper.

"In David's room. If Cody and Mr. Moll would have found it earlier while they were inspecting his room they would have accused him of larceny and probably would have expelled him," I said trying to make them understand the seriousness of the situation in vain.

"How can this be? David told me that he found Cody's papers under the table in the lab. If that was true how this piece of paper ended up in his room, he told me to trust him. Did he really steal Cody's papers?" Jack started murmuring as if trying to convince myself of his actions.

"What are you guys talking about? What papers? When did all of this happen?" Rudy questioned in confusion.

"Jack, I think somebody was trying to set David up," I said to Jack raising my eyebrows.

Suddenly, Rudy said something that made me and Jack look at him in surprise.

"What are you guys talking about? I know where that piece of paper came from," said Rudy snatching it from my hand.

After giving a brief look to each other Jack and I responded in the same instant, "Where?"

Rudy noticed the anxiousness in our eyes and clenched his teeth before replying, "This paper is more than a month old. David asked me to get it for him and so I did him a favor by asking Cody. I never knew then that it could become a hazard. I thought David had returned it to Cody and that's why I never told Mr. Moll or Cody anything about it. In fact, I didn't even know that it was in our room before this moment," he said looking at me.

"Well, at least you could have told me about this," I said looking at him suspiciously.

"What do I know? You and David are like thick friends for all I know. He could have already told you about it. It's you and him who are doing all the concealing. What is this thing about David giving Jack Cody's papers? What are you guys hiding from me? What are you guys up to?" Rudy exclaimed pointing a finger at Jack and looking at me with anger.

"Listen, Rudy, calm down, okay? All of us know David could never steal anything from anyone. I just wanted to know how this piece of paper got into David's room. Now that I do this discussion is over," I said taking the paper from Rudy's hands and making my way out of the room.

"Jack, you coming?" I asked Jack as he stood there thinking something for a moment and gave a sign.

CHAPTER 6

"That's that then!" he said and started to walk towards me.

"One more thing. I don't want Mr. Moll or Cody to know about this piece of paper. It can get us into trouble," I said before leaving the room, showing the piece of paper to both.

"So, what would you do with the paper?" asked Jack as we made our way to the room.

"I'll give it back to Cody first thing in the morning," I spoke.

"Listen, John. I need to ask you something. If David never stole these papers, then how come he got his hands on them in the first place? I know he's my friend and I need to trust him—"

"David never stole them, Jack," I said cutting him in between. "I know it's difficult to understand whatever is happening around us, but that's the truth," I replied looking at my steps.

"John, you really have to consider your options. You can't be so sure about it after all," Jack said, trying to convince me otherwise.

"Yes, I can be. He was my friend, for god's sake, my best friend!" I said suddenly halting my footsteps, staring at him coldly.

"John…" Jack said softly.

"Jack, you have to understand that if he wanted to steal these papers he would have never given them back to Cody and if he really wanted to do it he would have done it a long time back," My voice being weak, I explained frustratingly and made my way to the room.

Jack followed me briefly.

As I reached my room I was perturbed by a lot of questions. As much as I wanted Jack to know that there was someone who was trying to set David up I couldn't let him know what was going on in my mind.

I could not trust anyone.

In a very short while or should I say in a week exactly, my whole life had changed. I had lost my best friend and was striving to complete my thesis. I had to complete my Ph.D. within the coming two years and without David, this was seemingly a very difficult task, as he was one of my profound advisers during the years that we had spent together. It felt like my whole life was falling apart.

At the same time, I was determined to find David's killer and the person who tried to set him up. I was very much distrustful of Rudy following the course of events. The fact that he knew about Cody's research and his regular arguments with David in the early years flashed before my eyes.

Being David's roommate, he would have definitely known what David was up and somehow, I started to think that David's research paper was the reason behind his disappearance. If that was true, being his assistant no one had a better chance than Rudy to have access to his research.

My thoughts again started to conflict themselves as I thought about how good friends we all had been for the last couple of years. Rudy would've not tried to kill him, I thought to myself.

Somehow, I made myself get out of the following position and concentrate on my research.

CHAPTER 6

Jack entered the room quietly assuming that I was still furious about the last argument that we had had in the corridor. He gave me a quick glance innocently as he ambled to his bed.

Making himself comfortable he said, "Hey, John. I had a problem devising the implications of the particle model you gave me earlier, do you mind helping me out with that?"

"Sure," I said with a smile looking at him.

"Hey, Jack. I didn't mean to be harsh on you earlier that time."

"It's just that I and David had been such good friends that I can't bear to listen to anything against him. I hope you understand," I said with a smile.

"It's ok, John," he said complimenting a smile back and patting my shoulders, trying to cheer me up.

"Thank you, Jack. I don't know what I would have done without you," I said, cursing myself for not telling Jack what was going on, in my mind. I wish whatever I was doing was right.

Soon both of us got busy working.

The next day in the morning I decided to go tell Cody about the paper I had found earlier in David's room, the one Rudy had told me about. I apologized to Cody for missing this last piece of paper.

I also found myself guilty of doubting Rudy for the disappearance of David. Maybe things had taken their toll on me a little too unpredictably. I know somewhere inside he felt sorry for David the same as me. I decided to apologize to him.

As I reached his room and knocked on the door, I couldn't help but notice that he took quite a while to reach out and open it.

He looked nervous as he opened the door. Without saying anything to me he returned to his study table.

I could see a little of David's notes lying around here and there next to his table and yet again the feeling of distrust filled my thoughts. *What is he doing with David's notes? Is he searching for something? Maybe his research—*

My thoughts got disconnected as he turned his face toward me and inquired, "What are you doing here, John?"

"Isn't that supposed to be what I should be asking you?" I answered him with a retrospective question.

"What do you mean?" he said in haste.

"What are you doing with David's work? What are you after?" I couldn't control myself, my curiosity getting the best of me.

"I don't know what you're talking about, John," he said with confidence. He looked at the notes around him.

It was unlike Rudy to be touching David's belongings as I noticed they were old research papers going a long way back. I knew David didn't like to share his work with anyone.

"I know you are after his research, Rudy. I know you're the person responsible for his disappearance," I said this time in rage looking straight into his eyes. I was trying to look through his fake innocence.

"Are you out of your mind, John? Last time I checked, you were doing all right, what's wrong with you? Why are you acting so weird?" he said with a sympathetic tone in his voice.

CHAPTER 6

"Just answer me! Don't try to change the subject," I said trying to ignore whatever he was saying.

"John, I was his assistant and all that I am trying to do is to complete his incomplete work. I think you've completely lost your mind and you need to get a hold of yourself," he said, trying to calm me down.

Now I was pushed back a little but I was sure that he was up to something. I needed to get the right perspective on things. Without saying anything much I left the room.

As I left, I mumbled to myself, "John, control. Control yourself..."

Soon after that incident, I started to keep a distance from Rudy. He was persistent to find the reason behind my ignorance towards him, so he tried to speak to Jack about it. I told Jack not to pay any heed to him and with time he too stopped talking to him.

Something inside me kept telling me that there was something wrong about him. Later Jack told me that Rudy often used to talk bad about David behind his back and he had repeatedly seen him giving David jealous looks. I told Jack to keep a keen eye on Rudolph and tell me immediately if he finds something suspicious going around.

1972

Then came the day it was decided to demolish the Throop Hall building because of the crack that was left by the earthquake. The Throop Hall was one of the earliest and finest architectural heritages of the Caltech campus. The artwork and the sculptures that designed and outlined its walls and pillars were peerless. Its existence meant a lot to us.

Many were heartbroken by its knockdown. Nonetheless, it happened. A year had passed since we had been keeping an eye on Rudy. Nothing had happened that would have made my belief stronger in my pursuit to find him guilty. I had started to think whether I was wrong in my judgment.

A few days later, after the Hall's razing, I found Rudy taking a stroll on the campus and my gaze reached the wrist of his right hand. I stood there taken aback by what I had seen.

He was carrying David's glasses. The same spectacles that he used to wear, I couldn't have missed it for anything. They were the same spectacles he was wearing when I first saw him in the stadium. Years had passed but I was sure.

Without wasting a single moment, I ran towards him. Grabbing him by his collar I made him turn around.

He was startled by my sudden and absurd behavior.

"Where did you find these?" I asked him, snatching the glasses from his hands. He could see the pale look right on my face.

He kept looking at me partially cause of the bitter tone in my voice and partially because we had not spoken in a long time. Amused, he softly replied, "They don't belong to me… they belong to Jason Clement."

"What?" I asked him, swiftly recollecting about the note that I had found a year back the day David disappeared. *Jason Clement… J. C.* I remembered that I had not told anyone about the note since then.

"He came by in my room last night and we were studying. He forgot them in the room when he left."

CHAPTER 6

"You are lying to me, Rudy," I asked again just to confirm.

"No, I am not," he said almost moving away from me. "You got what you wanted. Now just leave me alone," he continued almost shouting, making his way, leaving me all by myself.

I stood there thinking for a moment. My resolute now was to find Jason Clement and I had to do that fast.

Lost in my own feelings I didn't see Jack running towards me as he approached me. Another piece of shock awaited me. When he came closer, I noticed he was out of breath.

"What happened? Why are you panting so heavily?" I questioned glancing at his informal attire.

"John, yesterday Rudy…he…" he started to say.

"Rudy what, Jack?" I asked restlessly.

Giving me a frightened look, those words came hesitantly out of his mouth.

"Yesterday, Rudy tried to kill me."

CHAPTER 7

Both I and Jack had been feeling like we were being followed every day since last year. It didn't matter whether we were in our rooms, taking a walk or giving classes. That feeling never stopped.

Turning my attention towards Jack, I tried asking again. At first, I didn't know what to say. "What are you talking about, Jack?" I said in confusion and shock.

"As I went into my room last night, I saw a shadow trying to creep up on me in the darkness and then a dart shot through the window. It just missed me," he said, showing me a bullet-like dart which seemed poisonous at once.

"But how can you be so sure that the shadow belonged to Rudy?" I asked trying to substantiate the incident he had been through.

"Because I got this," he said with confidence showing me a bracelet which was often seen by me and him on Rudy's wrist.

"You were right, John. You were always right," he said smiling at me.

"The thing is not about me being right or wrong, Jack. The real thing is that we are in trouble," I said profoundly.

CHAPTER 7

"Do you think we should talk about this to Mr. Moll?" Jack asked, terrified how things were turning out.

He knew things could get nasty, but this was turning out to be too much for him to handle. The situation was getting out of my hands as well. At the same time, I was determined to find whoever was behind all of this. Now that Rudy was one of them. I wanted to be sure if there were more.

"No, we can't let Mr. Moll know about any of these happenings. Rudy is close to him and if we do, the culprit will get vigilant and can slip out of our hands. We can't let that happen," I said, looking at Jack.

First, I had to get in touch with Jason Clement at any cost. He was the only one at this point who could solve the riddle behind David's disappearance. It was also important to know the truth behind Rudy's actions and the attack on Jack. I was running short of time.

Somehow, I didn't yet feel right to tell Jack about Jason Clement and the note that I found a year back in the basement. I hastily made my way to the closest college faculty register that I could find. Soon I found it.

Hurriedly going through the names inside the register I paused at the one that I was searching for. Next to it was written the room number and the names of his research advisees, one of them being Rudy.

In a few moments, I reached his room and knocked in anticipation thinking I would be able to get my answers regarding David's disappearance.

I stood there in vain as nobody came to answer the door. As I tried to push open the door, I realized that it was already open.

Stepping inside I noticed a prolonged absence, somebody had been away for quite a long time. It was getting late and I had to reach back to my room.

As I started walking back and noticed the familiar feeling of being traced. I tried to be as quiet as possible. I was willing to come back the next day. I decided that it would be the first thing I would do the next morning.

While walking back to my room I had a chance encounter with Cody.

"What are you doing here, John? I hope the final thesis is coming up just fine there is not much time to go for our doctorates, you know," he said trying to pick up a friendly conversation.

"Everything is going fine. Hopefully, I'll be done with it very soon," I said excusing myself out of the talk and made my way back to my room.

"Bye, John. Take care," he said waving his hand as he took my leave.

"You too, Cody," I said without turning my face back.

I was too engrossed in my own thoughts to have a word with him. I was thinking more about Rudy and Jason Clement.

The very next morning, as I got up I decided to make a visit to Jason Clement's room, I noticed a note kept on a side table beside my bed.

As I opened it to go through its contents, with dizziness still engraved within my eyes, my eyes were left wide open.

The note read,

CHAPTER 7

I know who killed David. Meet me outside Caltech, at Rialto Theatre, 6:00 pm. Come alone – J.C

I immediately looked for the piece of note that I had found a year back and getting my hands on it, I opened it quickly.

Meet me at 4:00 am inside Throop Hall – J.C.

It was the same handwriting.

Instantly twin feelings stamped my nervous system – the feeling was cold and painful. As the moments passed the feeling of pain grew harder and harder.

I was saddened by the fact that David was no more. This had become evident to me by the note. At the same time even as I knew this, I was now more willing to find the murderer than I ever was.

I went to Jack and told him to stay away from Rudy until I see him again.

"What do you mean till next time, John? Where are you going?" he asked desperately trying to figure out what I was up to.

"Don't worry, Jack. I will be all right. I just need to take care of something, I'll see you soon, take care," I said patting his shoulders before I took leave. I could have taken Jack along with me but as mentioned in the note I had to do this by myself.

I was more than sure that today I was about to find who was behind the death of David and whether Rudy had been a true friend all this while.

I was thinking about what Rudy had told me the other day while he was taking a stroll on the campus. A strange notion crossed my mind. Rudy had told me that he was in his room the last night. If that was true, then how did he manage to attack Jack?

More disturbingly, how did Jack manage to get a hold of Rudy's bracelet? If Rudy at all was with Jason Clement the same night Jack was attacked, then either Rudy's or Jack's stories was untrue. It could also be that Jack was mistaken.

How can anyone be at two places at a single time? All of this was confusing me and only one person could give me the answers I searched for.

As I reached closer to **Rialto Theatre** that evening, I noticed how the crowd was at its minimum and there was a strange silence unlike the aura of the place. It was one of the famous places within the territories of southern Pasadena. Always crowded and always full of happening and joy.

As I entered the theatre, I saw a man sitting in a completely empty row. I knew it was Jason.

I reached him and closely yet quietly sat next to him. Before I could speak anything he said, "There were gunshots. I saw a faint figure."

"What are you talking about? Tell me everything that happened to David. Everything," I said, getting restless.

"There is no time. I don't know who is behind all this but as the earthquake ended that day there was someone else there. There were gunshots and I had to leave. However, there was this faint figure I saw… It was—"

I heard two powerful gunshots aimed from a close range before he could complete his sentence. At once I ducked onto the floor.

CHAPTER 7

I could hear painful mourns coming from Jason and someone sitting close. I looked towards the seats to my right and saw someone of my age lying on the ground, helplessly counting his last breaths.

I pulled Jason down before he could get hit by another bullet. His eyes were fixed on me as if they were trying to say something to me. I could see a small pool of blood forming next to his abdominal region of the body.

Lying there for a few minutes making sure that there was no one around, I quickly crawled along with him to a reasonably safe zone.

My eyes looked at his feeble condition and before they could read anything else, his dying voice clutched my attention.

"John… the papers…" he muttered.

"Jason, I need to get you to the closest hospital as soon as possible," I said panicking in the helpless situation.

"John, there is not much time… Rudy, he is… he is…," he said, mumbling his last words. He grabbed my hand trying to gather strength in his last moments.

"Rudy… not… Cody… innocent," he said before passing out.

I waited for a while to make sure that the murderer was gone and that it was safe for me to come out in the open.

From a distance, I could hear a few people running across their way toward where I was. I had to get out of there. If they saw me with him, I could get in trouble.

I quickly searched his pockets for any final clues that I could get. I found a document in his deep right pocket. Taking it out I quickly stood up and made my way out of the theater.

I looked back a few times to make sure I was not being followed. Seconds later, a guy spotted me. They might have thought I was the one who fired the gunshot. I ran as fast I could, clinching the last piece of document that I had gathered from Clement's pocket.

They chased me along for a couple of minutes within the parameter of the theatre. I saw there was a narrow gap behind a cola refrigerator. I camouflaged myself behind it.

After searching for me for a while, they gave up. I just prayed to god that they had not seen my face. This could get me in a lot of trouble.

Upon their departure I slowly moved out, looking everywhere making sure that no one was around anymore.

I opened the file. It had a paper, a fragment related to David's research – Quantum Interpretation of Many Worlds. His handwriting was evident.

There had to be a link between Cody's paper and David's paper. After all, this began with him and his research. There had to be someone who had been keeping an eye on David's research for a long time. Rudy is the only fair suspect I could come up with.

My doubt about him being the person behind David's murder and now Clement's death was now getting even more positive.

Jason Clement was an advisor to both him and Cody.

Before I could think anymore, I knew I had to get out of there. The police could be here any moment. If they would find me on

CHAPTER 7

the sight of murder, I could get arrested. I made my way back to Caltech.

After the news of Clement's death reached everyone, I started to keep a close watch on Cody and Rudy.

Both Rudy and Cody were equally depressed by Clement's death as both were really good friends of his. Clement's advice had often fetched them immerse success in their study in the past years.

Jack was not quite happy with how things had turned out. He always had a very funny nature with a really good sense of humor. David's disappearance and now Clement's death, adding to it the attack he had faced a day before had left him thinking about his life.

"John, are you sure that Clement's death was in some way related to David's disappearance?" Jack said thinking something deeply.

"I am more than sure, Jack," I said looking at him with confidence and thinking about the document that I had received during the last moments of his life.

"John, we need to take care of ourselves," he said looking at the document which was titled *Quantum Interpretation of Many Worlds*.

"I understand that. But we also need to keep a close watch on Rudy and Cody, those were the last two words Clement spoke before he died," I said simultaneously looking at Jack and the document.

"I guess you're right, John. But can't we talk about this to Mr. Moll?" Jack said trying to think of a solution.

"I wish we could, Jack. But we don't have any proof. Moreover, if they get to know I was on the death scene when it happened, I can get into serious trouble," I said thinking about the whole event. "From what I can see, there is only one thing to do. You keep a close watch on Rudy and I'll see if Cody has any more skeletons hidden in his closet," I continued trying to explain to him what he had to do next.

It was sometime later during the same year that my efforts started to show some results.

One morning as I was following Cody I found him sneaking out of Caltech. I made sure that he didn't notice me by maintaining a safe distance from him. Walking along the way for a couple of minutes, he kept looking back. I think he was trying to make sure that he was not followed.

I followed him to the market where there were stores and shops which faced each other. Most of them were closed, awaiting their owners. It was unlike for someone to come to the market at a time like this. The atmosphere was quite numb. There were not many people walking around, only a couple of bystanders.

I watched him take a few steps toward a coffee shop. Finally, his footsteps came to rest. He saw a chair kept just a few meters away from him. Removing the dust with his bare hands he made himself comfortable on it.

I waited and gazed at him from a distance to see what happens next. The waiting had started to bore me a lot. Also, it was quite cold in the morning and the cool wind had started to blow hard on me.

After fifteen minutes of unfortunate restlessness, I saw a man coming towards him. He had a long, dark-violet coat covering him from his shoulders to ankles. This camouflaged his physique almost completely from my bare eyes.

CHAPTER 7

His face, as I could see from a distance, was unfamiliar to me. His cheeks looked wobbly when he sat on the chair. I can only assume he was heavy or maybe he had a considerably good build. He had average height and was definitely not a fellow mate of Cody from a different town. Had it been his friend, even coming from out of town he would have called him at Caltech itself.

Soon the waiter came, holding a tray with two warm cups. I think they were coffee.

Damn!! I wished I was having one of those.

Just as he bent forward to grab his cup of coffee, a metallic shine, scarcely escaping the depths of his right pocket reached me. I was confused and curious for a while as to what it could be.

It was not a moment before I realized what it was from its outer structure. It was a gun. A gun which I thought was heavy and loaded.

That's enough for now, I thought and made my way back to Caltech.

What is Cody up to? I thought to myself as I reached the entrance. Now for some reason, I was sure that he himself was the one who tried to set David up last year. Maybe the guy sitting next to Cody was responsible for Clement's death. There was no other possible reason why he would meet such a dangerous person.

Slowly it was all coming back to me. Cody was responsible for setting David up in the first place. He knew if he himself complained to Mr. Moll, nobody would suspect him.

Was he the one who was behind the attack on Jack? There had to be someone else who was accompanying Cody in his plans. Although I had found the puppet I still had to find out who was pulling the strings.

Before I knew I was back in my room.

I saw Jack sitting nervously waiting to tell me something. As he saw me enter the room, he looked at me with unease.

"What happened, Jack? What is it?" I asked staring at the frightened look he had on his face.

Picking up a few papers from a study table he handed them to me. They belonged to David. They were the same papers I had found in David's jacket the day he had gone missing.

"These are some of David's research papers on quantum theory," he said giving them to me.

Combining with the papers I had found in Clement's pocket, it could produce David's research.

"There are still a few papers missing," I said, still reading the papers that Jack had handed over to me. "The other missing papers must be with that guy who was keeping an eye on David. We must find them," I said with curiosity, thinking that the rest of the papers must be with Cody.

"I already did," Jack said, raising my excitement but sadness still dripping from his face. "I found these in Rudy's room. I have been sneaking into his room for quite some time now, looking for clues. Yesterday, I found this," he said, handing me a piece of paper.

It was the missing paper from David's research.

I looked at it astonishingly as I compiled it with other documents. *This would almost complete David's research.*

CHAPTER 8

"Where did you find this? This is an important discovery," I said in exhilaration and stimulation.

"I told you, it was in Rudy's room," he said thinking something deeply, trying to wipe away my enthusiasm.

"But that would mean…" I said suddenly realizing why he was so sad and frightened all this time.

Looking at me he realized that I had understood the gravity of the situation.

"Yes, Rudy was there when David disappeared," he said confidently. He looked at me for my reaction.

Things had taken a different toll all together and I was now even more puzzled about what was happening. I explained to Jack what I had seen today, I told him how I had seen Cody with a man having a gun.

I also told him about the note that I had found near David's jacket. I told him everything about Jason Clement. I showed him the notes I had found in the pocket of David's jacket the day he had gone missing and the similar one that Clement had given me.

After hearing me out, Jack became furious, "How could you, John, how could you hide all these things from me? That too for so long, all this time I thought we were friends! I guess I was wrong."

"This is not the time for us to fight about what has happened, Jack," I said, trying to calm him down. "If what you're saying is true then I'm afraid both Rudy and Cody are responsible for David's death. We need proof to accuse them guilty," I said almost getting to a conclusion. "We will have to be quicker, Jack. We can't let them know we are on to them. We will have to be more precise about our next turn. Also, to find the proof we will have to do this slowly, doesn't matter how much time it takes and we have to avenge David's death."

1975

It had been three years now that I and Jack had been searching for some evident proof against Rudy and Cody.

It was also the time when developments focused on the fusion between Quantum Mechanics and Relativity to achieve the UFT (Unified Field Theory) reached new heights.

One such important fusion was summarized by M thesis. It was a recent discovery suggesting that the most important elementary particles were one-dimensional and had a string-like, elongated structure, rather than atoms and molecules which had a traditional spherical form attached to them.

The proposition came in the form of many M theories. The span of M theories lasted for about twenty years. This was approximately from around 1972 to 1992.

The essential thing to know about the "M" theory is that it was the first to assert that all particle behavior and their existence were due to the vibrations of elementary strings. However, the theory

CHAPTER 8

really had no practical evidence backing it up. Still, it promised to show some interesting implications for the future.

While in Caltech, it had become quite an active field of research. But my mind was still on the document I had retrieved from Clement. There had been great escapes through the years, the attacks that we both faced all this while had made us strong. Depressingly, we still had to find some hardcore evidence against Rudy or Cody. The struggle for the truth must be persistent, that is what David used to say. I could not ignore his absence.

Both I and Jack are now used to a professorship. We lived a regular life.

I noticed the attacks that we faced in the last six months had increased to a great extent. They had also become more life-threatening. In the beginning, they were more like accidents trying to justify themselves as though we were killed by chance. Now it had more to do with guns and bullets.

I also understood that Cody and Rudy seemed to act like they didn't know about the things that were happening with me and Jack. I preferred to keep it that way; I didn't want Cody or Rudy to know that we were suspicious of them.

There was also something else I explained to Jack. "Jack, I think Cody and Rudy are trying to extract some piece of information they think we have," I said softly as he was sitting in the staff room and I didn't want anyone to hear us.

"What makes you say that, John?" he replied amusingly trying to understand my point as it seemed unclear to him.

"The thing is, Jack, if they wanted to kill us, they could have done it a long time back. The very fact that we are still alive is because they have kept it that way and the only reason for that could be to assume that we have some essential information related to David's research," I said trying to explain it to him.

"You may be right, John. But it can also be that we have been lucky," he replied judgmentally.

"Not this lucky," I said smiling.

"John, I have found that Cody is in touch with a lot of police officials in the town and it could be that the people who are attacking us are in law themselves. We have to be careful now," Jack said, looking at me.

"Hmm…" I muttered, thinking something.

The next day I found a note in the locker in which I used to keep the records of my students and it looked different. It was completely unexpected. The last time I saw something like this was when a note was given to me by Clement.

I slowly took it out. My mind was running like a bullet train as it was trying to anticipate what and by whom it was.

At first, I couldn't believe what it said but soon an adrenaline rush of joy passed through my body. It was like a miracle I never expected to happen.

There, it was in front of me….

Hey John…, I'm alive.

John, you need to keep this information to yourself. Otherwise, I can get into trouble. There is an address below memorize it and then destroy this note. — David.

CHAPTER 8

I quickly memorized the address that was written below. Later that evening I took the note and burned it with the help of the apparatus that was in the lab.

It was the best day of my life.

David was alive and for all I could know, in good health.

I considered sharing this information with Jack then later I realized that it was too important to be shared with anyone. The news could spread like fire even through an accidental slip of the tongue. No, that was risky. I couldn't tell about this note to anyone, not even Jack.

Jack later noticed that I was looking happier than ever. He tried to ask me unsuccessfully, but I had already made my decision. I remained quiet to his questions, trying to stay as unperturbed as ever. After some time, he stopped noticing my ignorance.

I told him that I had seen a girl a few days back in the market and that I was feeling happy about that. As a matter of fact, I did see a girl a while ago when I was purchasing some stuff from the market the day before. She was warm and beautiful and my attention was completely taken away by her presence. After she left, I wished I could see her again.

I told this to Jack so that he doesn't feel that I was hiding something from him. He had become a really good friend; not that he wasn't before, but after David went missing, it was good to have him around.

Things looked better than ever now. I was now happy that I would be able to talk to my best friend again.

A few days later I wrote a letter to the address I had memorized.

I started by asking David how he was. Later, a million questions followed like where he was, how he ended up there, what happened the day the earthquake hit the institute and finally why he never tried to get in touch with me again. Everything which came to my mind after all these years I penned down briefly, waiting for him to write back.

Meanwhile, Jack and I were attacked again. We were buying something from the market when suddenly a car tried to run us down. It was a narrow escape but now we both had become quite used to all these attacks that were happening around us in the past couple of years.

On a funny note, Jack got agitated as soon as he realized that my eyes were searching for a face restlessly.

It was the same woman I had told Jack about. I was hoping that I could see her again. I desperately wanted to see her face again. To Jack, this was all very amusing.

He furiously argued, "We have just escaped an attack on our lives and here you are, going nuts for women! Are in your senses?" he said, almost yelling furiously.

"Oh, come on, Jack. This girl is different, I am telling you," I said, trying to understand what he was saying.

I was completely engrossed in my search when he pointed out that it was getting late. "We have to leave, John," he said looking at the evening sky getting dull.

But my mind was focused on a completely different issue. When I had written the letter to David I had mentioned an address for him to write to back to me. It was one of the shops in the market itself.

CHAPTER 8

I did this so that nobody would detect that I was in touch with David. It was also the last place anybody would expect. So, every once in a while, I used to check in at the store to confirm if there has been any response from David.

Even today I was going to do the same but Jack was with me, so I had to tell him to carry on. I told him that I would catch up to him in no time.

"Why are you not coming?" he asked me in a lazy tone.

"I need to pick up some stuff. I'll be right behind you," I said pushing him to carry on before he could come up with any excuse to stay behind.

As soon I entered the store, I got the good news. The storekeeper knew about my anticipation and this time as I entered the store, he invited me with a smile.

"There you go," he said handing over the letter to me. "You have been waiting for this for quite some time, isn't it?" he said looking at me with humor.

I quickly opened it. There were so many things I had been waiting to discover. I started reading, standing there.

It really is good to hear from you, John. I see here that you have a lot of questions. I won't complain. I knew you would be worried, John. The address that you have here is where I am now, why I'm here is something you would know by now. I was being stalked, John. They were after my research, they still are. This was the reason I disappeared from Caltech. I had to bluff that I was dead. Now it seems that they have got to know that I am still alive. I am sure that there would be people behind you too. That is why you have to be careful, John.

One more thing which I wanted to tell you is whoever is behind this, it is a student or now a faculty member in the institute. You must leave the institute as soon as possible. I do believe your life is in danger for now. I'll keep writing, goodbye.

NUMERICAL ENIGMA

[The contents of this letter should be kept between only us, at all costs.]

The letter by David was a relief amid the terrifying incidences that were happening around in my life.

The thought of Jack feeling happy to know about David's escape crossed my mind, but I decided to keep the conversation of the letter with myself only, till the time was right for Jack to know about it.

Also, I thought of telling David about the events of the last couple of days in my next letter.

As I was returning to Caltech with happy thoughts, a familiar smile grabbed my attention.

It was the same girl I had been looking for. It was the same warm smile that melted my soul. This was turning out to be a very lucky day except for the attack that had happened to me a couple of minutes ago.

She had beautiful, blue eyes with a bright face. Her dress had imprints of flowers of different colors on it and she had a smooth, local accent.

Before I could know her name or walk towards her she took her belongings and left the store.

I was confused as to what to do next. Then, in an instant, an idea passed my mind. If she was a local, people here would know her and her family. So, I went to one of the shopkeepers and inquired about her.

The man at the counter told me that her name was Clair and she was the daughter of one of the owners of the storekeepers within the area confined to the south block of Pasadena. I bet the man

CHAPTER 8

got a hint about my feelings for her. Getting to know this little piece of information about her was almost like bliss for me.

My feelings for her started to become stronger. I thought of telling David about her in my next letter.

Later, as soon as I entered my room, I started looking for a pen and paper. Finding a blank page, I rushed to the library where I could find peace. It was known for its silent music, the one that inspired people to become one with their selves.

Calmly putting myself on the chair I felt comfortable. I slowly started putting my thoughts on the paper.

Hey, David. It was good to see your reply. Yes, after you left, things have been a little bumpy for me and Jack. There are a few important things that I need to tell you. First, Clement is dead, and second, I think I know who is behind all these evil happenings. I and Jack seem to think it is Rudy and Cody who tried to set you up.

I continued writing telling him how I had seen Cody sitting with someone who had a gun. I paused before telling him how Jack and I faced an assault in the beginning and about the missing bracelet and papers which were found in connection to Rudy.

I decided not to tell him about the girl I had seen at the market. I planned to tell him about that in the next letter. For now, there were other important things to discuss.

I wish David could throw some light on the events that happened with Jack and me, something that we both had faced bravely in the last few years. So, I waited patiently for his next reply.

Soon a few days later he replied…,

All this is bad news, John. Clement was the only person who could lead us to the culprit, I'm sorry for him. What you said in context with Rudy and Cody was shocking. Keep a close watch, John; I have a bad feeling about this. Make sure you move out of Caltech as soon as possible and try to take Jack with you. John, the papers you found in Clement's pocket are very important although they are just a part of my major thesis which I'm working on right now, they are still important. What I'm working on right now is in accordance with the search for U.F.T.

The interesting aspect of the paper is, if you haven't noticed how quantum mechanics is based not on single but multiple outcomes in conclusion to the working of reality on subatomic levels.

The quantum theory thus alternatively suggests ideas that there exist multiple universes for each corresponding outcome.

Though without any proof, this concept of quantum has become of great interest to me. I'll keep updating you about my findings. Please do tell me how things are going in Caltech from time to time. It's been a while since I left that place. I miss it, John, more than anything else. At the same time, I need to tell you a few important things on a more personal note, will do that in my next letter. Take care, John.

I could see now why Rudy and Cody were trying to extract something from me and Jack. They assumed that we knew something about the U.F.T. that David was working on. It was the same reason they had tried to set him up. I was happy to tell David about Rudy, Cody and Clement.

I realized I had a number of questions in my mind like why Clement was dead. Or why David really had to leave? There was so much more to know, so much more to discover.

David told me that he had given his research thesis to Clement during the last hours before he left Caltech but he didn't say he gave anything to Rudy. The attacks were now becoming stronger and stronger; I decided to leave the institute as soon as possible along with Jack.

A few days later I told Jack about my decision and he was more than happy to come along. The last two years had been a hard

CHAPTER 8

ride for him. He would have agreed to go to the Bermuda Triangle considering the situation here. Anything would have been better than this.

In my last letter I wrote David from Caltech I explained how the M theories were making their presence felt, featuring the "strings" one-dimensional nature. It had become the talk of the town.

I also told him about Clair. He was particularly happy for me and that was evident from his next letter.

Good to hear you have found a girl for yourself, John. It would be surprising for you to know something on a similar note has happened with me. This was the personal thing I was referring to in my previous letter.

About M theory, yes, it is surely the thing of the future, but I am least concerned that it is the UFT. You see, John, in the recent development of my thesis I have found that string has a unique problem with its bases.

It is because of this one-dimensional elementary particle that the theory has an abnormal and unique nature to blend itself to fit any application of particle physics, big or small. This is explained by the present theories of quantum or relativity.

It does so by showing not a single definite method for its conclusion but suggests that it can be done in multiple ways in theory. What I'm trying to say is, in principle, it lacks objectivity.

David's answers were quite interesting. What he was trying to say was just as in quantum mechanics we have multiple outcomes, in M theory we had multiple ways to conclude how the behavior of a particle or the particle itself came into existence. This in turn is disastrous because there has never been a theory that has ever supported a thesis as well as a hypothesis at the same time.

In the future, attributes of two M theories may differ completely, still, both will be supported by the string. Why does this happen?

This is where it lacks objectivity. Of course, David already saw this coming.

David's letter was intriguing enough for me to ask him what his take on UFT was. I also asked him about his girl and how he met her. I knew his next reply would be interesting.

It was also time for me and Jack to make a move out of the institute. I told Mr. Moll that it was a pleasure to be a part of Caltech but, it was time for me and Jack to move on.

Rudy was not very happy to hear about our departure, I did not care about him nonetheless. He was still a major culprit in my eyes.

I had still not told Jack about David, that he was alive. I was sure he had a hint that I was up to something.

There was another essential thing I needed to do before I left. I wanted to get married.

I decided that the next time I see her I would ask her out. I knew it was a bizarre thing to do but I know it was time now. I told Jack about this and he was a little skeptical about the idea. Then later, he told me to go for it.

I found out where she lived from the same shop owner who had told me her name.

Determined to marry her, I went to her place to meet her folks. Though in matters of the heart I have seldom known the art, I knew there was something different about her.

I told Jack to accompany me to her house. As we reached her house, I was getting cold feet.

CHAPTER 8

Her father opened the door and greeted us with a warm welcome. As we came at ease, I told Mr. Jacob, her father, that I was in love with his daughter.

He asked me some basic questions like who I was, what my profession is and particularly about my family as well. I must say, although I was confident there was an uneasy feeling of nervousness flickering inside me.

But soon as Mr. Jacob called Clair and his wife, Mrs. Jacob, and we started talking, I started to feel comfortable again.

In the end, it turned out to be a fair deal. I asked Clair if it was okay with her to get married to me.

Her reaction was bliss to me as she admitted that she too had a thing for me when she saw me for the first time in the market. She also told me that she had seen me eyeing her a long time back. The shop owner who told me her name was her uncle and she had known about my feelings for her for some time now.

She also told me she felt contented as even her family was happy with me and my family background, my father too being an owner of a store. We both belonged to Pasadena. I think a lot of things fell right into place.

Before I knew I was married and on my way out of Caltech.

At first glance, I was not happy about the thought of moving from Pasadena. To convince her, I had to tell her about the threats that I and Jack had been facing all this while before I met her.

I omitted talking about David.

As soon as I, Clair and Jack restarted to a new destination I decided to write a letter to David telling him about my marriage to Clair and shifting to a different location.

I had still not received the reply to that previous letter. I was a little worried. Having faith in him I knew he would be all right.

Scientists or theorists do not have the chauvinism of faith that is because they are born with a rational mind. Nonetheless, most of them come around to believing in god once they reach old age.

I shifted to Sacramento and a week after I arrived here, I received a letter from David.

Congratulations, John. I got the news of your marriage, you'll be happy to know that I too have decided to propose my lady love soon. Her name is Julia. She's the daughter of one of my father's friends. She is a lawyer and a good one too. After she is done with this one particular case we plan to get engaged. We wanted to get married now but, I don't want to risk her life. You know, John, how things have been after I left Caltech.

Anyway, about your question regarding the UFT. Well, John, I think anyone who knows about it would be eligible to point out that the UFT would have one very basic and important aspect attached to it. It would be a "knack", it would have for proportions.

Anything that we can understand, anything that we can predict has a uniform pattern. Things that are in order become easy to comprehend. On the other hand, random events seem complicated and difficult to understand. What I'm trying to say here is all patterns are proportions.

Therefore, I'm concluding that since the quest of UFT is to find that ultimate pattern that would help us to understand the mechanics of this reality, it would also be an ultimate proportion. Thus, my search now for UFT has shifted to find that ultimate pattern or proportion.

This letter by David was by far the most interesting. He was keen to point out that everything in the theory of relativity and

CHAPTER 8

quantum mechanics had a pattern. For example, in relativity, the planets, moons and other heavenly bodies had their own definite orbit. It was the same in quantum mechanics, as in the electrons having a precise uniform orbit around the nucleus.

In each of the following cases, the pattern or proportionality was governed by a constant. In the case of relativity, it was the gravitational constant G and in the case of quantum mechanics, it was the Planck's constant h.

Now the real test was to find the ultimate constant.

CHAPTER 9

1980

It has been five years since the last attack. David and I have been sharing ideas ever since his first letter in 1975. Recently he told me that he wished to get married now. I had been encouraging him to do the same for quite some time now. He was keen to ask Julia whether it was all right for her to quit waiting. He was sure that nobody was on his trail anymore, but it turned out that he wasn't completely right about that.

There was someone keeping an eye on me. I had an idea that there was somebody stalking me. They still suspected that I had something important. Even Jack had experienced a near-death event just when he had started to believe that he was out of danger.

It was a similar accident-type attempt on his life, a car trying to run him down. Later when he told me about this, I was more than convinced that the fight was not over yet.

Still, I tried to keep these things concealed to myself as I didn't want David to get all worked up. I knew he had been on his toes for more than five years now. Now, just when he was about to get the love of his life and about to get married, I did not want it to startle him. Besides love just happens once. One cannot stop

CHAPTER 9

living just because of fear of death. Death is inevitable; sooner or later it will come.

David got married to Julia in 1980. I was not there to witness the wedding as I knew I was being followed and I couldn't take the risk. Other than David, Clair too didn't know anything about what was going on with me and Jack in Sacramento. I told Jack to keep his mouth shut as well until I had made sure that it was the right time for Clair to know everything that was happening around her.

The sharing of ideas with David never stopped, in fact, David's search for the UFT had now become an obsession for him.

In his letter, he wrote of being excited about another piece of information.

John, I'm sure by now you too would have been trying to find a theory with an ultimate constant. It has been five years since I last wrote to you about the UFT having the ultimate proportion (pattern). I am sure you might have got my hint about the constants, as these are the constants which balance and preserve the proportions and the proportion in turn reveal to us the patterns. I am now convinced that such a constant or proportion (pattern) will have a universal quality like its counterparts G and h.

Thus, I believe under all the complex theories of our universe, lies this simple yet mystical ultimate proportion (pattern) or constant.

David now was talking about how proportions (patterns) were related to constants and vice versa. He meant that finding the ultimate proportion (pattern) also meant finding the ultimate constant.

He moved on to say that such a constant or proportion (pattern) had to be universal just like a rainbow, to put it more precisely, a spectrum of light. No matter from where you watch it, the spectrum of light will always remain the same, so just as the spectrum of light produces different images for the human eye, like a rainbow and everything around us, the ultimate constant produces chaos and complexity in a universe.

In the end, he mentioned that just like we penetrated light and found its spectrums, we have to penetrate the complexity present in our world. Only then we would be able to find that ultimate constant.

In the coming years, I was compelled to find a better explanation for everything that David was trying to say. My interest in the ultimate proportion (pattern) or constant was more deviated to the remnants of M theory. It was the time that the string was explaining everything in physics.

Of course, all of this was in theory. But I must say I was quite impressed with its accomplishments at least on theoretical grounds. I didn't know then that it would become the theory of the future.

Jack used to continuously nag me with his questions regarding the M theories. He, for his part, had greater belief in it. For all I can say, even more than me. He still didn't know anything about David. I was waiting for the right time to tell him, he would be glad to know that David was alive.

Later, I got to know that somebody had broken into his apartment in the night again. Incidences like these pushed me to share my secret with him but I controlled my emotions. I knew whoever they were, they were still after us.

Meanwhile, I kept asking David whether he was experiencing any attacks now or not. Somehow, I was more worried about him. He was getting very close in his research about UFT. More than anybody I knew.

CHAPTER 9

There were a lot of developments pioneering in the field of M theories too. Within the last couple of years, there had been a number of M theories devised. Essentially, they all had a similar base, the elementary particle being the one-dimensional, elongated strings. The difference was in the types and their combinations. Each M theory had a different type of string or otherwise had a combination of one or more strings in them.

David was excited about the growing popularity of the strings in M theory, but his research was guiding him elsewhere.

In his next letter, he wrote….

John, I found that the string in M theory, though very helpful in its structure, still has a number of loopholes regarding its conclusions of our universe. Firstly, I would like to bring to your attention to that, on paper, each of the M theory hypotheses can be described by its own one-dimensional elementary string, in a different way.

That makes the string a highly imaginative and adaptive idea in terms of hardcore logic, even though an interesting one. On the other hand, practical evidence of the string would no doubt prove me wrong, but would also bring us closer to the ultimate constant.

This, as of now, seems highly unlikely.

Even though I was silent about these ideas, I tried to ask Jack what he thought of the string. To him the string theory was the UFT; there was nothing more to it.

"Look, John. I think for most of my part, the string is the ultimate thing. It works fantastically in theory and fits our understanding on most levels of relativity and quantum."

David on the other side was convinced that there were still a lot of loopholes in the string theory that would be clarified in time in the coming years.

I was confused about whom to believe. Although I never doubted David's ideas, this time I felt he might be going off track.

The string had beautifully established itself everywhere theoretically. It was sure to reveal the ultimate constant as my colleagues believed. I too could see it making itself comfortable in my papers on particle physics.

According to David, the string could easily simplify the complications of any theory, whether it was relativity or quantum mechanics. The effect of these implications now had started to become visible.

In the next letter, David wrote to me a strange thing.

John, I have had a change of heart, I have started to believe that the string might just be real. However, there is something more interesting that has grabbed my mind. I'm somehow convinced that the string theory is not the key to UFT.

I am convinced even after finding the proof of the string, it will not reveal the ultimate constant. And I had a vision that the ultimate constant lies on the boundaries of the frontiers of science but it's a reflection which reaches far beyond science itself. Therefore, the string, even though able to fuse relativity and quantum, will not yet reveal the UFT.

This letter by David startled me. It was unlikely for him to talk so unconventionally about science. I was more than sure that he was onto something.

He was enthusiastic to tell me that he might have been wrong about the string in M theory and future might just hold the answers regarding the adaptive nature of the string. Even though that was possible, he was more than confident that the string was not the answer for the ultimate constant. His ideas originated from the fact that the ultimate constant was so sophisticated and elegant that even if it was present in the scientific realms of our

CHAPTER 9

understanding, its reflections had to be seen everywhere around us, even in the concepts of life and death.

This, to me, at first sounded philosophical but then as I gradually began to look at other theories and inventions. I realized what he was getting at was in fact, the truth.

Even the ultimate constant had to have a similar background as relativity. Relativity, even though its applications are far too complex when studied in detail, its basic nature is to be seen everywhere around us and the same goes with gravity. Today, everything that we observe, whether it is at rest or in motion, is relative. Even the conversation that we have, philosophy, and everything have relativity in some context or another. David was trying to establish a similar fact by stating that the ultimate constant like relativity was even more delicate and sensitive. Thereby stating that it was everywhere around us.

The only thing left for us to do was to open our eyes and look for it. Unfortunately, as I should say this had been going on for more than a decade.

It might sound simple at first when I'm referring to David's research but it's not. It should be interesting to know that otherwise whatever the ultimate constant David's research was pointing at in its basic form was simple. As it was known by everyone in my circle, under surface complexity lays simplicity.

Later, I asked him why he was trying to shift his interest beyond science intentionally, trying to fully grasp what he was after.

He was quick to reply.

John, I see that you have misunderstood my intentions. My aim is to search for the ultimate constant within the limitations of scientific knowledge and data available to me. All I am saying is that since we have been unsuccessful in that, over and over, it might be that we have missed something. Most people in our field try to rely on everything scientific. I believe, for once, we should look at life, for science has now become part of it.

It was just like I had thought. Even though David was sticking to science, he was just following his unconventional methods. It was something that he had always been famous for. It had been some time since I had seen David but talking to him through the letters I realized that he hadn't changed one bit.

I later told him in my reply that I was just pulling his leg, talking to him about his previous letter. He said that he knew and was just playing along. He thought I had known him too long to think that he would leave science and become a philosopher.

Considering the present scenario, things now had become quite peaceful for him. He was now married and nobody was trying to stalk him.

Jack, after a few days, came to me with a piece of news. He said that he had seen Rudy and Cody a few days ago in the city. I was afraid that they both might be catching on to us. More than me I was worried about Clair. I didn't tell her anything about what Jack had told me. I made sure that the letters David had written to me were in a safe place. I had not told Jack anything about them too.

I told Jack that we were moving out of this place and I gave Clair a hint to start packing at the same time. She gave me a confused look but soon realized that I was serious.

I later wrote to David about my departure from Sacramento not giving him much of a reason. I didn't want him to get conscious. More than that, I knew he was living in harmony, and I didn't want to interrupt his peace.

CHAPTER 9

Both I and Jack arrived back in Pasadena the same week. I updated David as soon as I got there. He was excited to know how everything was going down in the city.

I too was kind of happy to get back to my family and home. Clair was more than happy to see my mom and dad. Jack too was happy to make a few trips back and forth to my place. He had taken a place on rent close to my home.

Soon, she mixed in well with my folks. Clair was mostly engrossed in the house doing some domestic work or another. She enjoyed talking to my mother. In Sacramento, she had become quite used to living by herself, taking care of the house. But now, she was happy to mingle around with my family and to pass time talking about day-to-day things.

I, on the other hand, was back to my letters to David. I gave him some excuse for leaving Sacramento, not telling him the fact about Jack seeing Rudy and Cody there. I then came to the point about the present universal constant and what he thought about it in general.

He replied…

John, there are at present four important constants; c (speed of light), G (constant of gravitation, h (Planck's constant, the constant of action) and e (electric charge). It is now believed that the future of cosmology might reveal a few more, but there exists one ultimate constant. This constant would only be found by intimately combining all the Universal constants as I mentioned. There would be a few others that could be found later in the future. I, though, seldom agree that this combination would possibly point toward the string being the ultimate constant.

As for what I think it would be something more than physical.

I came to understand David's point of view much better now. His ideas for contradicting the present scenario of physics which were persistently supporting M theory to be the UFT seemed genuine. According to him, the string in M theory was important but not as important to become the ultimate constant.

Moreover, he was hell-bent on assuming that the ultimate constant was anything more than a physical quantity; that it was beyond measure. One could not get its pure value, just like the speed of light, gravitation, electric charge and the Planck's constant. We could see their functions and measure them but could not obtain their pure value. The same was true for the ultimate constant as well.

The letter he wrote next was even more profound.

John, as I have progressed, I have come to think that there must exist an ultimate function for such an ultimate constant, just as the universal constants have theirs in the reality. Like I had previously said that the constants are nothing but conserved and preserved proportions (patterns), it would in turn suggest this ultimate constant must be showcasing its ultimate proportion (pattern) into reality as well.

Only its function can reveal its existence. It must also be present in all theories retrospectively, but for now, this function is hidden from us.

This was very exciting. David was signifying that just like we see planets revolving around each other as a function of gravitation, energy fluctuations in bodies as a function of the Planck's constant, special relativity as the function of the speed of light and electricity as a function of electric charge, we must also try to search for a function of ultimate constant.

Just as we could measure their functions but not the universal constants themselves, it simply meant that none of the pure values of the above universal constants could be deduced numerically. It could be the same for the new ultimate constant that would be found in the future. There was also another significant thing David poses, and he says that the ultimate function is also hidden in the

CHAPTER 9

theories of quantum and relativity. This is because the ultimate constant is a central part of UFT and UFT is the culmination of all theories. Therefore, the features of the ultimate constant will also be hidden in quantum and relativity.

Later in the midst of his next letter, he put forward his exceptional view about the so-called theory of string, that it is not the UFT.

John, it is my intention to tell you that the string is not the so-called UFT. I'm now sure of this for I now understand that the UFT is sort of the theory of everything.

My idea stems from the fact that the string, in my opinion, does not pose as the ultimate constant. Although it is an elegant piece of work for the bases of science, it fails to reflect on the much broader scale of reality as the UFT should do.

The following notion is summed up in a saying by Max Planck...

"SCIENCE CANNOT SOLVE THE ULTIMATE MYSTERY OF NATURE. AND THAT IS BECAUSE, IN THE LAST ANALYSIS, WE OURSELVES ARE A PART OF THE MYSTERY THAT WE ARE TRYING TO SOLVE"

David was sure that the M thesis, though very helpful for science, failed to answer the basic conceptions of human understanding that reflected in our life activities. He was clever enough to understand that the ultimate constant was not just the tool for science and theorics but an inevitable necessity for the existence of life.

An idea later appreciated by a lot of theorists was that the ultimate constant was not just confined to time; it defined the nature of time as a whole for the entire universe. Just as relativity was essential for the understanding of the universe, that ultimate constant had the same thing to offer in terms of our lives. It would change our conceptions of life and death to bring us a new picture of science into our horizon. The ideas of Max Planck and other scientists were opposite to those to which David was pointing.

Max Planck was a man of logic. He was profoundly interested in the objectivity of things and therefore the conclusions he drew were of a similar type. For him, UFT was a thought that was impossible. This was because as to his knowledge, logically science was too big for a single theory to comprehend.

Planck gave a famous statement to one of his students when the student asked him whether it was possible to achieve the UFT or not.

To this Planck had replied,

"AS TO YOUR QUESTION ABOUT THE CONNECTIONS BETWEEN THE UNIVERSAL CONSTANTS, IT IS, WITHOUT DOUBT, AN ATTRACTIVE IDEA TO LINK THEM TOGETHER AS CLOSELY AS POSSIBLE BY REDUCING THESE VARIOUS CONSTANTS TO A SINGLE ONE. I, FOR MY PART, HOWEVER, AM DOUBTFUL THAT THIS WILL BE SUCCESSFUL. BUT I MAY BE MISTAKEN."

The answers to David's question were still to come. Yet, he was close to achieving his goal.

In the coming years, he wrote and he wrote. Then in 1984, he found something of great importance.

John, I think I have found a missing link for the UFT. From my study and understanding, I now believe that the string in the M theory will lead to many other theories, those that would essentially be of similar nature to its core string. These theories would then be combined to form one uniform string theory.

However, by my study of the ultimate constant, I believe that this uniform string theory will not lead to the UFT because it would lack the knack for proportionality, as I had told you before in my previous letters. John, I have found that the function of the ultimate constant

CHAPTER 9

has to stand for all of the universes if there exist any other than the one that we are in, for the same reason that it (the ultimate constant) has to be pure. It has to be beyond the realms of human measure. Just like in the case of a fine structure constant, which is a pure value formed by the combination of other universal constants h, c and e.

Also, I have a feeling that it does not stop just there. It will also have something more to offer.

For now, I fail to understand what it would be. To tell you the truth I don't even know what it is. However, I do know it can prove the existence of other universes. Thus, my search for now is shifted to Quantum Interpretation of Many Worlds ever more so powerfully.

David gave a hint of the fine structure constant, its value being a mystery in astrophysics. Its value is a pure number without any dimensions obtained by the combination of universal constants. It is yet to understand why the value of fine structure constant is the way it is.

He was implying that there would be more of such pure values that would be discovered in the future but only one would serve to be the ultimate constant. According to him, the ultimate constant in action has to be a result of something directly and intimately connected to the cosmos, parallel universes or maybe something divine.

Maybe, after all, Einstein was always right. Indeed, *God does not play dice*.

CHAPTER 10

The very next year something unexpected happened; something that I thought never would. My parents died, leaving me and Clair all by ourselves.

1985

David was on a morning walk with Julia.

"Julia, I had been waiting to tell you something important. It is an important aspect of my work also. I wanted to apologize that I have not been spending much time with you," David said, holding her hand.

"It's ok, David. I know, I can see in your eyes that you have been working hard. Just relax," she replied, caressing his face.

"Julia, it is just that I'm in the middle of an important breakthrough in my study and research and its implications can have profound consequences on the way people look at this world," he said, trying to explain to her how and what he was after.

"You don't have to say anything, David," she said, now bringing herself even closer to him. "I know how you have been struggling all your life for this. It is all right and I am always there with you, no matter what," she continued, trying to comfort him.

CHAPTER 10

"You know how it's been with me before I met you. I told you about the attack that happened to me and how I have been driving around since then," he told her letting her fall in his arms.

"I know, you told me," she said softly, thinking something.

"It's only when I felt that there was no one on my trail that I decided to marry you but now…" David stopped walking, thinking about something.

Julia looked up at him and saw that there was an unfamiliar worry on David's face.

"What's wrong, David? You can tell me," she said, now becoming a little nervous.

David found a bench and slowly walked towards it. He sat there quietly, deep in his thoughts, still not looking at Julia.

"What is it, David? Please tell me, you're scaring me now… please," she said quickly coming towards him and making herself comfortable beside him.

"It is just that…" David said, hesitating.

"David."

"They're back, Julia. They're back to complete what they started. Someone tried to kill me yesterday evening as I was on my way back home," he said, looking into her eyes.

"What? What are you talking about? Nobody knows that we're here except your friend John," she said looking more scared than ever before.

"There were gunshots and everything, I just drove and drove till they left my trail and all I was thinking about was you, the moments that I had spent with you," David said, thinking about the whole incident.

There were tears in Julia's eyes, she was really scared now.

"Please, David, we have to do something. This can't be happening to us, these are the best years of our lives," she said, almost breaking into tears.

"I don't know after five years why all this is coming back to me," he said, holding her tightly in his arms, trying to wipe away her tears.

"Does John know anything about this?" she questioned.

"No, not yet, I haven't told him. But I have to, before it's too late," he replied swiftly.

"But what if you get into trouble again?" she said worriedly.

"I won't, I promise. But I have to inform John. He's the only person around whom I can trust."

Julia fell in David's arms trying to feel the warmth of his chest, finding her worry disappearing slowly down there in his strong arms.

Meanwhile, at the same time in Pasadena, a faint sound of a baby girl giggling could be heard around. It's been some time since my folks left for heaven. It was only me, Clair and our daughter now.

Yes, I had become a father of a beautiful princess who filled a space in my life and made me experience the joy and happiness of fatherhood. Clair and I called her Laura. All of us were living

CHAPTER 10

a happy and wonderful life completely unaware that a bullet was about to come rushing through the window.

I was busy reading a newspaper next to my study which seemed silent and Clair was busy cooking something in the kitchen.

"Yes, they had attacked our house!"

I quickly took Laura out of the cradle and looked for cover. An iron cupboard was the nearest and safest place I could find. As soon as I took cover, I saw Clair rushing from the kitchen after hearing the gunshot toward me.

They were still firing, my heart screamed out to Clair before I yelled frantically to her, raising my arms, "Clair, take cover! Hurry!"

To my horror and ache, I was too late. A bullet had gone right through her body. She fell to the ground almost confused from the pain she felt and my voice she heard.

I stood there unable to utter a word, holding Laura tightly in my arms as I saw her looking at us painfully. In a way telling me to save Laura, I saw my love in her eyes.

She was motionless, bullets were flying in and blood was gushing out of her body. I could only curse myself for not being able to reach out to her.

Somehow, I kept Laura under the cover of the cupboard and reached out to Clair, I quickly pulled her under the cover of the cupboard.

She was taking her last breaths. She held my face and whispered, "Take care of her and yourself," she said, struggling for breath and looking simultaneously at me and Laura.

"I love you," I replied, crying and breaking down in tears.

"I love you too," she said before she passed out.

I stayed beside her for I don't know how long before a bullet passed inches away from my right ear. I soon knew I had to do something to get this over with.

I saw a telephone link straight up. It was a couple of meters away from me. I quietly made my way to it, letting Laura lay safely under the cover of the cupboard.

As soon as I reached it, I pulled it, and made an emergency call.

The firing was somehow restrained. I felt a bit relaxed. I paused for a moment and looked at Clair again. The fact that she had gone was still difficult for me to grasp. In a brief moment, I realized that Laura was everything that I had now and I had to take care of her.

I slowly got up making sure that the danger had subsided. I walked towards Laura and picked her up in my arms. I was completely in tears; she was everything that was left for me now.

Soon police officials arrived. They questioned me with their inquiry and assured me that the people behind the attack would be soon avenged. To their question if I had any suspicion on anyone around me, I told them about Rudy and Cody.

Jack came to me as soon as he heard about what had happened. He never asked me much; he knew there was too much pain. He just stood quietly by me, allowing me to speak my heart out. I felt it was pretty much compelling. On the other hand, he felt happy that Laura was unhurt. He saw her and smiled.

CHAPTER 10

I later narrated to him what had actually happened. I told him that I was happy for Laura was still alive but at the same time, I would miss Clair forever.

"Everything will be alright, John. Trust me, time will heal everything," he said, consoling me knowing that the death of Clair had left me heartbroken.

That was the only thing he ever told me. He wasn't so good with people facing depression. Now when I come to think of it, he was the same with Rudolph during the time when he was depressed in Caltech. It was ok. He was doing whatever he could to keep things going.

I knew either Rudy or Cody had something to do with the events that had changed my life forever. I remembered seeing them a few years back, maybe we were always been on a trail but I never noticed. Jack also reminded me of the attack that had happened to both of us. That how the car had tried to kill us.

I felt guilty about how much I had tried to tell Clair about it, but I couldn't. I just loved her too much.

Then a few days later I just realized something....

Maybe if I was attacked, David was not safe either. It was true that I had not told anyone of his location but just that these were grave times. I didn't want to take a chance. So, I decided to write to David about everything that had happened and wanted him to keep on his guard.

I wrote...

David, I am here to inform you with a broken heart that Clair is no more. I was attacked in my apartment. I must also tell you that this wasn't the first time it happened. I tried to protect her with all I had, but I failed.

It is also my concern that you and Julia should take another residence anywhere else where it would be the best for you and her.

I don't want what happened with me to happen with you, David. Therefore I plead, please listen to me. Go away as soon as you can. I know that you are very close in your study to finding the ultimate constant. This study should not go into the wrong hands, whatsoever. For all my life, I have listened to you. For once, please listen to me.

I had not told anyone of David's letters and his location whatsoever. Now, after the attack on Clair, I was disturbed and worried about David. I had a bad feeling about all of this.

Actually, 'the bad' had already happened and 'worse' was about to follow.

Soon David's letter arrived and I had been waiting for his reply since Clair had passed away.

John, although I read your letter, I still can't believe all that you mentioned had been a reality, it's like the worst nightmare ever. I hope you will recover from the loss. I know it's difficult, John, but now you have to take care of Laura. You have to be strong, John.

I'm always with you. Thanks for informing me about the upcoming danger. There was something I wanted to tell you lately. I had been attacked, John, just a few days earlier than it happened with you.

I wish I can make it alive out of this with Julia. I won't lie, I'm scared, but at the same time, I also want to find out who is behind all of this. I promise you, John, whoever it is, he will not make it out of this without getting the punishment he deserves for these dreadful acts.

There are times, John. I know how you feel, if things could have been different. I'm here to tell you all of this has happened for a reason.

I have found something important, a letter written by Einstein in 1945 to his friend and colleague, Ilse Rosenfeld. This letter almost proves what I have been searching for. Einstein

CHAPTER 10

was searching for that pure constant but couldn't find it, however, I still have to work on the details of the subject.

I would soon be sending you this letter. It is written in two parts.

After reading David's reply, I felt mixed emotions. I felt happy that David had found the missing link for his theory. Also, at the same time, I got worried for him as he mentioned the attack that happened to him and Julia. Whatever the consequences of the theory David was working on, for me, his and Julia's life was more important.

Life is lived but once.

I just hope things would just turn out well for both of them.

David, in one previous location almost died. The ripples of those events at Caltech were still seen as most of them at Caltech had assumed him already dead.

About the proof that he had found, I had no clue what he was talking about. I was too much in the trauma of Clair passing away. Later, to identify with his ideas I asked David to explain to me about how and when he would be sending me the next letter.

During all this, Jack had now become a very essential friend and partner to me. Everything that I did, he was sure to accompany me.

A few months later, I arrived at a certain conclusion. I told Jack that I was about to take a teaching job at Caltech once again. This time, however, Jack was not keen on following in my footsteps. He was working on something related to the string and I didn't want to be selfish. So, I did not force him.

Soon, I was back at Caltech, teaching my favorite topics. That was when I met Cody.

It was one afternoon I was making my way to my classes. Suddenly he grabbed me from behind.

"Hey, John. How are you doing, brother?"

I thought he might have left the university, but I guess I was wrong. He was still very much here.

"Cody!" I said with surprise, my face almost cold from the scene I had seen years back when I had seen him with a man with a gun. I also saw him in Sacramento when I was working there. During then even Rudy was there. I bet they both had known about me all this while. "What are you doing here?" my words almost became offensive thinking about the fact that I might be talking to someone who killed my wife.

"Hey, relax, John. I am just a teacher here like you are and just glad to see you around after such a long time," he said, getting scared by the look on my face.

"Whatever, I need to get back to my class. I am getting late," I said. I just didn't feel right talking to him. His words felt deceiving and fake. I was sure he was the one behind all of this, but sadly I had no proof.

Somewhere down I was just a little happy now that I would be able to get back my revenge after all. This was all that I had on my mind.

I told David about this. He replied to me telling me to stay away from him for a while. He had now shifted to another location. It was a new place. I think it was somewhere in London.

CHAPTER 10

He told me that he had been busy lately thinking about the details of *Quantum Interpretation of Many Worlds*.

In his letter then he briefly stated…

John, I think if I try to search for the many worlds (parallel universes), the ultimate constant would inevitably reveal itself as it is the only thing that would give a hint about the other worlds.

The ultimate constant is the only common link between all the worlds (parallel universes). Thus, it is my quest to find it through a paradox.

David meant to say that the many worlds practicality in life could only be discovered by the means of ultimate constant. This was because it was the only common link between all the worlds (universes). Hence, simply put, it had to be common. Therefore, to search for other universes would be a search for the ultimate constant itself.

I, on the other hand, was now keener to read the letter that David had found, the one written by Albert Einstein. He told me he would send it to me in the next letter explaining what he had discovered. David had told me about the letter having two parts and that he would let me know about the second part soon.

Soon his letter arrived. The first part was the key to his research. It was the last letter I received from him.

"With the question of the universal constants, you have broached one of the most interesting questions that may be asked at all. There are two kinds of constants: apparent and real ones. The apparent ones are simply the outcome of the introduction of arbitrary units, but are eliminable. The real [true] ones are genuine numbers which God had to choose arbitrarily, as it were, when He designed to create this world. In my opinion, now is - stated briefly - that constants of the second type do not exist and their apparent existence is caused by the fact that we have not penetrated deeply

enough. I therefore believe that such numbers can only be of a basic type, as for instance π or e."

John, this letter clearly proves my point that the ultimate constant will be one of the pure (real [true]) types, one that would be beyond measure. The one Einstein failed to find and discouragingly stated that they do not exist. It would only comprise numbers and numbers alone.

I was astonished by the evidence.

David was on his way to proving the holy grail of theoretical physics.

CHAPTER 11

12.12.2007, Pasadena, California,

10:45 PM.

Professor heard a movement, a sound outside his room. It was like he was pushed out of his memories.

It was the last letter David sent me. It was supposed to be composed of two parts. Professor remembered.

Professor only had the first letter with him today. The other was in his lockers with the rest of his letters. A locker nobody had a clue about, except a single individual.

Again, he heard the sound. *At this time of the night it is definitely them*, he thought.

Professor had felt that similar stalking feeling today. By now he was quite familiar with it and there was no mistaking it that they had come to retrieve that letter.

Before he could react to the gunshot, he reluctantly touched his belly and soon found that moist feeling engraving him with the last breaths left in him.

They must have known that I have figured it out. They are after the letter…There is no way I can hand it over to them. I need to get this in the right hands.

The Professor quickly grabbed the letter. He looked around trying to search for something to write with.

Laura was disturbed suddenly and woke up from her deep sleep. The sound of the bullet awakened her. She knew that there was something wrong. She looked around for something that would be suitable for a weapon.

She picked up a hard showpiece kept on a showcase in one of the corners of the room and without wasting another moment made her way quietly upstairs. With every step, she was praying for her father's goodwill. Coming close to the corridor, she looked at both ends.

There was nobody there. Finding a clear way she ran to the Professor's study, she knew at this hour he would always be spending his time there. He would often go to sleep reading his papers.

Today, somehow, she knew something was terribly wrong. As she entered the room, she saw the Professor laying there counting his last breaths.

"Dad! NO!" she screamed and ran towards him. Holding him in her arms she saw that the Professor was holding something in his hands.

Soon, she heard some footsteps closing in on her.

"Laura, you must find Alex and give this to him," the Professor said, looking dimly with love at his daughter.

CHAPTER 11

"Dad, please… don't," she said almost whining, her hands were now smeared with Professor's blood.

"You have to hurry, Laura. They're coming," the Professor said heavily as the footsteps were getting closer.

"Dad, but…," she said trying to make her body move.

As the Professor took his last breaths, he forced her to get up.

"Go…" he said before his eyes vanished in the silent darkness.

Laura, for a second, didn't know what to do. Then suddenly an idea came to her. She moved to the pick up the receiver kept on the study. To her disappointment it was dead. Laura could now hear men talking outside the room.

They must be in the corridor, she thought as she was quickly searching for a place to hide. In a short second, she slipped under the corner curtains.

Holding the letter tightly in her palms she saw two men entering the room. They had guns. One of them saw the dead body of the Professor.

"Search him," came the voice of the other one who was standing at the door, it looked like he was guarding him.

"He doesn't have it," said the man in disappointment.

"It looks like a little birdie was able to get to him before us. She might have run away with it. We should inform the boss," said the man standing close to the door, the hint of cold cruelty dripping from his words.

Laura knew she was in a lot of trouble and her only way out of this now was to get out of her own house. She waited with patience for the two men to leave. She tried her best to keep her emotions intact.

Immediately she had a brain wave. There was a ladder on the rooftop that led to the back of the duplex.

As soon as the two men left the room, she simply made her way running through the corridor out to the terrace. She was wearing a dark purple nightgown; she knew it would be hard for anyone to get a hold of her for now if she managed to stay in the dark.

Reaching the top she looked out for that long ladder. Finding it quickly, she stepped down towards the ground. Her feet were moving quicker than ever. There was no way she could let the men who killed her father catch her.

Coming to the ground she realized that the rain had stopped. She quickly glanced at the letter one more time before keeping it safely in the soft pocket of her gown. She looked up at the sky. It seemed clearer for now.

There was a kind of small forest in the back of the duplex. She went through it to find herself coming on a crossing of the main highway. There was a lot of traffic. The cars seemed to move at the speed of light. There was no way she was getting out of here quickly. She cursed herself for not having her cell phone with her.

She knew she couldn't turn back. That was too big a risk for her to take. She looked briefly at the bracelet she was wearing. She thought if she could let anyone give her a lift in the middle of this terrible night.

CHAPTER 11

Just then she saw a car coming towards her. It stopped next to her. The owner came out. Before she could say anything, she walked up to the car.

"Look, miss. I'm in great danger, please help me, I beg of you," she said nervously, almost crying now.

In the darkness, the woman's face was barely visible. As she came closer, Laura couldn't help herself running to her and giving her a smashing hug.

It was Rachel, her best friend.

"Laura, what's happening? What are you doing here at this time of the night?" she asked her comfortingly, seeing that she was in a mess.

"I'll explain everything. Let's just get in your car for now, please," she said, begging her.

Rachel took a good look at her before replying. "All right, get in the car," she said with partial sympathy and partial confusion in her deep voice.

"Thank you," Laura said with a faint smile in desperation. She looked back as she started to drive the car. She was making sure that she was not being followed anymore by anyone.

"So, why are you hiding?" asked Rachel while driving, offering a bottle of water sympathetically.

"Drop me at the nearest railway station. That would be very helpful," Laura said with a little confidence.

"How did you end up in the middle of the road at this time?" Rachel asked again in confusion.

"I was attacked along with my father," Laura said a bit reluctantly.

"Are you kidding me?" Rachel said, suddenly letting the car come to a halt, looking at her. "Are you all right? If you want me to head for the police headquarters, I can take you there," she said trying to comfort her.

"No, that won't be necessary. Just take me to the station, please hurry," Laura replied in stress, occasionally touching her forehead.

"As you say," Rachel said, starting the engine again.

Laura was now numb. She didn't know what had hit her in the last couple of hours. She was heartbroken, her father was the only person she had. Today he died. It was so sudden that she was just trying to convince herself that all of this was a nightmare. Her father died giving a piece of note which she was unable to comprehend.

He had told her to find Alex. That name never came to his mind, not once in the last one year and yet in his dying moments, his will was to find him. She remembered how her father had brought him home one day. She was young and so was he. At first, she felt her dad had brought a brother for her only to find out later that he was delivered to them only for a short while.

After a few months, he left because Professor had found a better place for him. He would visit once in a while every month and she would get to see him only then.

Soon Alex had become a beautiful friend. But one day, he had an argument with the Professor about something and she never got to know what it was. She tried to question the Professor, but he won't tell her.

CHAPTER 11

After a while, Alex stopped coming to their place. She longed to see him but couldn't. Soon years passed and the only time she spoke to him was through phone conversations. For the last couple of years, she moved to New York and city life caught up with her making her conversations with Alex brief and rare. She had to move on in her life. The studies became her priority and then there were new friends who came along.

Time seemed to pass so quickly and now a year had passed since she heard his name. It had been a long time. She never thought Professor was in touch with him anymore. She was hell-bent on finding the answers to her questions from Alex. She thought of looking at the piece of paper – the letter her dad had given her.

She wanted to open it, but now was not the right time. She wanted to be alone to read it with all her composure.

Soon, she arrived at her destination.

Coming out of the car she said, "Thank you, you have been an angel."

"Never mind, take care," Rachel said, offering her some money. "I wish I had more," she said, thinking something with a smile.

"Thank you," Laura said again helplessly, she knew how much she needed the money now.

"Get on the first train you get and flush out of here. I'll try and get some more cash from the ATM," Rachel said, getting out of the car and moving away from her trying to find something.

"I will," Laura replied with confidence again with a faint smile.

Laura was soon looking for a phone trying to talk to Alex. She also needed more money. Rachel knew this, therefore, finding the nearest ATM she took out some cash and came back to her.

"Now explain," Rachel said as she handed the cash into Laura's hands.

In a quick second, Laura explained everything that happened to her to Rachel.

After hearing her story, Rachel wanted to help her as much as she could. She looked at her before replying, "Wait here, I'll be back in a moment."

Laura stood there at the station, trying to figure out where all of this was heading. She thought of Alex and how in all these years he would have changed so much. His face seemed so blurry to her now. So much time had passed since the last time they had spoken together. A collection of all the fights and pranks they have had together passed her disturbing mind.

She soon felt relaxed and a little dizzy by all of it. The sleep that was broken by all the happening was getting back onto her. However, she knew she could not close her eyes, not for one second till she was on the train by herself.

Soon, Rachel arrived. She shook her a little as Laura sat there resiliently.

Laura was startled when Rachel called her from behind. She handed her the tickets and gave her a hug. "Make sure you give me a call when you reach there, right?" Rachel said as she saw her get on the train.

"I will, I promise," Laura replied with a smile to her best friend.

CHAPTER 11

Rachel gave her a flying kiss as the train started to move.

Laura was now off to Los Angeles. That is where Alex was.

He was studying there. The last time she had heard from him was from a common friend called Ben. That night, she didn't have the time to inform Ben about anything that she had been through. She knew he was a friend who could be trusted just like Rachel. Even Alex could count on him.

Then again, she felt it would be better to meet Alex and decide about it. If she was in dilemma or whenever she was in any kind of confusion it was Alex who would come to her aid. She remembered how once Alex had taken all the scolding for her when she had broken a glass. They were very young then. Remembering that incident brought a smile to her face.

Alex was adopted by the Professor and the Professor treated him like a son. For as long as they lived together or when Alex used to come to visit, never did the Professor show any difference in his love for him and her. There were times when the Professor looked worried and out of place. This is when Alex used to cheer him up.

Professor used to sit with Alex, explaining to him the ideas and magnificent theories of great inventors and scientists. Even Alex had a thing for it, now that she looked back and recollected the longstanding conversations between her father and Alex. He used to always question her dad with the most difficult and imaginative curiosities in his little mind then.

Laura was more into law and crime. She had been interning in New York at a private firm. She had studied many crime scenes and cases, but she never thought she would ever end up being part of one.

NUMERICAL ENIGMA

Taking the letter out of her pocket she realized she might be in the middle of some random conspiracy. She suddenly realized she had to look at the contents of the letter.

She quickly opened the letter.

It was sent by someone named David and it had a note written by him along with the letter compressed with it.

The letter was written by Albert Einstein in 1945 to someone named Ilse Rosenthal...

With the question of the universal constants, you have broached one of the most interesting questions that may be asked at all. There are two kinds of constants: apparent and real ones. The apparent ones are simply the outcome of the introduction of arbitrary units, but are eliminable. The real [true] ones are genuine numbers which God had to choose arbitrarily, as it were, when He deigned to create this world. In my opinion now is – stated briefly – that constants of the second type do not exist and their apparent existence is caused by the fact that we have not penetrated deeply enough. I therefore believe that such numbers can only be of a basic type, as for instance π or e." "=D-" "ϕ"

16.259.72.97.2.7.

After looking at the document she turned to the note.

Here it is – this letter is proof of my research, of what I have been looking for. It has another part which I think you received earlier.

I hope you get my hint.

After reading the notes she felt ever more confused.

Then all of a sudden something written in the letter by Einstein caught her eye. It was the "ϕ" and "=D-". Also, there was a series of numbers.

CHAPTER 11

They were not part of the letter. Her father had added them to it. She could immediately recognize the writing. At first, she didn't know what they were. Then it came to her, the Professor during his last moments had left some kind of clue for Alex and her before his death.

Now, she had to find Alex before it was too late.

CHAPTER 12

"Alex, where are you?" a voice startled a young boy who was quietly concentrating on his temperament. It was his coach. "It's time to get into the game, we have to win this and remember, it is your last game for the season. Show me what you've got, son."

Alex got up from the bench that was filled with substitutes.

It was the occasion of the final league match of the season for American football.

"Alex is here," a guy shouted to his fellow mates and suddenly there was a frisk of joy that flowed through his teammates.

"Alex, glad you made it," said one of his teammates, offering him the helmet.

"What's the situation here?" asked Alex, a boy in his early twenties, looking at each of his teammates.

A few cheerleaders were eyeing him from a distance.

"Bob, get your head back in the game," Alex said, finding that Bob's attention was taken a ride by the cheerleaders.

CHAPTER 12

"I think that she has a thing going for you there, Alex," he said with a smile.

"I don't care about that. When you're on the field, I want you all on the field. This is your quarterback. C'mon, do you understand?" Alex said, giving him a cold stare.

In a quick second, he explained to everyone what they needed to do to win the game and everyone returned to the field with a different feeling of enthusiasm.

"Now you're talking, man," said Bob, giving a look to Alex as he took his position with a wide smile on his face.

"All right everyone, ready?" yelled Alex to the formation of his team as he was about to give the final call.

No sooner they got back in the game, it took a turn in their stride unlike the expectations of their opponents. The end was that Alex and his team won the match by three points.

All teammates shook hands with their opponents and later a few of them thanked Alex. After all, he was at the top of his game.

Alex was someone who would perform skills in the field of football as well as science. His notions about ideas in physics had won him a lot of awards in and around his circle of friends and the colleges within the city.

He was quite famous being a bachelor and given his reputation, a lot of girls tried to hit on him. He never paid much heed to anyone, except Alice, a girl he had met in his senior year. Back then he had thought she was unlike any other girl he had ever been with before. It had been more than two years now that they had broken off and she started to date some other guy. It was a guy who played professional football for the Yankees.

The breakup fueled his rage and he was taking out his frustration on the game. Soon he decided he would become the best college football player in the history of Los Angeles. Now there he was, making his way to the top of the list. The thought about Alice still perturbed him, no matter whether he won or not. It was a feeling of despair.

He was having a hard time understanding why Alice left him. He later realized that it was due to his passion for physics. He remembered how he had missed so many of her parties and hangouts because he was busy with one assignment or another. It was beyond him why Alice wouldn't accept this fact about him. Maybe it was hard for her to understand. Alex could never explain this to her anyway.

While spending time with Alice and his studies, he had completely forgotten everything about Professor Gable. He had not spoken to him for a long time. Since his last conversation had happened, he had been fighting with himself to give the Professor a call.

Today he decided he'll do just that.

The game he had just won gave him a lot of accolades, credits and even fans. But there was still this silence inside him that failed to disappear.

He thought he couldn't take it anymore, so he called the Professor. But there was no answer. He felt empty yet again.

"Hey, Alex. Are you all right, man?" said a voice from a distance, it was Bob.

"Yeah, I'm all right," he replied, trying to sound OK.

"Alex, you don't look so good. What is it, man?" said Bob, trying to get him to talk.

CHAPTER 12

Alex was a reserved kind of person. He never spoke much and he felt close to only a few people in his life. The people he felt close to, he could trust them with his eyes closed and his mind shut. He could tell everything and anything to those people.

"I'm all right, Bob. Don't ask me that again," he said, almost getting irritated.

"I was just about to say I think you should give a call to Ben. You guys are like good friends and I'm just saying this 'cause you don't look so good to me," said Bob, trying to be as honest as he could.

Alex gave him a look, trying to read his gestures. *Maybe he was right, maybe I should give him a call. It's been a long time and I do feel like talking to someone*, he thought and made his way back to his apartment, bidding goodbye to Bob.

He came into his house, and the landlady Mrs. Crawford saw him as she was coming out of her apartment.

"Alex, where is my money? Give me my money," she came towards Alex, almost screaming and losing her breath.

"It is not the first of the month," he replied weakly.

"I'm sorry, I forgot. By the way, there was a call for you by someone named Laura, she seemed tense. I think you should call her back," she said trying to feel sorry for asking him for the rent, keeping the same teasing tone she always had.

Laura!

"Did she leave a number to contact her or something?" Alex asked in curiosity.

"No, she didn't," Mrs. Crawford replied in disappointment.

"Before I could ask her, she disconnected the phone but I can tell you this, she sounded desperate," she said again with an easing tone.

It had been years since I last heard from Laura, Alex thought. She had not thought of calling him all this while. All of a sudden, she wanted to see him. There was something terribly wrong. He had a bad feeling creeping up on him for the last few days. He had to find out what was going on.

"Thank you, Mrs. Crawford," he said before entering his room.

He quickly undressed and took a shower. Coming out of that he got dressed again and started to search for his cell phone. His room seemed to be a mess. Though it had always been like this, today he was even more disappointed with his carefree nature.

With great struggle, in the end, he found his cell phone. To his disappointment again it had no battery. After thriving, rushing and randomly throwing his stuff around, he found the battery. He quickly put his phone to the charging point and waited for it to get charged.

In the next few minutes, his patience got the best of him. Taking the cell phone away from the charger he disconnected it. Realizing that so little battery is left and only a few moments before it gets switched off, he made a call to Laura.

Her cell was not responding. After a couple of minutes, he tried again. Still, there was no progress.

"What is going on? Maybe it's just bad luck," he thought to himself before making himself comfortable on his bed.

Then thinking something he decided to make a call to Ben.

CHAPTER 12

He and Ben had been very close friends since childhood. So, he would talk to Ben every time there would be a situation. However, this time it was for a different reason. He wanted to ask him if Laura had tried to contact him.

Within seconds, he was talking to Ben.

"Ben, long time no see, man. How have you been?" Alex said, cheering his voice.

"What is it, Alex? What is the favor you want?" he replied in a flash.

"How do you know that I want something?" Alex said in confirmation.

"I know you for the last five years. You never called me unless there is an emergency of some shot. However, being your best friend, I think I deserve a little more than that. But that's OK, and now, what is it?"

"Yeah, right. You are always right, Ben. As long as you have known me you are always right. All right, listen, have you heard from Laura lately?" he said smiling, feeling a bit relaxed to hear his best friend's voice on the other side after a long time.

"Of course, it was only last Christmas that we spoke."

"Ben, I'm not joking, have you heard from her?" he said seriously.

"Okay seriously, you want seriously. Dude, it's been a year since we both spoke to her. Why are you asking about her all of a sudden?"

"'Cause, she called me and I'm trying to figure out why," Alex said sharply.

"Why don't you give a call to her, you have her number, don't you?" Ben said trying to give him a solution.

"I already did, you moron. But I couldn't reach her, her cell is not responding. That is why I called you to confirm if she had tried to contact you," Alex said, trying to explain.

"All right, I see that you are taking this way too seriously. If she wanted to contact you, then she will. Just relax, sooner or later she will find you," Ben said confidently.

"Maybe you're right, Ben, I should just sleep over it for a while," Alex said, in a relaxed tone.

"I think you are probably right," said Ben, about to hang up.

"I was unnecessarily taking too much tension. Goodnight," Alex said before disconnecting the call.

Alex was trying to sleep but somehow he couldn't. The thought that Laura was somehow trying to get it to him kept disturbing him. Also, it had been quite some time since he had seen the Professor and her.

He bid goodbye to the night, but the Professor kept coming back to him. He thought how rude he had been to him that day and somehow he felt guilty about all of that. He decided that he would let Laura know of his feelings when he would meet her. Probably they both could go to the Professor later.

He had left the Professor's house years back when he found out that the Professor was not his real father as he had told him once. The thoughts startled him and he decided to leave the house swearing he would never come back again.

CHAPTER 12

But another truth was still eating him. No matter what he thought, the Professor would always be his only family. Therefore he knew that no matter what, he had to speak to the Professor somehow really soon. He decided that it would be the first thing he would do the very next morning.

Suddenly, the phone rang.

Before he could move and pick it up it stopped ringing. He looked at the number but couldn't recognize it. When he called back at the same number there was no reply. He thought of it as a wrong number and decided to go to sleep.

As he was about to go to sleep he looked at the locket the Professor had once given him when he was really young. He remembered how jealous Laura had gotten of him because of the locket. He wanted to give it to her but the Professor objected telling him that he should never give it to anyone or let it out of his sight ever.

Yes, that was what he said, Alex remembered the words of the Professor quite clearly. Thinking about Laura and Professor he went deep into sleep.

The next morning, as soon as Alex got ready and was about to move out, there was a knock on the door. They were two men who looked like Federal agents at the door.

"Are you Alex?" said one of them.

"Yes, I believe you have the right man," he said and questioned briefly. "Why?"

"Mr. Alex, I am sadly obliged to tell you that your guardian Professor John Gable has died in an attack last night. His daughter Laura is now nowhere to be found," one of the men standing said, showing his official batch.

Alex stood there numb. He didn't know what to say. He couldn't believe what he heard; all he could muster with significant courage was to ask them, "What?"

"Alex, we want you to inform us as soon as possible if you'd hear from Laura," said one of the agents coming inside, confronting Alex to his bed.

He made himself sit next to him comfortably.

"Look, we will leave you now but here is a number. Please don't hesitate to call us if you feel that you have some important piece of information," the officer said giving him his card and putting his wallet back in his pocket.

Soon, they were gone.

Alex lay there on the bed for a while before he broke down.

He knew now that he would never be able to convey his guilt to the Professor. He felt so sorry about everything that had happened.

Suddenly, he felt the determination growing within him. He made a promise to himself. *No matter what I will find your killers Professor, I will find them. The unknown number, could it be?* Alex remembered the unknown number which had flashed across the screen of his cell phone earlier.

It was Laura…

CHAPTER 13

Alex heard a knock on the other side of the room. It came from the kitchen. Realizing there was no entrance from that side he quickly made his way toward the sound.

It was Laura trying to climb in through the window.

He opened it for her. "What are you doing here? Are you all right?" Alex said, giving her a tight hug as soon as she was comfortably inside. He had been worried about her for quite some time now.

"I'm OK, Alex... I'm OK," she said, responding with a hug.

"What happened?" Alex questioned her softly, knowing whatever it was, it was bad.

Laura quickly explained to him the whole incident about the night that had changed her life. She told him about the letter and the note. Also, about how her friend Rachel who had helped her to get to him.

"That's why your number was not reachable," Alex said, looking at her.

Laura now felt a sense of comfort with Alex. She told him how she had tried to get in touch with him from different locations.

"OK, that explains the unknown number in my cell phone last night," he said taking her to the room.

She asked him what was it that they were going to do next.

Alex was quick to respond by telling her that the federal agents were there and they had told him everything about the murder of the Professor.

"We need to find out who is behind this, Laura. But I can't do it alone," Alex said, looking at her deeply.

"I am with you, Alex," she said in confirmation.

"OK, the first thing we need to do is to get out of here," Alex said, picking his things up. He got a few essential things like his wallet, his cell phone and a lock. He simply moved his eyes around the room making sure that there was nothing left.

Moving out he locked the door.

"Where are we going?" asked Laura nervously. She was worried if they were going against the law and everyone would end up thinking that they are the culprits.

"Nothing will happen. Just trust me," Alex said.

While moving out he gave a call to Ben and explained to him quickly about the whole situation. Then he decided to meet them in an hour at Los Angeles station. Ben's father was a rich man therefore he had a number of resources at his prejudices. Alex told Laura why they needed Ben and explained to her how Ben could play an important role in their search for the truth.

Laura thought it to be a good idea. She too was eager to meet him as it had been a long time since she had met Ben. *It would*

CHAPTER 13

be fun to see him again, she thought, forgetting the gravity of her situation for a moment.

In no time they were making their way to Los Angeles station. After reaching there and waiting for a couple of minutes, Ben arrived.

He looked a little worn out, but he was still happy to see his old friends.

"I'm so happy that you are here to help us, Ben. What would we do without you?" Laura said with a smile.

"No thanks required. After all, that's what friends are for. So, what's the story?" Ben said as all of them made their way to the platform.

"Well, you've already heard mine. I think now you must hear what Laura has to say," Alex said, looking at Laura.

Laura told Ben about everything that had happened to her—how she had escaped from the duplex and her story up until she met Alex. "I was about to call you before, but then I thought meeting Alex was more important. I mean, that was dad's last wish," she said, looking at Alex.

Ben looked at Alex. "So, in fact, it all sums up to this little piece of note," Ben said taking a look at the letter in Laura's hands.

"I guess it does…" Alex said looking at it too.

"One more thing, why didn't you inform the authorities in the first place?" Ben inquisitively asked.

"Well, I don't know. I just did what came to my mind first, I was in a completely different state back then. I hope you guys understand," she said worriedly looking at Alex and Ben both at the same time.

"Yes, of course…. Of course," Ben said holding her hand trying to comfort her.

"It's just that all of this was so sudden. Besides we don't know who is behind this, if he is a man of power or not," Laura said trying to evaluate things.

"Seems you're right," Ben said.

"It is only men with power that would have access to such information like what your father had, which is in this case in this letter," he continued.

"But what is in this letter?" asked Laura, now almost confused.

"Well, I say let's take a look," Alex said.

He opened the letter…

"With the question of the universal constants, you have broached one of the most interesting questions that may be asked at all. There are two kinds of constants: apparent and real ones. The apparent ones are simply the outcome of the introduction of arbitrary units, but are eliminable. The real [true] ones are genuine numbers which God had to choose arbitrarily, as it were, when He deigned to create this world. In my opinion now is – stated briefly – that constants of the second type do not exist and their apparent existence is caused by the fact that we have not penetrated deeply enough. I therefore believe that such numbers can only be of a basic type, as for instance π or e." "=D~" "ϕ"

$$16.259.72.97.2.7.$$

And went through the note…,

CHAPTER 13

"Here it is, this is proof of my research. It has another part of which I think you received earlier.

I hope you get my hint."

"Well, this seems like one of your father's colleagues," pointed out Ben moving his finger to the sender's address. That was where the name was—David.

"I think we should start with trying to understand what this letter says," Alex said.

"So, what does it say?" asked Laura with curiosity.

"It seems that some of the greatest theories of science and physics have some fundamental constants," Alex said, trying to explain.

"And what are these constants?" asked Ben in between.

"To start with simple ones like gravitation and speed of light, however, it is important to note that gravitation is a bit different."

"How different exactly?" asked Laura, looking at Alex.

"Instead of gravitation on Earth it represents gravitation in the cosmos," Alex said trying to explain things to both Laura and Ben.

"So how many such fundamental constants exist?" Ben started to question.

"As of now, there are about five, the constant of gravitation, speed of light, the Planck's constant, electric charge, and magnetic and electric constant. Previously they were even fewer."

"You mean to say previously there were fewer constants," said Ben, trying to understand what Alex was getting at.

"Yes, see, there was the speed of light, the Planck's constant, electric charge and the constant of gravitation. But all this doesn't matter."

"Why do you say that?" asked Laura.

"It is because they're not pure," Alex said, again trying to explain.

"What is your point?" asked Laura impatiently again.

"The point is that the ultimate benchmark of physics which is known as the UFT has only one ultimate constant."

"But why only one?" asked Laura.

"It is because this one ultimate constant would be able to describe all forces of nature. All those we know presently."

"So, you are saying that this letter is a clue toward that ultimate constant," Ben said, raising his eyebrows.

"Yes, it seems so," Alex replied with a smile.

"Go on. What else do you see in this letter?" Laura said, returning Alex's attention to the letter.

"It also states that whatever this ultimate constant is, it would be beyond measure."

"Beyond measure? What do you mean by that?" Ben asked again.

"It simply means that it would have to be pure without any dimensions," Alex said, forcefully.

"Please, I am lost here," Laura said.

CHAPTER 13

"Everything that can be measured has a dimension in length, mass or time. According to this letter, the ultimate constant will have none. It will be pure," Alex said, slowly trying to make her understand.

"So, you mean to say it'll just be a number."

"Exactly," Alex said with enthusiasm.

"So, how do we know what this number is?" Ben said.

"There has to be some clue. Wait a minute, take a look at the note," pointed out Ben.

Here it is, this is proof of my research. It has another part which I think you received earlier.

I hope you get my hint.

"It says that this guy David, whoever he was, was working on a research paper on a particular theory to find the ultimate constant," Alex said, smiling.

"If we find him, we might find that ultimate constant," he continued giving Ben and Laura a smile.

"Well then, where do you suggest we begin?" Laura asked.

"If this guy David was a colleague of the Professor, we must go back with him a long way," Alex said.

"We need to get to Caltech to know his identity," Laura said.

"Bang on!!" Alex said.

"We need to move fast if the man who killed the Professor is behind this ultimate constant just as we are. We need to commute faster, let's take my car," Ben said.

Soon they were moving out of the station and back to Ben's car.

"Hang around, there is no way we can get to this information now. Besides, we don't want anyone to know we're up to something," Alex said, trying to be careful.

"Caltech opens tomorrow morning, I would go and fetch the records as soon as possible," Laura said.

"No, wait. Not you, you are being tracked. I'll go. Ben, you stay with Laura. I think that would be the best thing to do," Alex said looking at Ben.

"I think Alex is right, Laura. Let him go, we don't want any risk," Ben said.

"Where are we going to stay tonight?" Laura said.

"At my place, of course, that is, if you don't mind," exclaimed Ben, giving her a smile.

"No, I don't thank you," Laura said, smiling back at him.

"Alex, now that you have left the college hostel the agents might feel suspicious of you and would try to get a hold of you. You will have to maintain a low profile since we don't know how much power the person who is behind these events has. The law might just be in his hands. We never know," Ben said, trying to explain to Alex the gravity of the situation.

CHAPTER 13

"Ben is right, Alex. We have to be together and reasonable while we do this and right now a lot of lives are in trouble," Laura said with a little bit of worry in her voice.

"There is something else that is bothering me," Alex said.

"What is it?" asked Ben and Laura together.

"Why did Professor choose *me* to read this letter?" Alex asked, looking at Ben and Laura.

"Well, of course, you guys were close and you are the only one who can understand physics very well," Ben said, beginning to come to a conclusion.

"I don't know. I don't think that's enough, there has to be something more," Alex said, thinking something deeply and looking at the letter.

Suddenly Laura realized something. "Yes, there is something more," she said in excitement.

Alex immediately looked at her. "What is it?" he asked Laura.

"You see these symbols next to π," Laura said, pointing towards the letter...,

"With the question of the universal constants, you have broached one of the most interesting questions that may be asked at all. There are two kinds of constants: apparent and real ones. The apparent ones are simply the outcome of the introduction of arbitrary units, but are eliminable. The real [true] ones are genuine numbers which God had to choose arbitrarily, as it were, when He deigned to create this world. In my opinion now is – stated briefly – that constants of the second type do not exist and their apparent existence is caused by the fact that we have not penetrated deeply enough. I therefore believe that such numbers can only be of a basic type, as for instance π or e." "=D-" "φ"

16.259.72.97.2.7.

"They were never included in the letter, the Professor has written them. I recognized them by his handwriting," she said enthusiastically showing Alex the two symbols…

"φ" and "=D-"…

"Yes, of course, how could I have missed them and the series of numbers, they have to be some kind of a clue leading to something," Alex said, feeling hyper.

As soon as he looked up to share his excitement, he saw Laura and Ben's eyes were frozen over something hanging from his neck.

It was the same locket that the Professor had given him when he was young.

Between the golden strings hung a φ shaped diamond.

CHAPTER 14

"What is that?" Ben and Laura said astoundingly.

Both of them looked at the locket with grace and humility anticipating what in the world it really meant, as nothing was making any sense to them. But that is how it was always supposed to be. The Professor was smart.

Alex thought of it as an object that he was meant to keep to himself. All this time he had it with him and he didn't know what to make of that, keeping it with a sense of achievement. *You always made me think that I was special until the moment I discovered that I was just an adopted child.*

Both Laura and Ben tried to make the best possible sense of what the locket was meant to do. Could it be opened? Or was it just a lucky charm?

Alex couldn't think of the locket as anything interesting until he saw a small gap within the diamonds. At last, he thought it was best for him to keep his mouth shut for the time being and return to the present issue.

"It is important to first find out who this David is. He was the one who had been writing to the Professor all this time," said Alex.

He was in a way trying to deviate the situation by shifting Laura's and Ben's attention from the locket.

Both of them understood quickly that there was not much time left to get things moving.

"What is the plan of action?" Laura said, simultaneously looking at Alex and Ben.

"I think the best thing for me to do will be to go to Caltech the next morning. I think that is the best place for me to find out more about this guy David," Alex said, looking at them, thinking something deeply.

"Are you sure you want to go alone?" Laura said.

"I'm cool by myself. If you tag along, it will be trouble for both you and me. Don't forget, people can get suspicious, so we need to be careful," Alex said, trying to reason why he alone could go to Caltech.

The next morning, Alex was quickly making his way to Caltech. *Why was the Professor dead? Who was David?* These questions were hunting him inside and out.

As soon as he reached Caltech he stood there for a moment, absorbing the atmosphere of the place. He looked out for someone to inquire about the students of Caltech. One of the men walking around guided him into the office where one could get the information.

Alex quickly made his way toward the direction the man pointed. It was the office where the records of Caltech alumni including the professor were kept.

CHAPTER 14

He took a deep breath before asking the woman who seemed busy typing something on a computer.

"Excuse me, I'm looking for a small piece of information regarding a student in the batch of 1964," he said, trying to remember precisely which year the Professor was there in Caltech.

"Well, if it's not too much trouble, may I ask what is this regarding?" she replied looking straight back at him.

"It's for a close friend. His father expired recently and has left something of grave importance to an old friend. The friend was a research student here in Caltech," Alex said, quickly making an excuse.

"I'm sorry, it is against the rule to give any information to a stranger without the permission of the principal. However, if you want to get the information, try to get a letter from the faculty or an official letter from the principal," said the lady, now looking back at her computer.

Alex moved away disappointingly. There was not much he could do.

Walking a few meters away Alex made himself comfortable on a sofa. The lady at the desk kept staring at Alex for some time and then turned back to her work.

A few moments later, an old man sweeping the floor said something to him. It took Alex a moment to notice him before he heard his voice.

"What was the name of your friend's father who expired?" asked the old man, now coming closer and looking at Alex humbly.

"His father's name was Professor John Gable," Alex replied softly.

"Of course, I remember him, he was in the first year then," he said, looking at Alex.

"Do you know anything about this guy named David?" Alex asked him curiously.

"Of course, he was his best friend but..." he paused thinking something deeply.

"What happened?" Alex asked curiously.

"He was the student who died in 1971 by an earthquake that hit Caltech that year. He was working on a theory, something called Many Worlds, if I'm not wrong and yes, a few years later there was another guy named Jason Clement who got shot," said the old man, trying to recollect memories of those years that had passed him by. "Now if you must excuse me, I should go back to my work," he said, returning to sweeping the floor with his broom.

Alex stayed there for a few moments trying to grasp exactly what the old man had just told him. Then something occurred to him.

Getting out of Caltech, Alex rushed back to Ben and Laura as soon as possible. They were surprised to see Alex in such a hurry.

"Where is the letter?" Alex said hurriedly, barely holding his excitement.

They gave Alex the letter quickly, trying to understand why Alex was so tense and what was he trying to understand by looking at the letter.

"This can't be... How is it possible?" Alex said to himself and then turned to Laura and Ben.

CHAPTER 14

"What is it? Can you tell me why you are acting so crazy, Alex?" Ben said, not able to control his excitement.

"It is the date on the letter, can't you see?" Alex said in a high pitch, his voice box barely able to contain his normal tone.

"Yes, I can see that it's 1975. What's wrong with that?" Ben said, looking at Alex in confusion.

"When I went to Caltech they told me that David died in 1971 in an earthquake that hit Caltech that year," Alex said, looking straight back at Ben and Laura.

"But if he was dead in 1971 how can he write this letter?" Laura said looking back at Alex with confusion.

"That means, he never died in 1971 and the letter is proof of his life."

"You're missing another point," Laura said looking at the letter and Alex, her face turning a little serious now.

"What is it?" Alex questioned her. Ben too came closer to hear what she had to say.

"If David was truly alive in the year 1975 then what happened with dad and this letter is proof of the fact that somebody has been trying to get his hands on him and my father for a long time, almost since the time David disappeared from Caltech."

"You mean, from the year 1971. If that is true then this has been going on for a really long time and we are in a mess."

"I'm afraid you're right. We are in mess and for that matter, a big one. But that is not the question, the question is what do we have to do next. Where will we find our next clue?" Ben said, trying to argue.

Alex was himself very confused and his thoughts were going random and then an idea hit him.

"One minute, pass me that letter. I need to see something," Alex said taking the letter back from Laura's hands, trying to look for something and looking at all the sides.

"Here it is. This is what I've been searching for," he said, showing Laura and Ben the name of the city that was written in small capital letters at the left corner of the back page of the letter.

Newbury House

10-13 Newbury Street London EC1A 7HU

BLOCK **1-9-4** HOUSE **8**

BEHIND BLOCK **1-9-7** HOUSE **7**

"So, this is what you've been searching for," Ben said looking at Alex with a smile.

"Yes, this is where we are going now and maybe we can find something more about David when we reach there."

Soon after they reached London within a couple of hours by flight. The flight was on time and so they reached their destination quickly.

Unfortunately, time was against them. Therefore, without wasting a single moment all of them reached the address written in the letter.

CHAPTER 14

It was improbable to find anyone awake this late at night. As the taxi came closer to the address, they realized it was an old London building, fairly heightened and the apartment from the ground looked beautiful. They stared at it, unperturbed by the cold wind which was blowing on their faces.

Getting out of the taxi they stood there looking at the building for a moment.

Ben knew they had no time. They made their way to the apartment in the building.

Opening the door slightly, an old lady looked at them densely. It was unlikely for someone living there to see new unknown faces at this hour at the doorstep.

"What do you want?" asked the old lady with a sense of horror in her voice.

"I'm sorry to disturb you, Mrs. McAdams, but it is really important for us to talk to you. It will take just a couple of minutes," Alex said mildly.

"My husband is not here. I'm sorry," said Mrs. Mc Adams, trying to resist.

"It's alright, Mrs. McAdams. We can talk with you. We are friends of Professor John. It won't take long, just a few questions and we'll be gone in no time," Alex said looking at the lady with desperation in his eyes.

"Then it's OK, if it is just for a couple of minutes," said Mrs. Mc Adams, pausing for a moment before opening the door for them to come in.

All three of them came inside and they made themselves comfortable in her living room. It was not late that Alex spoke.

"Mrs. Mc Adams, we're here to know about one of the tenants back in the year 1975. His name was David."

"What do you want to know about him? To be honest, it was quite a long time back and I don't know if I can really remember…" she said looking at their faces.

"Mrs. Mc Adams, tell us anything that you know. Anything that you can remember. Do you remember David's last name? If you could tell us even a little, we would be very grateful," Alex said humbly, looking at the old lady.

"Well, if I remember correctly, back then he was married to a girl called Julia. They were so happy until that day…" Mrs. Mc Adams started to speak.

"What day?" all three of them said at the same time.

"It was in the year 1985, the day I heard some gunshots. That was the day that David and Julia were murdered," she said, looking at the kids. Then turning away, her voice became a bit cynic and low.

"Murdered?" exclaimed all three of them.

"Yes, I think he was working on some scientific paper. It was very important and there were people who wanted to get their hands on his work," she said trying to recollect her memory.

"Do you have any idea who these people can be Mrs. Mc Adams? Any idea at all?" asked Alex, becoming a little proactive.

CHAPTER 14

"I'm sorry, child. I have no idea who these people were but they definitely knew him. How else could they know anything about his work?" said Mrs. Mc Adams, reasoning.

"She is right," Ben said, looking at Alex and Laura.

"Can you tell us anything more, Mrs. Mc Adams? Anything that comes to your mind, maybe something important that David told you before he died?"

"Wait a minute, he did pass on something to me to give to his old friend John. Do any of you know John? This was a really long time back so I forgot all about it. But thanks to you children that you came and reminded me," she said with a smile.

"Yes, Mrs. Mc Adams. John Gable was my father. David and he were best friends," Laura said, coming forward in desperation, looking at her.

"Were they? Then I must give you what David gave to me," she said, walking away from them.

"Mrs. Mc Adams," Alex tried to stop her.

"Please wait here. I'll be back in no time," she said as she made her way into another room.

Alex, Ben and Laura looked at each other with excitement. They couldn't wait to see what David had passed on to Mrs. Mc Adams. Maybe it was a clue to help them find whoever was behind these hideous crimes.

Soon, she returned with what looked like a key, a really old one for that matter. She walked up to Laura and gave it to her.

"Here it is, it's the key for locker number 438 placed in a bank close to this place. Here's the address," she said, handing over a piece of paper that had the address on it to Laura.

"I'm afraid that's all I can do for you, children," she said with a smile.

"Oh no, Mrs. Mc Adams. You have been really helpful all this time and on the behalf of all three of us I thank you from the core of my heart," Laura spoke.

All three of them made their way out of the apartment giving Mrs. Mc Adams a hug and promising to see her again soon.

"All right, there really is no doubt these events go back a long way. Also, it goes without question that the bank will be closed and we should check out the locker first thing in the morning tomorrow," Ben said, looking at Alex and Laura.

"Yes, I think you're right. But we need a place to say for the night," Alex said, looking at Laura.

"Well, I can spend a couple of dimes. I think there is a place close by, hopefully, a hotel. Maybe we can check in and stay for the night and tomorrow morning we can leave for the bank," Ben said, looking at Laura with a smile.

"I wish I was as good as you Ben," Alex said, giving him a friendly grin.

The next thing they knew they were in the hotel room. It was quite a cold night and they were really tired.

However, none of them could rest as all were thinking about the locker and its contents. Of late Alex got tired and thought he

CHAPTER 14

should give Laura a visit. *Maybe she isn't sleeping either*, he thought and made it to her room.

He was right. Even in the middle of the night, Laura was wide awake. She opened the door with a faint smile.

Alex asked Laura if she wanted to go and check out if even Ben was awake or not. Laura was kind of cursing herself for not letting him know that she was worried. Sometimes she just thought of keeping things to herself.

Looking at how cold Laura was feeling, Alex offered her his jacket. "This will keep you warm for some time at least," he said, rolling it over her shoulders as they walked towards Ben's room.

As they thought, even Ben was not sleeping.

All three of them stayed there, trying to discuss the possibilities of the near future.

"Mrs. Mc Adams said that whoever attacked David and his wife knew him. That means whoever is behind us would do anything to get his hands on this key," Alex said, showing the key to Ben and looking at Laura.

"You're right and he would stop at nothing before he gets his hands on us, we have to be really careful," Ben said, trying to make things a little bit serious.

"But this also means that whoever killed David is the same person who killed my father," Laura said, almost raising her voice unintentionally with rage.

"Calm down, Laura. We know that they knew David and Professor very well and knew what was David up to, just like Mrs. Mc Adams said. So, we have a lead here," Alex said with determination.

"And I have a way to find out who that person is. I might know someone who knows what's going on with us and can help us find who the culprit is," replied Laura with an idea striking her mind just at the right time.

"What? Who?" Alex and Ben asked at the same time.

"Uncle Jack," Laura said with a smile.

CHAPTER 15

The next thing they knew, they were rushing on their way to the bank and locker 438, in the early morning.

On the way, Laura called Uncle Jack but was unable to get through for some reason. *Maybe he was in some kind of a meeting*, she thought and decided to call later.

"What's wrong, Laura?" Alex asked.

"Nothing. It's just that I am unable to get to him, he seems to be busy in some kind of a meeting or maybe his cell phone is out of coverage. It doesn't matter, I'll try again later," Laura said disappointingly.

"It's OK. We can call him later. Let us first focus to get the contents of the locker," Alex said swiftly, looking at her.

Soon, they were at the bank where the locker rested. There was a guy standing at the reception that came over to them.

"Yes, may I help you?" the man said softly.

"Yes, we are looking for locker number 438. Can you take us there?" Alex said, coming closer to him.

"Here, this way," said the man, telling them to follow him.

He left them on the destination and parted ways saying, "I would leave you to it, sir."

All three of them stood there before Alex stepped his foot forward to open the locker. As he was unlocking the locker, Laura and Ben looked at each other in anticipation of what could be inside it.

Alex opened the locker. There, it was staring at him, a black diary.

He quickly took it out and simply made his way out of the bank looking at Ben and Laura closely.

As soon as they were out Ben and Laura asked him swiftly, "What is that? Show us," they said in excitement.

Alex took out the diary and showed it to them.

"This must have been David's. We should open it, it might contain something valuable about the constants that the Professor was trying to tell us," Alex said, opening the diary and going through its pages.

At a certain point, Alex came to a stop, there was an article written by Albert Einstein in the year 1926.

It had a similar symbol marked on it: "ϕ"

<u>In the Thirteenth Edition (1926) a wholly new topic, "Space-Time," was discussed by the person most qualified in the entire world to do so, Albert Einstein. The article is challenging but rewarding.</u>

"I experience the moment "now," or, expressed more accurately, the present sense-experience (Sinnen-Erlebnis) combined with the recollection of (earlier) sense-experiences. That is why the sense-experiences seem to form a series,

CHAPTER 15

namely the time-series indicated by "earlier" and "later." The experience-series is thought of as a one-dimensional continuum. Experience-series can repeat themselves and can then be recognized. They can also be repeated inexactly, wherein some events are replaced by others without the character of the repetition becoming lost for us. In this way we form the time-concept as a one-dimensional frame which can be filled in by experiences in various ways. <u>The same series of experiences answer to the same subjective time-intervals."</u>

"I see now what the Professor is trying to tell us and I think I know why the Professor wrote those symbols in the letter," Alex said, glancing below. "It was to define the nature of the constants. The symbol is the representation of proportion (pattern) like a divine proportion," Alex said, looking at Laura and Ben. "I think what the Professor is really trying to tell us was that all the constants have this simple proportion (pattern) and so must the ultimate constant."

"What do you mean?" Laura said.

"What I'm trying to tell you is that all constants are nothing but proportions," Alex said, looking at Laura and Ben, trying hard to make them understand what he was getting to. "The divine proportion symbolizes that any quantity divided by three-quarters of its whole part would give this divine proportion," he said, clarifying his point.

"So, what is this divine proportion anyway?" Ben said.

"It is 1.618. It is found to be common in all aspects of nature. I'm surprised that you both don't know anything about this," Alex said, looking at Ben and Laura.

"So, it is a pure number?" Laura said looking at Alex.

"Yes, it is. But it is not the ultimate constant because it is not a force and does not describe the unification of the other forces of nature. Like I told you, only the ultimate constant would be able to define all the forces of nature."

"So, you mean to say it will be able to place all the forces of nature that you know presently on a common platform," Ben said confidently.

"Exactly, there has to be a common link between all the constants of nature to lead us to that ultimate constant," Alex said, looking at Laura trying to explain to her what he said a few moments ago.

"So, you mean it's more than just mathematics and numbers here," Ben said with a smile.

"Yes, it's physics, it has to be a force," Alex said, smiling back at Ben.

"You know, if David has found this ultimate constant like you think he has, then this quest is bigger than anything that I ever expected," Ben said, looking at Alex excitedly.

"You're right, Ben. We need to get to the bottom of all this, this could change the way we look at our lives. This guy David was a genius," he said, looking at Laura.

She too had now started to get the feel of all that was happening around her. The back of her mind was still strongly clutching on to the sorrow of the Professor's unexpected death.

"However, the complete essence of the letter is incomplete without the understanding of the second symbol and we are yet to grasp the meaning of that one," Alex said in disappointment.

CHAPTER 15

"That's alright, Alex. We can get to it later. Let us concentrate on the present issue first," Ben said, looking at Alex.

"So, what do you think this common link can be?" asked Ben.

"That's what we have to find out. But to find that common link between all the forces we'll have to find the ultimate constant," Alex said confidently to Ben.

"So, you mean to say that this guy David knew what that common link was between all the forces of nature known to us," asked Laura, trying to understand the conversation between Alex and Ben.

"To know the ultimate constant, you would have to know the common link between all the forces of nature. So, if he knew about the ultimate constant then he knew about this common link between the forces of nature as well," Alex said, looking back at Laura.

"Check this out," Laura said, looking into the pages of the diary and suddenly interrupting the conversation between Alex and Ben.

"It says here that David had written letters to the Professor from the year 1975 to 1984," Laura said simultaneously looking at the letter and Alex.

"Maybe he was trying to tell the Professor about the ultimate constant and that link between the forces of nature. We need to get our hands on those letters as soon as possible before anybody else does," Alex said looking at Laura and Ben.

"So, these clues might just lead us to the location of those letters," Ben said, feeling quite a bit excited from the way things were unraveling.

"Yes, that might be true. Whatever it is we have to get to the letters before anybody else does," Alex said in determination.

"What if you're wrong? What if David didn't know about the ultimate constant?" replied Laura worriedly.

"If he didn't, then the Professor did and something tells me both he and the Professor were trying to figure out the ultimate constant and in the process of doing so there was someone who was trying to take credit for the discovery," Alex said, trying to reason with her.

"So, that is the reason the same person is behind us now and the Professor might have seen it coming. That is why he gave you the letter, Laura, and told you to find Alex," Ben said, looking at Laura.

"I think you're right. More so I was the only one who knew about your location, Alex," Laura said, looking at Alex.

"That explains it. The Professor then wants you to get to that constant and I'm just glad I'm here to help," Ben said with a smile.

"Laura, do you have any idea where the Professor could have been keeping those letters that David was writing to him?" asked Alex yet again.

"No, I have none. When it came to work, dad was always confined within himself and he never told me anything about David," Laura said disappointingly.

"And you have any idea where he used to keep his belongings? He might have some kind of safe or something within the house, haven't he?" Alex said, questioning her humbly. He knew she was still disturbed by the Professors' death.

CHAPTER 15

"I think he has one within the library. But I don't know the combination of the lock," she said in disappointment.

"When was the last time the Professor opened the safe in front of you?" asked Alex, trying hard to make her remember anything about the safe.

"It doesn't matter, it was a really long time back," she said, shaking her head disapprovingly and trying to clash with his judgment.

"Laura, you have to think. 'Cause, it doesn't matter how long ago it was. The Professor couldn't have changed the code, there is still a chance," Alex said a little forcefully.

"Wait, it's a four-digit combination. I think it was one…" Laura said, trying hard to recollect the code.

Alex then stood there for a couple of moments waiting for Laura to remember the next few digits. Unfortunately, she couldn't.

"I don't remember… I'm sorry," she said, looking at Ben and Alex.

"Let it be, Alex. What else can we do? We have to think of other options," Ben said, looking at Laura sympathetically. "What else do you know about the divine proportion? Maybe the next clue is hidden somewhere in the number itself," Ben continued, this time looking to Alex.

"I don't think so, Ben. There is not much to be said about the divine proportion and its values that appear is in mathematics. There is no explanation for it," Alex said, trying to explain to Ben that there has to be something more.

"How did you come to the conclusion between the relation of divine proportion and the constants in the first place?" asked Ben.

"I thought I had already told you, didn't I?" Alex asked confusingly.

"No, you didn't. Now, would you please explain how you knew that the Professor was trying to link the divine proportion to the constants?" Ben asked again.

"I need the diary, where is it?" Alex said, looking for the diary which was with Laura.

"Here it is," she said, handing it over to Alex.

Alex quickly flipped through the pages to find the article by Albert Einstein that he had seen earlier in the diary.

Finding it, he looked at Ben and told him to come closer.

"You see, this article talks about time as 'experiences'. I don't know much or what to make of it. But it sure makes a point about proportions," he said to Ben and Laura.

"You see, this article was written by Albert Einstein in 1926. It has the same symbol and the article is trying to say the same thing as the Professor was trying to explain to us through the symbol of divine proportion (pattern). This article talks about time as a series of experiences. Note that the last line of the paragraph is underlined," Alex said, showing them the article and the last line of the paragraph that was underlined.

Ben looked at it closely.

<u>In the Thirteenth Edition (1926) a wholly new topic, "Space-Time," was discussed by the person most qualified in the entire world to do so, Albert Einstein. The article is challenging but rewarding.</u>

I experience the moment "now," or, expressed more accurately, the present sense-experience (Sinnen-Erlebnis) combined with the recollection of (earlier)

CHAPTER 15

sense-experiences. That is why the sense-experiences seem to form a series, namely the time-series indicated by "earlier" and "later." The experience-series is thought of as a one-dimensional continuum. Experience-series can repeat themselves and can then be recognized. They can also be repeated inexactly, wherein some events are replaced by others without the character of the repetition becoming lost for us. In this way we form the time-concept as a one-dimensional frame which can be filled in by experiences in various ways. <u>The same series of experiences answer to the same subjective time-intervals.</u>

"Yes, I can see that," Ben said.

"It is trying to say the same thing, things can only be predicted when they are in proportion or to say has a pattern – like a series with the same subjective time-intervals," Alex said, looking at Ben.

"So, if all constants are proportions, then what you're trying to say is that, these constants which we know of presently are predictable," said Ben, a little confused by what Alex was getting at.

"No, not to everything we do in our daily lives but in science only as they help in predicting certain notions of the fields they represent like in relativity, quantum or electromagnetism. However, in the case of ultimate constant this, may differ," Alex said, trying to explain to Ben.

"What do you mean?" questioned Ben.

"The ultimate constant is a reflection of all reality. If it is found it may as well change our beliefs in the way this reality functions, by providing us with important insights about how this universe works. This is one of the major reasons people have been trying to find the Unified Field Theory because it may lead us to the ultimate constant," he said trying to make the picture clear to Ben.

"Alex, you really think that this is possible?" Ben said, looking at him.

"I don't know, Ben. But if it wasn't, we won't have found ourselves in this mess in the first place," Alex said, looking back at him.

"So, what do we know from this?" Ben said, simultaneously looking at the letter and Alex.

"Well, to be honest, we don't know much 'cause this article is just a part of the special theory of relativity," Alex said confusingly. "It may be referring us to learn something more about the special theory of relativity," he said, thinking something deeply.

"We have to be precise about this, Alex. We can't afford to waste time," Ben said, trying to remind him of the situation.

"I know that we're running out of time. But there's nothing that I can do any more than this," Alex said, looking at Ben helplessly.

"What are you talking about, Alex? We can't give up now. We have just started to make sense out of all this," Ben said, trying to encourage him.

"Wait a minute, it says continued on page 41," Laura said, looking at the page the article was written.

"What? What are you talking about?" Alex asked, looking at Laura, who in turn was now looking at the article carefully.

"Didn't you follow the mark? You're supposed to continue to page 41," she said, aggressively looking at Alex.

"What mark? What are you talking about?" Alex asked, walking towards her.

CHAPTER 15

"This mark," she said, showing Alex the page of the diary.

Ben and Alex came forward to look at what Laura was pointing at.

She was right. In his hurry to understand the contents of the article, Alex had forgotten the mark that was written at the lower right corner of the page.

It was telling them to continue to page 41 of the diary.

They soon fled to page 41 and found that E=mc² was underlined with a "ϕ" over it.

There was something written next to it.

Draw number two, article eight Page 96… A.E desk

As Alex understood the gravity of the message, he was shocked.

Laura and Ben asked him what was wrong and he told them what he had in his mind. "We need to see page 96 of that file kept in that drawer," Alex said, looking at Ben and Laura and telling them they're on the right track.

"But I don't understand. A.E desk? What's the meaning of this?" asked Ben, looking at him trying to understand why Alex was so shocked.

"The file is kept in the drawer of that desk. The equation E= mc² under the mark "ϕ" was created by Albert Einstein. A.E is Albert Einstein," he said looking at Ben and Laura, still in a state of shock.

"You mean we have to…" Ben and Laura asked at the same time.

"Yes, we need to break into the residence of Albert Einstein."

CHAPTER 16

Laura and Ben looked at each other in amazement. It was unlikely that the events would lead up to something so deep and confidential.

By the time they checked out from the hotel while speculating and discussing the article in the diary, it was already late evening. So, without wasting another moment they got a taxi and left for the airport, making their way to Princeton, New Jersey.

Laura looked at Alex occasionally to find him lost in thoughts. "Alex, while talking about the proportionality of the constants you said that the proportion reveals a pattern in nature. Does this mean that the patterns have something to do with the file kept in the desk?" asked Laura, thinking something swiftly.

"What do you mean?"

"I am asking if the file contains the final constant," replied Laura in anticipation.

"It might, but we will know the complete picture only when we open that file," Alex said, clarifying his point of view.

"But how are we supposed to get inside the residence?" Laura asked in confusion.

CHAPTER 16

"Yes, I mean, why would anyone allow us inside?" questioned Ben suddenly.

"I have a friend in Princeton who is working on Einstein's theory of relativity. He might be able to get us a brief tour of the study," Alex said, remembering his friend.

"Yes, of course. Once we are in, Alex and I would sneak into the study which might work," Laura spoke.

Soon, Alex was speaking to his friend about the tour. "Hey, Ron. This is Alex. Do you remember, we met at the science conference last year? I need a small favor from you. Well, you know how big a fan I am of Albert Einstein. Can you help me and my friends to get a brief tour of Einstein's residence in Princeton now that you're there?" Alex said, counting that Ron would be able to grant him this favor.

"All right, Alex. But it depends on when you want to do this?" Ron said, agreeing.

"You tell me, man, whenever you say," replied Alex, smiling while still on the call.

"How about we do this tomorrow morning? To be honest, that is the best chance I can give you with my uncle leaving for a few hours. I am going to be free for a little while, you can come by with your friends. But you better make it quick here, you have only 24 hours," Ron said, telling Alex about the time in advance.

"I will give you a call once I reach there," Alex said with a smile.

"Take care," Ron said before he hung up.

Laura was curious to know what they were going to do next. However, the flashing smile which caught her attention briefly was enough to tell her now that things were going according to plan.

"All right, here is what we are going to do. Ben, you stay on guard on the tour. More so make sure that you create a distraction so that I and Laura can slip into the study. Now we know the location of the file so it's not going to be too long before we find it," Alex said, explaining the situation to Ben and Laura.

"How long it's going to be for you two to return?" asked Ben, making sure there were no doubts left.

"We will try to make it as soon as possible but if there is a problem give me a signal," answered Alex.

"What signal?" asked Ben in confusion.

"Make sure you give me a miss call on my cell if a situation arises. Then I and Laura would quickly make our way out of there," Alex said, improvising the plan.

"Okay, sweet!" Ben said with a smile, happy with Alex's plan.

"All right, let's make our way to the airport before it's too late," Laura said, interrupting the conversation, noticing they had arrived.

"Yup, let's do that," Alex said, making a move followed by Laura and Ben.

As soon as they reached the airport, Laura saw that the flight they had to board was still a few hours away. *It would not be until midnight that they'll board the flight,* she thought.

CHAPTER 16

"Why don't you try calling Uncle Jack? He might be able to throw some light on the things that have been happening around us," Alex said, looking at Laura comfortingly.

"I have been trying since yesterday but his phone is somehow out of reach," Laura said helplessly.

"Are you thinking what I am thinking?" Alex said, grasping the expression on Laura's face.

"I hope not," Laura said reluctantly.

No matter what Alex said, she was still amused by the letter and the fact that they were being followed. She was also quite aware of the danger that might be heading toward the three of them.

"Hey, Laura. Let's go, it's time," Ben said, coming towards her.

As she was lost in her thoughts, time had fled without a hint.

She quickly boarded the flight following Ben and Alex and made herself comfortable beside Alex. Ben had to make himself comfortable a few seats away from them.

"Empty your mind. We need to concentrate on the task at hand," Alex said, realizing Laura was still thinking about Uncle Jack.

Laura gave him a friendly smile. She was in a way happy about the fact that she had Alex with her in this dreadful time.

Alex on the other hand had more than a few things going on in his mind. *Why the Professor wanted him to be a part of his plan?*

After a few minutes, he looked at Laura who was now innocently sound asleep. It was not long before that he too had started dreaming.

"Ok, get up. It's time," Alex opened his eyes to see Laura, her voice somehow felt sweeter.

"Where are we?" asked Alex waking up and looking around just to make sure everything was all right.

"We are about to land at New Jersey airport," she said to him.

"Hey, good you guys are up," Ben said, walking up to them. "By the looks on your faces, I thought you guys won't be up for a long time," he continued, noticing Laura raising eyebrows. "Yeah, actually, I thought I could use some sleep too. Anyway, we are about to land. Make sure you let your friend know that we have reached and pick a place to meet up," Ben said in confirmation.

"Yeah, I know. I'm already at it," Alex said, typing a message on his cell phone.

"Yup!" Alex murmured, confirming that the message had been sent.

As soon as they landed, they swiftly made their way to the nearest transport. Ben asked Alex confusingly, "Did you receive any message from Ron about where we are meeting?"

"He said to directly meet up at Einstein's residence as he has quite a few things to take care of today," Alex said, confirming his conversation with Ron.

"That sounds fair, the sooner we are done with this, the better," Laura said confidently.

"Absolutely, Ben, you know the plan," Alex said, calling for a cab and getting in. Laura and Ben followed swiftly.

Soon all three of them were making their way to their destination.

CHAPTER 16

As soon as they reached, Ron gave them a warm welcome. Alex introduced Laura and Ben to Ron.

"These are my very special friends," Alex said briefly looking at Laura and Ben.

"Sure, what do you do, Ben, Laura?" asked Ron, turning his head toward Laura.

"Well, Ben here studies with me in college," Alex said taking turns to look at Ron and Ben briefly.

"What about you, young lady?" Ron said looking at Laura.

"I am studying law in New York," she said, trying to relax with a bit of uneasiness.

"Both of them are my really close friends. I hope you don't mind me bringing them along," Alex said, expressing a little worry.

"Oh no, not at all. It is my pleasure to meet the fine young minds of today," Ron said with a smile hardly offended.

"So, shall we begin with the tour? Which place would you like to see first?" Ron said, moving forward.

"Thank you, Ron," Alex said.

"It's my pleasure," replied Ron with a smile.

"So, now, let me bring to your attention to the residence of Albert Einstein," Ron said as he proceeded inside the residence.

Laura didn't want to miss an opportunity which had appeared to her as soon as she saw Ron had shifted his attention toward her.

"Ron, can you show us the study?" she asked him politely.

"Well, I'm sorry, Miss Laura. Nobody is allowed to see the study. There are far more important documents there and I cannot afford to take such a risk," Ron said cautiously.

"Oh, that's alright. Can you tell us where it is? I have seen it a number of times in science magazines. I hope you don't mind," Laura said carefully making sure he wouldn't doubt her intentions.

"That's alright, my dear. It's on the left, the third room, when you take left from the end of the corridor," Ron said, pointing toward the corridor stretching out in front of them.

Laura looked at it longingly, trying to find a way to shift their attention so that she could get into the study.

After a few moments, Ben had an idea. Coming closer to Alex, he said, "Call me on my cell right now."

Alex looked at him in confusion at first and then he understood what Ben was thinking. Ben gave Laura a wink as soon as Alex gave a call on his number.

"Oh yes, she is here. Laura, there is a call for you," Ben said, offering her his cell. Laura accepted it with a similar mischievous smile which Alex and Ben had always seen on her face when she was young.

Laura understood Ben's plan. Ben and Alex would continue their tour and she would slip away to the study with the excuse that she was talking to a friend.

"Excuse me, you guys carry on. I'll be there just in a moment," she said casually looking at everyone.

CHAPTER 16

Soon Alex and Ben were far away with Ron and this was the right time. She quickly made her way to the study before she raised her voice to make an excuse. "I think I just need to go use the restroom, you guys carry on," she said as they turned around.

"But—"

Before Ron could say anything, Alex quickly responded, "It's alright, Ron. It will just take a moment, please move on," he said looking at Ron reassuringly and left to join Laura who had already disappeared.

Ben took Ron in his stride and started asking him random questions about the place so that Ron forgets about Laura and Alex. He wanted to divert Ron's attention. This would get just enough time for Alex and Laura to find the article. On the positive side, he always had his cell to give a call to Alex and Laura to get them out.

Meanwhile, they had already made their way into the study. She was about to open the desk when she heard footsteps closing in on her. She quickly moved behind the curtains.

Her heart started beating faster as the footsteps felt like they were coming closer to her until they were in the same room.

"Laura, where are you?" a voice grabbed her attention.

It was Alex. She quickly came out of the curtains swearing at Alex. "You scared the shit out of me."

"Stop wasting time and look at the file," Alex said, trying to calm Laura down.

"I was just about to go to the desk when I heard your footsteps," Laura said, showing Alex the desk.

NUMERICAL ENIGMA

"Yes, here it is. Let's have a look," Alex said with a gasping breath.

Laura was about to open the draw when Alex stopped her.

On the other hand, Ben was on the verge of counting seconds.

He looked at Ron nervously. Pointing at a shelf with an exclusive design, he asked, "Can you tell me a little more about this piece of furniture? I think my grandfather also has something of this sort made around in his house."

His attention shifted to Ron as he spoke.

"This is a Tibetan masterpiece, it is used to store liquor," Ron said with a grin opening the top of the shelf to view the bottles of wine. "I suppose you have not seen anything quite like this," he continued.

"I have seen the design, but no, I have not seen anything like it. This is unique," Ben said, smiling reluctantly and looking at Ron.

A few meters away Laura and Alex were struggling to find the draw which contained the file.

"Do you have the note that we found in the locker?" asked Alex moving quickly, and looking at Laura.

"Yes, it says draw number 5. But I can't find it anywhere in the desk, there are only 4 here," Laura said helplessly.

"Give me that," Alex said, trying to grab the piece of paper from Laura.

In the process of doing so, it slipped right under the desk. As Laura reached under the desk to get it back, something caught her attention.

CHAPTER 16

"Here it is!" she said almost shouting, making Alex jump right next to her under the table.

There it was, at the center of the table, only underneath it.

With anticipation, both Laura and Alex opened the draw.

Quickly opening the draw Alex took out the file and followed the instructions written on the note they had found in the locker.

"There it is, article 5.0," Laura said, pointing to what looked like an article in the file to Alex.

Alex looked at it briefly, trying to make sense of it.

<u>In the Thirteenth Edition (1926) a wholly new topic, "Space-Time," was discussed by the person most qualified in the entire world to do so, Albert Einstein. The article is challenging but rewarding.</u>

I experience the moment "now," or, expressed more accurately, the present sense-experience (Sinnen-Erlebnis) combined with the recollection of (earlier) sense-experiences. That is why the sense-experiences seem to form a series, namely the time-series indicated by "earlier" and "later." The experience-series is thought of as a one-dimensional continuum. Experience-series can repeat themselves and can then be recognized. They can also be repeated inexactly, wherein some events are replaced by others without the character of the repetition becoming lost for us. In this way we form the time-concept as a one-dimensional frame which can be filled in by experiences in various ways. <u>The same series of experiences answer to the same subjective time-intervals.</u>

"C" ⟵⟶ STRING THEORY

He quickly came out. Standing next to the table he stared at the article. Now looking for a pen and paper, suddenly he got a missed call from Ben.

"That must be Ben. Quick, we need to hurry! Hand me a pen and paper," Alex said helping Laura out of the table.

As soon as Laura found a pen and paper, Alex started scribbling something down from the article.

"What is the meaning of all this?" Laura asked, looking at Alex and wondering what was he up to.

"I don't know. All I know is we need to head to Geneva," he said, looking at the article and then at Laura exhaustingly.

"Alex, this is crazy. There has to be another way out, we can't just fly to Geneva," Laura started muttering in panic.

"We have to get out," Alex said keeping the article and the file back in their place.

"I don't understand," Laura said almost shouting.

"Neither do I, but you have to trust me. This article is linking back to 1926, something that happened almost 80 years ago, something important," Alex said with a shine in his eyes. *"80 years back, someone was way ahead of us. We just have to find out who that someone was."*

CHAPTER 17

As soon as Alex and Laura came out of the study, the first thing that got their attention was Ben and Ron looking at them from a distance.

Ron was rather amused by the look on both Alex and Laura's faces which seemed to him pretty grave for the moment.

As he quickly walked up to them, closely followed by Ben who was now trying to get a hold of his nerves, he spoke, "What are you both doing here?"

"Um… We were just trying to find our way back to you," Laura said gently, trying to back up the situation.

Ron stood there staring into the depth of her eyes, trying to judge those rapid blinks of her eyelids whether she was telling the truth or not.

Soon, he thought to himself it would be better to end the tour. He was smart enough to understand something wasn't right. He didn't want to invite any trouble.

"I am afraid our tour ends here," he said looking at three of them.

Alex was in fact happy to hear that, knowing he got what he came for.

"Actually, Ron is right. It's late and I think we should get going," Alex said, winking at Laura, making sure that Ron doesn't notice him.

Ben interrupted, "Yeah, I think I have had enough tour for the day. Thank you, Ron. Would you escort us and help us find our way out?"

"Please, this way," replied Ron.

Laura, Ben and Alex looked at each other just as they followed Ron.

Ron looked back a couple of times before he showed them the door making sure that all of them were following him.

"Wow, I think he got a little suspicious of us. Did you get what we came for?" asked Ben as they bid farewell to Ron.

"Yes, we did," Alex said taking out a piece of paper.

"What is that? Give me that," Ben said, grabbing the piece of paper.

In the Thirteenth Edition (1926) a wholly new topic, "Space-Time," was discussed by the person most qualified in the entire world to do so, Albert Einstein. The article is challenging but rewarding.

I experience the moment "now," or, expressed more accurately, the present sense-experience (Sinnen-Erlebnis) combined with the recollection of (earlier) sense-experiences. That is why the sense-experiences seem to form a series, namely the time-series indicated by "earlier" and "later." The experience-series

CHAPTER 17

is thought of as a one-dimensional continuum. Experience-series can repeat themselves and can then be recognized. They can also be repeated inexactly, wherein some events are replaced by others without the character of the repetition becoming lost for us. In this way we form the time-concept as a one-dimensional frame which can be filled in by experiences in various ways. <u>The same series of experiences answer to the same subjective time-intervals.</u>

"C" → — ← STRING THEORY

"What is this supposed to mean?" asked Ben, looking at Alex.

"I don't know yet. It was marked under the article so I figured it was something important, maybe the next clue," Alex said, looking down and simultaneously watching the traffic passing by.

"What do you mean maybe it is the next clue?" Laura said, strongly looking straight into Alex's eyes.

Alex gave a soothing smile back to her appreciating her enthusiasm.

"Now, wait a minute. Let's just get our facts right first. We have the letter by the Professor, one," Ben said counting on his fingers.

"Right," Laura said in confirmation.

Ben proceeded, "A note by this guy called David, who was the Professor's friend in Caltech, who is dead," Ben said counting two on his fingers.

"Done," Laura said, going with Ben.

"And now we have this article written by Albert Einstein, three," continued Ben.

"Don't forget the letter by the Professor was also written by Einstein," interrupted Laura.

"Yup, right. So, where does this leave us?" Ben said, looking at Alex.

"I don't know, let's talk about this on our way to Geneva," Alex said, raising his hand for a taxi.

"Geneva? Why the hell we are going to Geneva? It's going to cost me a fortune to get us there. You see that?" Ben said showing the word 'string' written and marked on the piece of paper to Laura.

"Yeah, Alex has a friend who is working on this theory called the string theory in Geneva and he thinks the word string is related to the string theory itself. He thinks his friend can help us understand the meaning of these marked words," Laura said, still puzzled.

"I don't understand," Ben said, feeling a bit helpless getting into the taxi followed by Laura and Alex.

"Maybe you will, if you stop thinking about your freaking money for a second," Alex said as he settled down frustratingly at his end of the seat, closing the door.

"Don't mock me when you can go around the world anywhere you like on my liberty just 'cause we are friends. You take me for granted," Ben said a few moments later as the three of them were about to board the flight.

"You are right, I give up. It's me who is filthy rich," replied Alex with a sign.

"Cut it out, you two. By the way, how did you survive by not killing each other while I was away?" Laura said, controlling her giggle.

CHAPTER 17

"Beats the shit out of me," Alex said looking at Ben who in turn replied to him with a wicked smile.

This time on the flight, Laura decided to sit in the middle with Ben and Alex on either side.

As the plane started to take off Laura felt a hard vibration hit her seat and she quickly grabbed Alex by the top of his palm letting her fingers grip the space between his knuckles.

"Relax, it's all right. It happens all the time," Alex said, trying to even her anxiety. Soon they were off to Geneva.

Laura and Alex were silent for the most part of their journey and Ben had started to become impatient.

"You two wake up, we have things to do here," Ben said, flicking his fingers next to Laura's soft earlobes.

It took a moment for Laura and Alex to grab complete consciousness of their surroundings.

"We got three clues and none of them makes any sense to me," Ben said, bending his head and staring at Alex.

"I don't know, man," Alex said, trying to ignore and still trying to make out how the hell he got himself in a situation like this.

"Of course, you do. You are good at this, it's physics, remember?" Ben said, cheering him up.

"He is right. You can definitely figure this out," Laura said, first looking at Ben and then turning her head swiftly towards Alex.

"You are the one who told us about the final constant and the huge impact it can bring on our day-to-day life as well as on modern physics. Do you think these phases relate to that final constant?" continued Laura.

"All I understand right now is only about the constants. I don't know what to make of it now other than the fact that we are looking for a dimensionless constant," Alex said, looking at Ben and Laura.

"Maybe looking at these clues one more time might bring some important fact to our attention," Laura said, trying to make Alex confident.

"It might. So, what do we have here?" reciprocated Alex.

"Well, first was a letter, of course, pointing towards the constants," continued Alex.

"Yup, you explained to me about how finding the universal constant can bring a revolution in physics," Ben said quickly, trying to move on.

"That is of course what this quest is all about. We have to keep that on our minds," Alex said, making a point.

"How do we find it?" asked Laura again curiously looking at Alex.

"Let's see, this letter also brought another clue with it, other than the constant that was the sign of divine proportion," Alex said, looking at the facts.

"The "ϕ" is the connection between the constants and the idea of proportion and then there are the patterns," Ben said, conforming. He remembered the conversation between him and Alex earlier.

CHAPTER 17

"That's right, but proportions are patterns. So, what is the pattern we are looking at?" Alex said, taking out the paper in which he had copied the phrases and staring deeply at the article.

"You mean there is a pattern in these phrases," Laura said, simultaneously looking at Alex and then towards Ben.

"Well, patterns are our key right now, to get close to our goal," responded Alex.

"You said that this article was about special relativity and it had something to do with time, right?" Laura said trying to recollect the conversation she had earlier with Alex.

"Not something. It has everything to do with time. Wait a minute, that's it! Time! Take a look at this," Alex said persuasively, suddenly getting excited from what just crossed his mind.

"You see this?" Alex said, pointing towards one of the phrases he copied.

<u>The same series of experiences answer to the same subjective time-intervals.</u>

"C" → — ← STRING THEORY

"Yeah, what about it?" asked Ben.

"It's a property, a characteristic of time. I think I just found out the link between the constants and this phrase," Alex said smiling, overwhelmed by his discovery.

"What is it?" asked Ben and Laura immediately.

"In this phrase, Albert Einstein is talking about time in special relativity and focusing on the characteristics of time. It might as well be focusing on a pattern in time and if that is the case, which

I think it is, I think I know what he is focusing on," Alex said excitedly explaining to Ben and Laura.

"What?" Ben and Laura asked together.

"All patterns are proportions, and proportions are constants. So, I think this phrase is pointing to a proportion in special relativity, to put it precisely…" Alex said looking intensely at Ben and Laura.

"A constant!" said Laura and Ben finally understanding what Alex was getting at.

"Absolutely, a constant which has played a fundamental role in defining the special theory of relativity and if we look back at the note in the diary we find it there as well in an equation under the equation $E=mc^2$, which means the constant this article is referring to and the clue Professor left us is the…"

"Constant of the speed of light," said all three of them together.

"I am sure about it," replied Alex.

"Hey, look here. This phrase has the letter c pointing an arrow with string written next to it," Ben said, pointing towards the phrase that Alex had copied.

"Yup, it would mean that he too is trying to establish a connection between the constant of the speed of light and the string theory," Laura said, looking at the piece of paper.

"Yeah, it would seem so, but there are numerous equations in which the speed of light and the string are connected," Alex said, looking a bit confused.

"Let's leave that for your friend to answer. I mean if he is in Geneva working on the string theory, he might be able to help us, right?"

CHAPTER 17

Laura said a bit exhausted from all the thinking but excited at the same time. It had been a long time that she had been with Alex. She knew all this was depressing, all the running around and passing away of the Professor, but somehow there was also an element of thrill she felt around her.

As soon as they landed in Geneva they were on their way to the lab. Laura got curious and asked, "What is his name? Does he know we are coming?

"I tried calling him a couple of times, but he was out of reach. His name is Dexter. I think we would be giving him a bit of a surprise," Alex said, ignoring Laura.

"I think it's normal considering the last couple of days have been nothing but surprises. Also, I wanted to ask you, when was the last time you met this guy?" questioned Ben, relaxing on the seat in front of theirs on their way to meet Dexter, trying to face away and looking out the window.

"It's been a while actually since the science quiz last year and we have been in touch through the internet all this while, he has a blog and I have been following it," answered Alex, sounding careless.

"Look, man. You are turning into such a geek. You better concentrate on football, the season is still on," Ben said trying to cut him off.

"Do you think this is the time to talk about football?" Laura said rudely, looking furiously at Ben.

"OK, I know we got better things to take care of," Ben said backing off from the subject.

"We are here, people," Alex said looking outside.

As they made their way to Dexter, Alex thought it was likely that Laura was right and he would be able to get the precise link between the speed of light and the string, then again Dexter would know better. Locating his whereabouts, soon they made their way to Dexter. Alex and Laura noticed something suspicious as they were walking. A scientist who was keeping an eye fixed on them.

"Guys, I think we are in a bit of trouble. There are people stalking us, we need to split up in order to confuse them," Alex said, trying to bring Laura and Ben up to speed with their current situation.

Both Ben and Laura felt a little nervous about Alex's plan. Nonetheless, it seemed inevitable at that moment.

"Laura, go with Ben. You guys, when you get to a safe location give me a call and I'll do the same," Alex said swiftly, again making sure the words came out softly.

As a junction approached Alex made his footsteps quicker trying to make sure he had the lead and was followed immediately, letting Laura and Ben converge to safety.

What he missed by not looking back became clear to him within moments as a bullet, passing inches away from him, hit the wall. So, the alarm went off.

"They have a gun!"

Now the situation was different and unlike a few minutes ago. Alex was now under a panic attack. Racing now for his life he knew he had to get rid of the men. The only way to do it was to outrun them or hide before their men breached the parameter.

Taking random turns, skidding and breathing heavily he turned back.

CHAPTER 17

"Shit!" he yelled pushing the people in his way, watching them as they closed in on him.

Alex was running around in jeopardy, trying to figure out a place where he could hide or at least get out of touch of their trail.

Looking around he immediately saw a narrow passage to his right and left. Taking a swift left and going around in a circle to dodge he quickly made his way to the right side of the passage and hid in one of the rooms along the passage.

He later saw, how the men behind him were confused and argued among themselves in dismay, trying to figure out which direction to take. Just as they made their way out of his sight, he gave a call to Ben and Laura trying to calm himself down and hoping for their wellbeing.

Laura picked up the cell, controlling her breath and asked Alex whether he was okay softly.

"Alex! Where are you? Are you all right?" she said whispering.

"I'm alright. What about you and Ben? You guys holding up fine? Try to confuse these guys and hide somewhere," Alex said, giving her a bit of advice on his behalf.

"We're doing the same, what next?" she said giving him relief.

"All right, listen. I am going after Dexter. I'll meet you guys in the parking lot along with him," he said, explaining the plan briefly.

"OK. I'll tell Ben. You better hurry, Alex be careful," she said before disconnecting.

As Alex made his way to Dexter he made his feet quicker by the second. He had to reach Dexter before the men could start stalking him again. He talked to himself, "Do these people know what we are after? Do they know about Dexter?"

All these questions were adding to his worry. He had to find Dexter soon.

To do so he had to make his way to the upper floor by climbing the stairs. Just as he did that, he heard some footsteps coming from above. They were the same guys from before, they had not noticed him. Alex had to hide somewhere again. With so little time on his hands, the only place he chose this time was going toward the basement.

His plan worked like a charm. The men ignored searching in the basement and continued to walk back to where they came from.

He was happy they didn't see him sneaking on them. Alex headed toward the upper floor. He was about to enter the door where Dexter was supposed to be when a familiar voice stopped him.

"Alex, what are you doing here?"

It was Dexter. There was a smile on his face for a moment before he realized the irony of the situation.

"We don't have much time." Alex carefully stepped up to Dexter and said, "I can answer all your questions later. But right now, you have to come with me," he said looking at Dexter in a way telling him to trust him.

"Those guys I saw just now, were they after you?" asked Dexter amusingly.

"Yes, but right now you have to come with me," Alex said again, making sure he understands the urgency of the situation.

CHAPTER 17

"All right, all right. Where are we going?" Dexter said, believing him.

"Just follow me. But before that, guide me to a shortcut to the basement," Alex said, thinking something.

"There is a service elevator which leads directly to the basement that might be useful," Dexter said, offering a solution.

"That sounds useful, where is it?" questioned Alex softly.

"It's that way," Dexter said pointing towards the opposite end of the corridor from the direction Alex came from.

"Okay, Dexter. You stay behind me," Alex said forcefully, making sure he understands.

So, they climbed inside the service elevator and made their way to the basement. Reaching it, Alex gave quick look around hoping to see Laura and Ben come out from their hiding.

"Yup, we're here," Laura said coming out, with Ben following her.

Alex came closer, hugging both tightly. Dexter on the other hand watched the reunion with confusion.

"Who are these people?" asked Dexter, disappointed by all that was happening around him.

"They are friends. I'll explain everything but before that, we need to get out of this place," replied Alex hurriedly.

"I have a car. It's in there," Dexter said making his way to the car.

All of them followed him without any question. As soon as they climbed into the car, they heard a shot. From the sound of it, it was close to the car. When Alex looked back, he saw the same men who were chasing him.

"Hit it," he shouted at Dexter before everyone became comfortable inside the vehicle.

In a flash and they were out of there. But Laura was looking back now and then making sure they were safe.

It was time Dexter lost his patience, "Would somebody here please tell me what the fuck is going on?" Dexter said in anguish.

Alex took out the piece of paper they found from the Einstein residence and showed it to Dexter.

"There is this piece of paper we found from Albert Einstein's residence. We are hoping you would be able to tell us what it means. We are in search of the universal constant for the UFT," replied Alex, stating his reasons.

Dexter gave a light laugh sarcastically before replying, "Ha-ha! UFT, did you say?"

"Look, we are serious, Dex. What can you tell us about this phrase?" Alex said sounding serious, showing the phrase on the piece of paper to him.

"I can't...., Wait a minute," he paused pressing the brakes of the car before he glimpsed at the paper again.

"What is it?" said all three of them astonishingly.

"This is not the first time I'm looking at this phrase." Alex was stumped by what Dexter asked later. "Has this something to do with a guy named David?"

CHAPTER 18

"I still don't understand," Alex questioned waiting for him to explain. "What do you know about David?" he continued.

"A few years ago, while I was still in high school, I came across this guy's research about multiple universe theory. His ideas seemed a little complicated but very interesting," Dex explained.

Alex and others were intrigued by Dexter.

"I saw this phrase in one of his old research papers," continued Dexter, perturbed by the look on the faces of the people in front of him.

"What can you tell us more about this guy?" asked Laura, thriving to get into detail.

"Look, I can't give you guys anything unless you people give me the complete picture," Dexter said uncomfortably.

He knew there was more to all to this than what met the eye. At the same time, he knew Alex won't have come to him all this way to Geneva if it wasn't important.

"All right, the Professor is dead and there are a lot of guys chasing us for this letter that we showed you. We think it is some sort of a clue which leads to the universal constant and the UFT," explained Alex, trying to keep it as uncomplicated as he could. "All we have now is this letter and a phrase from an article written by Albert Einstein in 1926."

"Yeah, I know that's the one you showed me," Dexter said in confirmation, now understanding the gravity of the situation a little.

"What we make of it as of now is that the Professor was trying to give us clues to find the ultimate constant. You see this?" Alex said, bringing the letter close to Dexter's sight.

"Yup, what about it?" asked Dexter curiously.

"You see the symbols at the end of the paragraph?" Alex said, pointing at the symbols.

"Yes, but they don't seem to be the content of the letter," replied Dexter, noticing the change in the writing.

"They are not, they were written by the Professor moments before he died. You see, he was trying to tell us something. We are still to interpret the second symbol but guessing from the context of the letter, the symbols are hints towards finding a divine proportion," explained Alex, trying to be as precise as possible.

"Right, proportion and patterns relate to the constant and in this letter, the first symbol of the divine constant should relate to the ultimate constant as you said. This could lead us to the UFT," answered Dexter with a smile.

"Absolutely, the next clue we got is this phrase and now you think it is related to David and his research. We think that the Professor and David worked as friends in Caltech," Alex said as Laura and Ben listened to their conversation attentively.

CHAPTER 18

"Yes, of course. What you have to understand is that I don't know much about this guy as you know, I know bits and pieces about his research but nothing about him personally," Dexter said helplessly.

"Shit!" exclaimed Alex in disappointment.

"The guy just disappeared during an earthquake years ago. The dude is a mystery man!" continued Dexter, trying to justify himself.

"He didn't die, he was alive," Alex said carelessly.

"Huh?" Dexter was amused.

"In fact, he was the one who sent this letter to Professor in the first place," Laura said, looking at Alex and turning toward Dexter.

Dexter turned the letter to the other side to read the date and address written over it.

"This is… I can't believe it!" Dexter said in shock.

"I know. For a few years after he disappeared from Caltech, he was still in touch with the Professor," Alex said looking at Dexter who was in a state of shock.

"What next?" he said with words barely coming out of his mouth. Dexter now understood the seriousness of the situation.

"I think this phrase has something to do with the constant speed of light," Alex said.

"We followed the clues that led us to break into Albert Einstein's residence. That is where we found this phrase written in a file, in an article written by him in 1926. Of course, you know already that," Alex continued, explaining to him the course of events.

"You broke into the study of Albert Einstein and stole an article?" exclaimed Dexter with yet another shock. "How in the hell did you do that?" asked Dexter, wanting to know more about it.

"We can talk about that some other time," Ben interrupted, looking at the phrase and then Dexter's simultaneously.

Dexter resumed looking at the phrase and then looked up at Alex, Ben and Laura. He began to explain. "It happened at the beginning of my research. The following phrase relates to a characteristic of time, the experience here in this phrase refers to the action or events that are repeated after a specific interval in time. An appropriate example would be the revolution of planets around the sun," stated Dexter, now and again looking at the attentive faces of Alex, Ben and Laura.

"Yeah, right. That is what the statement means. The same series of experiences answer to the same subject of time interval like each revolution of different planets around the sun again and again defined by us in years," continued Alex understanding the notion.

"Further, new studies in detail done in special relativity tell us this repetition of events happens due to a direct impact of the speed of light on time. It is due to this speed of light that each planet has its own day and night and specifically its own time," Dex continued trying to be as simple as he could.

"That's the part I don't understand, what you mean by a specific time?" asked Ben, trying to understand.

"Light from the sun takes time to reach each planet. That makes time a personal concept rather than a universal one. This is the main essence of the theory of special relativity. Why do you think countries have different times on either side of the globe?" Dexter said, feeling like a schoolboy explaining the concept to Ben.

CHAPTER 18

"Yeah, right. I get it," Ben said, finally understanding the point.

"Listen, Ben. There's more to it," interrupted Alex, trying to share something.

"I know what is bothering you," Dexter said, looking at the piece of paper and Alex again.

"You do?" exclaimed Alex in a bit of confusion. "The reason we came to you was to understand what this is about," Alex said, pointing towards the arrow linking the phrase to the string.

"You were right, Alex. This phase is trying to relate the speed of light to the string theory," Dexter said patting his shoulder.

"Yes, but I still don't know how to establish the link. I mean there are so many ways in which the constant of the speed of light can be used in the string theory," Alex said, sounding a bit helpless.

"Alex, it's not so much as to the number of ways. It is used in the string theory but what it does is the clue that you are looking for," Dexter said, looking at all of them one at a time.

"Of course, why didn't I think of it before?" Alex said beating himself up.

"Yes, now you get it, don't you?" Dexter said, judging from the expression on his face.

"The one-dimensional string in the theory! How could I miss that?" Alex said, smiling to himself.

"What of it?" asked Laura and Ben, shocked together.

"The idea of constant of the speed of light validates time as a personal concept in the special theory of relativity because of the vast distances between bodies in space. It does not have any influences on bodies which are closer in comparison to those which are millions of miles apart," Alex said, his mind analyzing certain notions quickly.

"So what does it have to do with the string?" Laura asked, questioning curiously.

"That's the whole point. What the speed of light does to special relativity is nothing in comparison to the way it influences the string," Dexter said, joining in.

"Can you come to the point?" Ben said, getting a bit frustrated.

"String is still a theory which is changing every day. Even as we talk now, there are new ideas and various notions thrown in from people across the globe working on the theory," Alex said continuing.

"Yes, but that is where the interesting part begins. As we come across new ideas and developments in the theory with each passing day we realize string is not an easy concept," Dexter said again.

"Its technicalities are highly complicated as it brings across the unification of quantum and relativity," Alex said, looking at Dexter and then toward Laura and Ben.

"But you said we are still looking for the UFT. Then how can this string theory unify relativity and quantum?" Laura asked, sounding a bit confused.

"Yes, but that is why string theory is still a speculation, as it still has some loopholes regarding its unification. However, it is the closest we can get to the unified field theory," Alex said, trying to make both Laura and Ben understand.

CHAPTER 18

"All right, but what is your point?" Laura asked, losing patience now.

"The technicalities of the string are complicated due to a single reason, its elementary particle the string," Alex said, looking at Dexter who smiled knowing what Alex was about to say next.

"And why?" asked Ben, realizing how badly Alex wanted him to ask this question judging by the way he was explaining the concept to Laura.

"It is because of its one-dimensional nature that gives the equations almost unlimited modulations in the theory. That is the main reason why the string theory itself has so many dimensions. There have been many number of dimensions taken into consideration but eleven is what scientist has come to appreciate as the most appropriate one for our universe," Alex said in excitement.

"I thought our universe had four dimensions, three in space - length breath and height, and one in time. That is what you told me earlier," Ben said, looking at Alex a little overtaken by his explanation.

"Yes, that is taken to be the case as that is what we observe as humans and by far it is the most convenient and conventional way the dimensions of our universe have been defined. However, only in the case of string theory we have an eleven-dimensional universe and this is because the 'string' in the string theory is able to fold space, thus giving rise to new dimensions," Alex said forcefully.

"That went completely over my head," Laura said in disappointment. "Please explain with more simplicity," requested Laura.

"Okay, close your eyes and imagine a ball bouncing and moving in different directions in a square drawn on a piece of paper and the same ball bouncing and moving within a cube drawn on the same piece of paper. Now which seems more complicated?" asked Dexter, trying to make a point.

"The cube, that is more complicated," Laura and Ben said together.

"Yes, this is because the square is two-dimensional whereas the cube having two dimensions on paper is actually three-dimensional. So it is more difficult for us to imagine bodies with three dimensions or more. I hope you got this," Alex said, hoping both Laura and Ben understood his point.

"Yeah, we got that," Ben and Laura said looking at each other and then toward Alex.

"All right, so it is easier for us to imagine a single string with one dimension but once we try to link multiple strings, things start to become more complicated as it tends to bring more and more dimensions into the picture," Alex said, confidently looking at them.

"And this is the process which happens in theory with the help of equations," added Dex, taking part in the conversation.

"So, you mean to say the way physicists have manipulated and combined the equations in the string theory eventually defines the dimensions of the string theory," Laura said with a glimmer in her eyes, finally getting the point Alex was trying to make.

"Exactly," Alex said, smiling at her.

"But that is absurd, another physicist can well end up deriving a different number of dimensions for the string theory and that would mean there is no fixed dimension," Laura said worriedly.

CHAPTER 18

"And I always thought scientists were supposed to be the brains of the country," Ben said mockingly.

"Don't come to conclusions, Ben. Laura is right, but things are not so simple really. Physics has a set of laws and they have a certain way of reality. The debate over the string is far from over. Like any other theory it has its advantages and disadvantages," Alex said, telling Ben in a way to calm down and not get judgmental.

"But what does this have to do with the speed of light?" Laura said patiently, now getting interested to know more about the string.

"Like I said, the string in the string theory folds the space with the help of the strings. This brings across drastic influence in the way the speed of light influences time," Alex said, thinking something deeply.

"What influence?" asked Laura in excitement. She had begun understanding this conversation.

"Unlike in special relativity where the constant of the speed of light makes time different for bodies which are really far away from each other, within the realms of string theory it makes time different for everything regardless how close or far bodies are from each other. This is still a theoretical belief like many others about the string theory but important for the constant of the speed of light," Alex said, finishing his final piece of the explanation.

"But why does it make time different for everything? I mean why disregard the bodies being close or far from each other?" questioned Ben, just trying to understand a little more.

"Can't say anything in detail, but I guess it is primarily because of the folding of space in theory which makes the true measure of distance between bodies vague. You can never really know how close or how far two bodies are in string theory," Alex said, erasing the doubt in Ben's mind.

"Right, so if you don't know the distance light has traveled between two bodies you can't tell the time. Yup, that makes sense," Laura said, feeling happy that she was getting along with all the geeky stuff.

Ben, on the other hand, was rather amused. Although Laura had understood most of what Alex was trying to say his mind was still unclear. He always enjoyed Alex more in his conversation about football. He saw Dex feeling restless. It was like he wanted to share something. Alex noticed this and decided to question him.

"You look restless, Dex. What is it that you want to say?" asked Alex.

"Like I said, I myself have been researching the subject for quite a long time now. What I think the connection between the constant of the speed of light and string gives rise to a concept of no time and it may well be related to David and superposition," Dexter said confidently.

"Superposition, but…" Alex said beginning to say something.

"Yes, I know it's a thing of quantum mechanics, but I remember going through some stuff about David and his paper. I think he was also trying to relate this idea of no time to superposition as both are one and the same. I'm sure you'll be able to find something," Dexter said, shaking his hand before moving out of his car.

"Dex, where are you going? What about your car?" Alex asked looking at him as he moved out of the vehicle.

CHAPTER 18

"You can take it. Bring it back to me once you are done, although an unlikely one. But this visit it has been a pleasure," Dexter said, bidding goodbye to Alex and his friends.

Alex shifted onto the driving seat and made himself comfortable. "Now, where are we heading?" laying his head on the back seat in exhaustion. "I am hungry. Are you guys hungry too?" asked Alex, looking at Ben and Laura as they nodded.

After driving for a while Alex noticed something close by, it was McDonald's. He woke Laura and Ben up; they both had fallen sound asleep and were not so happy with Alex waking them up after their conversation with Dexter.

"Let's go grab something to eat," Alex said looking at Laura and Ben with a smile.

Laura and Ben swiftly made themselves a little active knowing they had to hurry up. They still didn't know where they were heading but decided to keep it to themselves until after they had their meal.

While having their meal, Laura was the first one to ask, "Where are we heading now?"

"I don't know, I guess we have to research superposition," Alex said, conforming to Dexter's advice.

"So, you want to go with Dexter's advice?" asked Ben, looking at Alex.

"He knew about David, didn't he? That proves something," Alex said, trying to justify what he was thinking.

"What if he is not right?" asked Ben sarcastically looking straight at Alex.

"Ben, Alex is right. It's our best shot as of now," interrupted Laura, taking the side of Alex.

Alex was unperturbed. His mind was on what Dex had told him. In fact, he paid no heed to what Laura and Ben were talking about. He looked out the window from the table they were sitting on. Ben was on the window side.

Suddenly he looked at Laura and Ben who were busy arguing.

Laura was the first to notice the intimation in his voice. "What?" she asked, knowing Alex had got something important on his mind.

"Super position…" muttered Alex.

"What about that?" asked Laura yet again, this time Ben joining in.

"Superposition is related to "Quantum Mechanics Interpretation of Many Worlds". That's what the Professor and David were working on years back," Alex said to himself, with a spark in his eyes, remembering what the old sweeper told him back in Caltech when he was trying to know more about David.

CHAPTER 19

There was silence for a few moments before Laura spoke.

"How can you be so sure?" she asked reluctantly.

"It happened when I went to Caltech. I met this old man who told me about David. Not to mention when I was going through the article copying the phrase, I was so engrossed in it that I missed the title under which the article on special relativity itself was written," Alex said, almost yelling with enthusiasm.

"Then why did Dex tell you about superposition?" Laura asked, intimidated by what was going through his mind.

"Superposition is a part of quantum mechanics but it has more to do with "Quantum Mechanics Interpretation of Many Worlds". Listen to me, I am sure about this," Alex said, trying to convince both of them.

"All right, where this new idea of yours takes us next?" she asked Alex after a brief pause.

"I don't know I think we need to research a bit on *Quantum Interpretation of Many Worlds*," Alex said looking at Ben.

"I think the best way to do that as of now is the internet. Also, I think we need to keep on looking at the clues we have in our hands. We don't know if there is anything new we might find," Ben said, thinking something.

"Yeah, you are right," Alex said, understanding he might be right.

Alex saw Laura lost in her thoughts thinking about something. "Laura, what is it?" asked Alex.

Laura looked up, the voice of Alex bringing her back to reality.

"What happened? What were you thinking about?" asked Alex yet again.

"I was thinking of going back home," she said abruptly, sounding emotional.

"I don't think that is a good idea," Alex said, thinking about the officers who informed him about the Professor's death.

If they were to get their hands on Laura she could fall into danger, considering the present situation.

"Wait a minute, maybe we all should head back to Professor's place," Ben said, getting an idea and a brainwave.

"What are you talking about? There can be security all over the place. This is not the right time," Alex said, arguing.

"Think about the numbers in the letter, they look like index numbers of books kept in a library or they might be a combination for a safe. We might find something regarding *Quantum Interpretation of Many Worlds* in the Professor's study. It is a risk worth taking," Ben said, sounding sure of it.

CHAPTER 19

"I need to go back," she said, looking at Alex in a way telling him she had already taken the decision.

Alex looked at her thinking something deeply and turned toward Ben.

"OK, we'll go. But we need to be on our toes, get what is helpful and leave as soon as possible," Alex replied, making sure Laura understands every word.

Laura wanted to take a few of her belongings which reminded her of the best memories and times she spent with her father. Things which really matter and made a difference to her were still lying in her room back home. She thought of one of the snap she had in her room, one where she could be seen with her dad, the coat of her father and a few other things.

It is going to take some time to get back to Pasadena, I hope we are not wasting time, Alex thought to himself.

All three of them were now heading back to Pasadena. Laura was especially keeping quiet the whole time as they drove to the airport and on the flight. Alex thought of talking to her but on second thought it was better to give her some space. That would give her the time to sort things out and get a clear perspective. Actually Alex himself was going back to the Professor's place after a long time. He remembered being a child and the time he had spent with the Professor. He always considered him as a fatherly figure. However, things had turned out differently between him and the Professor. Alex was disturbed by the voice of the attendant announcing their arrival on the flight. Soon they reached their destination.

As they were making their way back to the duplex, Alex called Dex and told him that they were in Pasadena and the location of where they had parked his car in Geneva.

Laura sitting quietly, now spoke gently, "I'm glad to have your company," she said looking at Alex and Ben.

Alex and Ben looked at each other and gave her a faded smile knowing what she had been through for the last couple of days.

Alex soon had his senses back to what was going on with them. As they came closer to the duplex, with each passing moment, Laura felt an uncertain anxiousness flowing through her.

"I know how you must have been feeling. You don't need to do this," he said, looking at Laura, focusing on her eyes.

Laura smoothly allowed her fingers to slide into his in response, feeling the same completeness she had always felt.

However, this time it was more like she needed it. Alex noticed it and he knew what she was going through. It was like she telling him, "Yes, I have to find out who killed my father."

Ben was looking out through the window when something distracted him and he turned to Alex and Laura to speak his mind, "Look, there is heavy activity going on. There are guards everywhere," he said looking at Laura and Alex.

"I think he is right," Alex said, looking outside from his side of the window to confirm while holding her hand.

"This means there got to be roadblocks, we need to be more careful," Alex continued.

"Let's get down a few meters away from the duplex. It's better than going by taxi, walking down we will have more freedom and at the same time we will be able to keep an eye out for the guards. There will be security at every entrance of the duplex," Alex said, coming up with a plan.

CHAPTER 19

"That might be a good idea," Laura said, looking at Alex smiling.

At that time his smile felt soothing to her.

They were a few meters away from the duplex when Laura gave the signal. Ben was already anticipating it. They came to a halt.

Getting down on the sidewalk, Laura somehow felt familiar maybe because she had walked on it a hundred times with her father. She remembered how they used to take a walk so often in the morning when she was still young. Her father's voice marveling her with each word he spoke. How he used to guide her along the path explaining to her a thing or two about life. They were some of the happy moments but now times were different.

Now was a time she needed her father the most. Stepping on the sidewalk she tried to hear the same voice, the voice of her father and it came to her again, a voice from her heart. For a moment, she felt warm and peaceful.

"Laura, what's wrong?" Alex said, shaking her hand he was holding softly.

"Yup, nothing," she said coming back to reality from her memories.

"All right, now, let's just try to keep as much away from the lights as we can. We should be sheltered in the darkness. It would help us to keep our movements discreet," Ben said, letting Laura and Alex know of their situation.

"Let's go," Alex said as they began to walk towards the duplex.

Laura walked closely along his side still holding his hand.

"What is that?" Ben exclaimed as he came to grasp the view of the duplex.

There was security like bees around honey.

"All right, guys. We need to stay away from the fire, keep close," Alex said looking at the guards.

"We need to check out the positions of the officers to find a gap to slip through," continued Alex, thinking something sharply.

"Yeah, just like football, it's all about the timing," Ben said, smiling at Laura and Alex.

"We not playing a game here," Alex said mocking him, although it seemed more like an encouragement he was giving to himself.

"OK, let's do this. Ben, you keep a watch from here and I'm going to take Laura along with me to go look at the security on the other side," he said, explaining to Ben.

Without wasting any more time Alex was moving along with Laura to the other side of the duplex.

After reaching the other side, Alex spoke. "Which side do you think the security will be at its minimum?" he questioned, looking at Laura for an answer.

"I don't know. The last time I escaped was from the ladder behind the duplex, but they have security there now. What are we going to do?" she asked Alex.

"Oh shit!" exclaimed Alex suddenly, noticing something.

The next thing he did was to rush back to Ben along with Laura as soon as he could. Laura kept asking what had happened and why all of a sudden he had become silent. Ben got startled as Alex grabbed his shoulder from behind.

CHAPTER 19

"Jesus Christ! What's wrong with you?" asked Ben, almost lowering his voice at the last moment.

"Will somebody tell me what's going on?" Laura said, losing her patience.

"These people are not from law enforcement," Alex said, raising his eyebrows.

"What do you mean?" asked Laura and Ben, reacting at the same time in confusion.

"Look, they don't have any batches on their side arms. All officers have a batch on their side arms and these men are just dressed in their uniforms. They are not authentic," Alex said, quickly explaining why he was so charged up.

"He is right, I noticed it too," Ben said, quickly staring at one of the guys guarding the duplex.

The guard looked keen as if he was waiting for someone to show up.

"My guess is they are looking for us to show up, man. This makes it even more difficult for us to get in," Ben said in disappointment.

"And dangerous," Alex said, judging the situation.

Although she was tired and sloppy she wanted to get in the duplex desperately and just when she had lost all hope, the voice came back from her heart.

"I have an idea," proclaimed Laura with a faded smile. "Remember when Ben, you and I used to play in the garden, in the middle of the garden, there was a small wooden door leading to a passage," she said looking at Alex.

"Yes, of course. The one with the wooden door, circular, with the fish painted over it," Alex said, surprised by his own memory.

"You're right, the same one," she replied, nodding her head.

"We need a distraction," Alex said after a brief pause, looking at Laura and Ben.

"I got this. I'll follow you guys soon enough," Ben said with certainty, coming up with a plan.

"All right, let's do this," Alex said as all three of them made their way to the garden.

"Remember, it's all about the timing," Alex said to Ben just when they were about to execute their plan.

"You are not the only one who is good with the ball," Ben said with a smile, encouraging him to proceed.

Ben picked up a stone and threw it along the sight of the guy walking in the garden. As soon as he heard the sound, he ran towards it followed by the other guards. When Alex and Laura saw an opening, they swiftly made their way to the wooden door in the middle of the garden that Laura had mentioned. Within moments, Ben followed them and they were in the passage in no time.

"Where does this lead to?" asked Ben, whispering.

"To the hall," Laura and Alex said together, looking at each other with a smile.

"I just hope they don't have anyone guarding it from the inside," Alex said, crossing his fingers.

CHAPTER 19

As they walked along the passage, they came closer to the end. Soon they were below the hall of the duplex.

"Let me take a peep to see if someone is around," Alex said, lifting the wooden door similar to the one that they had come from placed in the garden.

"Thank goodness, no one's around, let's go," he said, slowly making his way out of the passage.

Laura and Ben slowly made their way up.

"Ben, you stay with Laura. I'm going upstairs to the study," Alex said, quickly making his way upstairs.

As Alex was making his way up, he remembered in flashbacks how he used to run around in the house. He had a sharp memory of the place. It helped him to get to the study.

Ben and Laura went ahead to her room looking for the picture she actually came back for. Ben tried to restrain her, but couldn't.

Alex was struggling to find the next clue that would help them understand things a bit more clearly. He searched every draw and cupboard, yet he could find nothing. All he could see around were books and random papers. There was nothing he could find to be of his interest.

Just when he had given up all hope, helpless and agitated, his eyes rested on something he didn't notice before.

The books on a certain shelf had a series of numbers which resembled the numbers written in the letter. Behind the pile of books on the shelf was a safe. He remembered Ben talking about a safe and the series of numbers in the letter being the combination.

He decided to give it a shot and bingo! it worked. Inside there was a book that stood out. Unlike most of them which were related to astrophysics, this one had something to do with the stock market.

Alex felt this was really strange as far as the personality of the Professor was concerned and what he did in his life. There was no need for the Professor to keep a book related to the stock market in his study.

He had known that the Professor used to gamble but not very often, just once in a while. Even that wouldn't explain why he would have a book on the stock market. From what he knew, the Professor never had that kind of addiction. His life had been a dedication to theoretical physics. Stock market? Never!

"Of course, it all makes sense. There was no way someone would have known about it other than me and Laura," Alex was talking to himself looking around to see if he had missed anything else. "The Professor would have wanted me or Laura to find it sooner or later," he continued talking to himself, still looking around. Then finally, he knew there was nothing else to find, he had looked into every corner of the room. The book was the only thing Professor was hiding. Now the question was *why*.

Alex fled through the pages of the book. Somewhere in the middle, he stopped, he thought he saw something. He was right, there was a name. "This could be our next clue," Alex muttered to himself as he took the book and made his way down to Laura and Ben.

As soon as he was with them, he noticed that Laura was holding a picture in her hands. It had blurred but he could make out her face and the Professor in it with an ocean in the background. From the look of it, it felt like they were standing on a cliff or something. He realized he had something important to say, "Look, this is what I have found," he said, explaining to them how he had found the book.

CHAPTER 19

"Look, there was this name written between the pages," he pointed out, showing it to Laura and Ben.

"I have heard this name somewhere," Ben said, thinking something hard.

"I know, it felt very familiar to me too, but somehow I can't remember it," Alex said equally disappointed.

"It's this millionaire who was in the papers a few weeks back, someone related to the stock market, Wall Street mentioned him in *Fortune*," Laura said reminding them.

"Yeah, they were talking about betting on stocks and in the interview he spoke about something called Chaos Cable," Ben said remembering what he had read and seen a few weeks back.

"What did you say?" Alex asked, suddenly realizing where the Professor's next clue might be pointing at.

"I don't understand," she said in confusion.

"Chaos Cable, what about that?" Ben said looking at Alex.

"We need to go see Russel Ryan," Alex said, thinking something immediately.

"What? That dynamics guy or what do you call it? I don't know," Ben asked, totally clueless.

"What's going on here?" Laura said, sharing Ben's emotions.

"I'll explain on the way, let's go," Alex said in a hurry, walking ahead. Then without saying a word, he ran back to the Professor's study as if he had forgotten something.

Remembering the men outside the duplex, Alex picked up a table clock from the Professor's study and ran back to Laura and Ben the same way he came up, only this time he was quicker.

"OK, here is what we are going to do," he explained his plan to Ben and Laura which, to them, sounded quite convincing.

All three of them soon made their way back to the garden from the same passage they came in from. They were silent for the most part making their movements slow and steady. Upon reaching the end, Alex picked up the wooden door of the passage slightly and threw the watch to a safe distance.

He waited patiently for he knew what was about to happen. Soon, all three of them heard the clock ringing loudly. It was their lucky day, Alex had set the alarm. He knew the guard would react to it. That is exactly what happened.

As the way became clear for all of them, they ran towards the sidewalk. They knew the darkness would aid their rescue. Alex kept holding Laura's hand and Ben followed closely. Soon, they were at a safe distance, away from the duplex. Alex was searching for the transport when he saw a car deliberately making its way toward them. For a second, he thought the men might have found them. However, it stopped soon enough and two opaque shadows slipped their way out of it. Soon, he knew the shadows he had seen were of a man and a woman making out in the drift of night. The three of them could make out now that they were smooching and cuddling one another. The guy had his hand on her waist, slowly trying to seduce her. They were pushing each other away from the car towards a parking space where Alex could only assume nobody came to at this hour.

"What are you doing?" asked Laura as she saw Alex move toward the car.

CHAPTER 19

"Wait here, I'll be back in a jiffy," Alex said animatedly coming to the parking space.

As he came closer he could hear their moans getting louder. He got a small peep of the couple. He was wrong; they were not a mature couple like he thought. They were teenagers. As he moved a bit closer he could see that they were not making love, they were making out in pure lust. He thought it was the right time to see if the keys are still plucked in the car. Alex knew it was impossible to get a cab at this hour of the night. He got back to their car and as he had thought earlier, it was his lucky day.

He picked up Laura and Ben and in moments all three of them were relieved. When they were young, Alex had Ben steal a car. It reminded Laura of all the pranks Alex had played back when they were still young.

"So are we heading to your friend? What was his name?" Laura asked, sliding the picture into her left jeans pocket.

"Russel Ryan, yes, that's who we are going to," Alex said, passing the book he had found in Professor's study to Ben who was sitting behind him.

"What am I supposed to do with this?" Ben said, unknowingly grabbing the book.

"Hang onto it," Alex said as he saw a radiant smile appearing on Laura's face.

"So, what about this Russel guy? Are you sure he knows something regarding the Chaos Cable?" questioned Laura with uncertainty.

"He is someone I met only in my college years; he was also the one who made me meet Alice. Back then, he was game for statistics, later he made dynamical systems his thing," explained Alex.

"Who is Alice?" asked Laura trying to sound carefree, yet Alex knew she was curious.

"She is—" Ben was about to say something.

Alex interrupted, "We can talk about that later. We need to know more about these dynamical systems now."

"Your geekiness is really getting on my nerves now," Ben said, getting a bit irritated by all the complicated terms he had come across in the past few days.

"Dynamical systems are systems which are simple at their initial state but later with time become complicated," answered Alex, starting to explain.

"You mean they are time-dependent," Laura said, adding what she understood.

"Yes, that is why people who study them have to understand probability and predictability. I got to know about all this from Russel as I had a thing for physics then," Alex said, feeling they were getting somewhere.

"You said the UFT had to be a theory of predictability," Ben said, suddenly understanding his excitement.

"Exactly, that is why I think we're close to finding it, but that is not all that's on my mind. Chaos Cable is a dynamical system and so might be the case with *Quantum Interpretation of Many Worlds*," Alex said, his mind now grasping how big the whole picture is.

"What do you mean?" asked Laura, sharing his excitement.

CHAPTER 19

"From what I know, Chaos Cable helps predict the workings of the stock market. I think *Quantum Interpretation of Many Worlds* might do the same for reality," Alex said, sounding electrified.

"So, what you were saying is we have to find a connection between Chaos Cable and *Quantum Interpretation Of Many Worlds* and Russel might just be able to help us find that connection," Ben said, understanding the most of it.

"No, what I'm trying to say is someone has already found the connection," Alex said, looking at Laura with a smile. Laura paused and stared at Alex before realizing what he meant. She took out the picture from her pocket and stared at it with a smile.

CHAPTER 20

"Where is he put up?" asked Ben, feeling a bit uncomfortable in the back seat as they had been driving for a few hours now.

"He stays in San Diego with his folks," Alex said strongly. He looked at Laura to find her sleeping peacefully. She deserved it as he recollected the events of the night.

"Do you think he would be expecting you?" asked Ben, knowing the last time he showed up in front of Dex, they had men chasing them like dogs.

"Yup, I called him earlier. He is pretty excited by what I told him, he won't mind us," Alex said, ensuring Ben.

"I think we should just put the pieces in the right picture before we end up discussing the whole lot of things that have happened recently with us," Ben said urgently.

"All right," Alex said, still paying attention to his driving.

"From the beginning," Ben said. "Let's start with the clues, there was this envelope by the Professor that he gave to Laura that turned out to be a letter from Albert Einstein to Rosenthal," preceded Ben. "Yes, only that the Professor had added the two symbols," Ben said, trying not to miss out on anything.

CHAPTER 20

"Yes, the symbols pointing towards the constants and "=D-" which we are yet to figure out," Alex said, remembering.

"Correct, then you went to Caltech to search for a guy named David whose address was on the envelope and found that he died. But that came to be untrue when we followed the address," Ben said strongly.

"Yes, it turned out he died years later. Also, we found the diary in London which then led us to the discovery of the paper in Albert Einstein's residence," Alex said, going along.

"OK, that was the next clue which led us to Dexter, the one with the special theory of relativity which related the constant of the speed of light to the string," Ben said confirming.

"So the "ϕ" in the Professor's letter was pointing at the constant of the speed of light. Next, we combine it with the string to manipulate dimensions, leading us to superposition and *Quantum Interpretation of Many Worlds*," Alex said, explaining a little.

"Yes, but you are forgetting something," Ben said, trying to say something.

"What?" he said cautiously.

"Even this guy David was working on *Quantum Interpretation of Many Worlds*," Ben said, remembering what Dexter had told them earlier and reminding Alex.

"Right, how can I forget that? Maybe David and the Professor both were working on *Quantum Interpretation of Many Worlds* and they might have found a way to get to the Unified Field Theory," Alex said, understanding things more clearly.

"So, maybe there was someone who wanted to know what they knew," Ben said, adding.

"And for the same reason, they are now behind us," Alex said, looking right at Ben.

"Of course, there is no doubt about it. But what about the Chaos Cable and *Quantum Interpretation of Many Worlds*?" asked Ben, coming ahead now and looking at Alex.

"That is our next clue, I think the Professor and David were trying to connect the two and my guess is they succeeded," Alex said confidently.

"How can you be so sure about it?" asked Ben, trying to understand what Alex was thinking.

"We are about to find out," Alex said as he took a turn, entering San Diego.

As soon as they reached Russel's home, Ben noticed it wasn't a big place unlike what he had imagined. Russel stayed in an apartment.

Laura stood up steadily to see Alex and Ben staring at her. Suddenly she got stunned by someone knocking on the window. It was Russel.

"What took you guys so long?" Russel said to all three of them as Alex pulled the window down.

"It doesn't run so well by the looks of it," Alex said, staring at the wheel.

"Why don't you guys crash at my place? My folks are out anyways," Russel said hurriedly. "And you can tell me about your thing that you spoke of on the phone," he said with a wide grin.

CHAPTER 20

Laura felt a little amused watching him smile.

All three of them made their way up to Russel's place. As they entered, Ben realized it was a super spacious and comfortable apartment.

"Why don't you guys make yourself comfortable? I'll be back in the jiffy," Russel said, walking down the corridor on their right to what seemed like his room.

He soon came back with a bunch of snacks and some water.

"I thought you guys might be hungry so I saved up some snacks," Russel said, offering them some.

Laura saw now that he was a little fat but more of a happy-go-lucky kind of guy.

"So, I know you guys don't have much time, so let's just get on with it, shall we?" Russel said, eager to answer some questions and hear Alex's story.

Alex explained to him the whole story, what he and others had been going through the last few days, about Dexter and the clues, everything.

Russel was more than excited to help them out. He felt this was his time to redeem his glory, given a chance to add useful information to help Alex find the ultimate constant.

"Why don't you tell us about dynamical systems?" asked Ben calmly.

"OK, I don't want to make it sound complicated, so give me a minute," Russel said, taking some time to think about it.

Alex and Laura looked at each other silently as he looked at them.

"All right, here it goes," Russel said, beginning to explain. "Have you guys ever heard of the butterfly effect?" he asked curiously.

"Yeah, the flutter of a butterfly's wing can cause a typhoon halfway around the world," Laura said, answering Russel's question.

"Yes, that is correct. But that is not what it literally means, it means a small breakdown in the vast system can crumble it eventually," Russel said, pausing before making a statement. "For example, take any machine. If there is any single part missing, no matter how much small it might be, its absence will shut the machine down," Russel said, trying to make things simple for Laura and Ben to understand.

"What does it have to do with a dynamical system?" asked Ben yet again.

"Well, all dynamical systems are made of such small parts, only that they are not parts. They are mathematical functions and though being simple functions in the initial state of the system they become chaotic with time," Russel said slowly so that Ben and Laura understood what he was saying.

"Give me an example of a dynamical system," said Laura believingly.

"Stock market, statistics, any system that has a vast amount of data input. Other than that there are simple dynamical systems too but they are of no relevance," answered Russel instantly.

"Why?" asked Alex, coming into the conversation.

"For two reasons mostly, there is not much data and they are predictable," Russel said, looking at him.

CHAPTER 20

"What type of dynamical system is Chaos Cable?" asked Laura, guessing what he might say.

"It is a complicated dynamical system as it studies and interprets patterns over vast data," Russel said turning towards Laura.

"You said patterns?" Alex said, suddenly grabbing Russel's attention.

"Yes, all dynamical systems are deterministic," Russel said, again looking at Alex.

"What do you mean by deterministic? Wait, can you please keep this simple? I understood when you said about Chaos Cable being a complicated dynamical system but what about these patterns you speak of?" Ben said, trying to understand.

"Deterministic means things which are predictable or at least probabilistic. Chaos Cable interprets patterns over vast data and helps in predicting when one would come across a similar pattern of data next," Russel said, making it almost clear what he was trying to say.

"How does it work?" asked Alex.

"As I said, theoretically, all dynamical systems are made of mathematical functions," Russel said slowly, answering their question one by one.

"And these functions become complicated and chaotic with time," Alex said confidently this time.

"Yes, essentially because of the kind of data that they are interpreting or should I say calculating," Russel said feeling good that all of them now understood what he was saying.

"So, as the data in the system changes the function changes. But how do we analyze and calculate such vast data, I mean—" Ben said but he was cut off by Russell.

Russell was pointing at something. As all three of them turned to what Russel was pointing at they all smiled. It was a computer.

"So, you insert mathematical functions with the help of the computer to analyze data," Laura said.

"Yes, but these mathematical functions are more like a set of instructions," preceded Russel when he was cut in between by Ben this time.

"OK, I know that one. It is called an algorithm," he said with a smile.

"Yes, Ben, you are right. It is called an algorithm," Russel said, patting his shoulder.

"What is an algorithm?" asked Laura, understanding most parts but a little confused.

"It's called a program," Alex said, bringing the point to her attention.

"So, why couldn't you say program in the first place?" she said sarcastically. "So, what does it have to do with *Quantum Interpretation of Many Worlds*?" asked Laura unintentionally.

There was a small pause before Alex spoke.

"Maybe just like Chaos Cable, even the theory Many World Interpretation Of Quantum Mechanics is predictable and has a function, one which is yet to be fully understood," Alex said, looking at Russel.

CHAPTER 20

"I don't know, it might. But even if it does, you are talking about a function – an equation that describes the mechanics of the whole world and predicts it, the complete reality, there is nothing that could predict what's going to happen in reality," Russel said, trying to think something.

"Why not? Even reality is chaotic, so there might just be a function of this dynamical reality," Alex said forcefully.

"Alex, you don't understand. Even if there is such a function, you cannot predict everything in this reality. It is too big, you won't be able to see it," Russel said, trying to calm him down.

"Alex, he is right," Laura said, trying to help Russel calm him down.

"It's not just that," Ben said suddenly with something coming into his mind. "It's not one world we are talking about. Remember, it's called quantum interpretation of *Many Worlds*," he said looking at all three of them.

"Although that theory has no proof, he is right and there is just no way you would predict the whole of reality," Russel said, agreeing with them.

All of them sat quietly for a while.

"All I know about *Quantum Interpretation of Many Worlds* is, it is made up of choices," Alex said, trying to convince himself.

"What did you say?" Russel said suddenly realizing something.

"I said all I know is, it's made up of choices. Remember, it's many worlds," Alex said again.

"You know what, Alex? I think you might be right," Russel said with a smile.

"What do you mean?" Alex asked confused about what Russel said.

"Look, all dynamical systems have trajectories in which the data tends to flow and the function finds common grounds in these trajectories to reveal patterns and then predict how the system will evolve," Russel said excitedly.

"You mean," Alex said, suddenly grasping what Russel was trying to say.

"Wait a minute," Laura said, now getting Russel's point.

"It will be interesting to see what happens when one substitute these trajectories with choices in Many World Interpretation theory. I mean, it can be one way to find such a function if even there exist such a thing," Russel said.

"What's happening? Why you both are so excited?" Ben said, feeling sorry for not being able to understand their conversation.

"Wait a minute, there is still something I need to understand," Alex said looking at Russel. "How does a function work in a dynamical system?" asked Alex.

"For the most part, it's a mystery but I did say most of it would be the law of averages. The function evolves with data, time and again to keep the system predictable," Russel said before taking a pause for a moment.

"Guys, instead of all this discussion maybe we can find the function in the book," Ben said, thinking that might be helpful.

CHAPTER 20

"That might work," Alex said, thinking how he never really searched the whole book completely.

It was a different situation then as his mind was on another track. Alex and Laura grabbed the book and began searching for something that looked like a function, an equation or something like that.

To their disappointment there was nothing that they could find.

"Maybe we missed something back at the Professor's place," Ben said, thinking that they might have to go back.

"No, we can't go back," Alex said, but he was interrupted by Russel.

"What's this?" Russel said, pointing at a page number and a single letter that was circled within the page.

It was so small that all three of them had failed to notice it.

As they searched furthermore, they found there were more like them. They wrote them on a single page, at first, they seemed random. Soon Alex saw through it.

CHAOS CABLE → RICHARD FEYNMAN

Alex knew where they would find their next clue.

"I know where we might find the function we are looking for," Alex said.

CHAPTER 21

Soon, next morning, they were heading close to a nearby library.

It had been a long time since Ben found himself stepping into the world of books.

Laura saw that Alex had his mind on something; she began to ask him where they should start this search.

"Alex, what you think should we do?" she asked, coming closer to him.

There was no answer. Alex was looking around the library lost in thoughts.

She asked him again. This time it broke the chain of thoughts that were running up his head and he answered reluctantly.

"Yeah! What? I don't know," he said.

"What were you thinking?" she asked calmly.

"I don't know why, but I think I want to know more about this guy David," he said, looking up at Laura with confusion.

CHAPTER 21

"We will, in due time. But I think it's more important for us to find the function as of now," she said gently.

"I think you are right. Maybe if we find the function it will tell us more about David," Alex said, hoping things would go well. "I think I'll check the books. Meanwhile you and Ben, why don't you go search the internet and let me know if you'll find something?" he continued, showing Laura the direction in which the computer was.

"Yeah, I think you are right. I don't think Ben can stand this place for long, look at him. He is so terrified with all these books around him," she said smiling as they both looked at him.

Ben looked at them from a distance. As Laura walked up to him, he was quick to react.

"This place is killing me, Laura. Get me out of here," he said desperately.

"Follow me," she said, turning around and giggling with deep caution.

Now Alex was searching for reference books and, on the other hand, Laura and Ben were comfortable going through stuff on the internet.

A few moments later, Laura came back to Alex. He was too engrossed in looking at the book in his hand to see that she was out of patience.

"Alex, we can't do this," she said, looking tired.

"What happened?" he asked, wondering.

"There is just too much physics and numbers and equations, I don't know what to do," she said, expressing her disappointment.

"I know I think you should take some rest now. How is Ben doing?" Alex asked politely.

"He has gone bonkers. He doesn't know what he is supposed to look for," she said, giving a sarcastic smile.

"I don't blame him," Alex said, giving a faded smile himself.

"You guys should grab some lunch. I'll join you in a few minutes," he said encouraging her to go along.

"Are you sure? We can wait for you," she said looking at him.

Ben came walking along from behind.

"Hey, what's going on here? Are we getting somewhere or what?" he said looking at Alex and Laura going through books.

"Let's go grab something to eat," Laura said, walking away.

"God, I'm hungry," he said looking at Alex and back at Laura.

There was a restaurant close to the library. Ben and Laura made their way to where it was. It was a Chinese restaurant.

As they went inside Ben said something to the lady who welcomed them.

"What was that? I never thought you spoke Chinese," Laura said, smiling.

"I never thought I did, until now," he replied flirting with his voice.

CHAPTER 21

"You are such an ass," she said, trying to discourage them.

Soon as their meal was served Alex joined them.

"Did you find something?" asked Laura, anticipating good news.

"Nothing much. But I was kind of thinking we should concentrate on his major achievements. Maybe that would lead us to something," said Alex, talking about Richard Feynman, swirling the noodles by his fork.

"How are we supposed to know which of his achievements will lead us to the function we are looking for?" Laura said, disagreeing.

"I'm sorry, Alex. This is not going to work," Ben said going with Laura.

"We know that it is in his works somewhere. We just don't know where it is," Alex said, trying to cheer them up.

"But that's our main problem," Laura stopped as she saw Alex had his attention on something else.

"What about symbols π and E? Don't you think we have missed something?" added Ben.

"No, π is a constant, 3.14 and it's the same with E being a mathematical constant. They have nothing to do with the function we are searching for, excuse me," Alex said, calling the waitress serving a nearby table.

"What do these numbers mean?" asked Alex to the lady quickly, pointing out the circled numbers written on top of the menu.

"It's the year we opened the restaurant, sir," she replied politely.

Alex looked at Laura who was smiling at him.

"Are you thinking what I'm thinking?" he said looking into her eyes.

"I think I am," she said, continuing to smile.

"What? What are you guys thinking? Would you just tell me already? You never tell me," Ben said looking at both simultaneously.

"The numbers circled on the top of the book are the years," Laura said, telling him to relax.

"What help would that be?" he said, puzzled by their discovery.

"We don't know yet what we are about to find out," Laura said, beginning to get up from the chair along with Alex. "Come on, get your ass moving already," she said looking at Ben.

Soon they were back at the library. This time all three of them were on the internet. When they combined the numbers with permutation and combination, they found they were converging to give two years 1977 and 1948.

They found that it was in 1977 that Chaos Cable was formed and it was in 1948 that Richard Feynman invented something called a 'Path Integral Formula'.

"What is this?" Ben asked yet again with most of it going over his head.

"It is the function which Feynman created for quantum mechanics. I don't completely understand it, but it has something to do with determining the position of the electron in quantum mechanics," replied Alex.

CHAPTER 21

"Excuse me, is your name Alex?" a voice startled all three of them. They turned to see who it was. It was a man who seemed to be in his mid-thirties. He was wearing formals; he seemed like security personnel to Alex, judging from his black and white attire.

"Yes, who are you?" Alex asked a bit taken aback.

"There is no time to talk, all your questions will be answered. But first, you must come with me," the man said without wasting any time. "Are they your friends?" he continued looking at Laura and Ben.

"Yes, they are. What this is all about?" asked Alex, determined to get an answer.

"Good, then you all must follow me, I believe your life is in danger," he said quickly walking away, telling them to follow him.

"Where are we going?" questioned Alex as they all took his trail.

"I have transportation waiting for you outside. We must hurry, they must be close," said the man, moving closer to the exit.

Just as they took a few more steps, a gang of men carrying weapons entered.

"Run, find another exit, all of you!" said the security personnel, without wasting another moment.

Within moments Cody's men entered, the man in the uniform quickly took his gun out and turned the table to take cover and all three of them ran in the opposite direction to find the door. As Alex ran, he could hear the gunshots behind him.

"Here, this way," Alex said, noticing the door.

Going through the back door they noticed there were other people who were trying to escape too through the back corridor. One of the guys pointed the way out for them. They were now in the back alley. It was empty and they could see the main road. It was a relieving sight.

"Maybe we can get to the car from there. That road can lead us to the front exit," Ben said, trying to escape.

"What if these men have already taken out that car?" Alex said, stopping him.

"We have to take the risk, it's our only chance," Ben said, panicking.

"Alex, Ben is right. We have to go now before it's too late," Laura said, understanding Ben was right.

"All right, now it's cool," Alex said, moving ahead.

Running as hard as they could, they came close to the front exit of the library. As they were trying to find the escape, Laura pointed out a white car parked on the other side of the road. There was another limousine parked next to the library.

"That black one might be the one from which the men came out to kill us," Ben said, sounding sure.

"I think you are right, but how are we supposed to get to the white car? If the men sitting in the black limo see us, they might even kill us," Laura said, quickly analyzing the situation.

"I think we have to make a run for it," Alex said, thinking there was no other option.

"But—"

CHAPTER 21

Laura stopped Ben before he could say anything. "Ben, we have to do this, we took the risk earlier when you said, remember?" she said, agreeing with Alex reminding Ben how they had entered the duplex earlier.

"Let's do this," Alex said, getting ready.

"Remember, run as hard as you can. Laura, you stay ahead, Ben and I will follow you," he said before Laura took a run for it. To their surprise, the door of the white car opened and all three of them found themselves safe inside the back seat in no time.

"Hold tight," they heard the voice as they felt a jerk on their backs.

The car accelerated swiftly through the road destroying a few wagons parked on their side in the process.

"We are being followed," Alex said, looking back through the rear window.

"Don't worry about it," he said as the car took some swift and edgy turns.

Finding a gap between them, the driver pushed the car into a passage he knew the limousine would not get through. It was not enough as they were followed by another four-wheeler of what looked like an SUV and this time there were gunshots.

"Hold on," said the driver again.

The chase went on for another few minutes when the man driving the car ran over a traffic light. It was a sleazy escape, within moments they could have died in an accident. Soon the driver took a couple of quick turns to get out of sight of those who were following them. In a few moments, all of them were safe but were shaken up by the event, it wasn't like the last time when they were traced back to Dexter. This time they were more men and more ammunition. Not to mention a life was lost. There was no way the man who had come to inform them about the threat would have made it out of the library alive.

Both Ben and Laura soon fell asleep, they had nothing to say. Alex too thought it was best for them to relax for a new tomorrow to come. God knows what they would have to face next.

Although he first felt it would be best if he would stay awake but later, he thought the guys who saved their lives wouldn't be that bad.

"Where are we going?" he asked, his voice getting a bit sleepy.

"To a friend," said the driver keeping the conversation brief.

"Which friend?" Alex asked feeling a bit dizzy.

"It would be best if you would leave your questions to rest till morning," said the driver telling him to relax.

Alex wouldn't say anything more, his eyes won't let him. The last thing he saw was the driver taking a turn towards the highway.

The next morning, Laura was the first one to wake up. She quickly shook Alex and Ben hard to wake them up.

Both woke up with a jerk as the memory of men chasing them was still fresh including the sound of gunshots.

"Where are we?" asked Laura to Ben and Alex, simultaneously looking at them.

She looked at her watch. It was more than eight hours that they had been traveling.

CHAPTER 21

It was supposed to be a nice sleep for them, yet it seemed to all of them like it had been only a couple of hours that they had dozed off for.

Alex was about to ask the driver when all three of them saw a road sign. It was huge, they wouldn't have missed it.

"What are we doing in San Francisco?" asked Alex, this time with a strong voice demanding an answer.

"You will know in a few minutes, don't worry about it," said the driver trying to sound as casual about it as he could.

"Alex, how can we trust this guy?" whispered Laura, coming closer to Alex.

"Relax, he saved our lives. He can't be that bad," whispered Alex looking back at her.

"How can you be so sure?" Laura whispered, looking at him.

"Yeah, you never know what we might get ourselves into," whispered Ben, joining as he had just heard Laura.

"I asked him where he was taking us yesterday when you both were asleep. He said he is taking us to a friend," Alex said, ensuring them nothing could be going wrong.

Ben and Laura kept their silence as they knew they were in a car and they couldn't do shit about it now. As they entered the city, it was full of enthusiasm and vigor. For once, all three of them felt a little alive after what they had been through.

Suddenly they heard the phone ring. It was the driver. He answered by flipping it over and controlling the steering with the other hand, "Yes, they are with me now, I am bringing them to you. I'm almost there, sir," he said in an obeying fashion.

He turned back and asked, "Do you guys want to eat something or you want me to take you to the final stop?" he said in a comforting tone.

Although they were hungry, Alex answered on behalf of all three of them, "No, thank you. Just take us to the friend you told us about," he said aggressively.

"Whatever you say," said the driver and disconnected the call.

As Alex looked outside, he was pretty sure that they were now in the heart of the city.

There were malls and multiplexes all around. After a few minutes, he was sure that they were entering a residential area.

As the car came to stop outside a private estate which looked quite lavish with a huge gate and a path that led them to the entrance, Ben and Laura noticed the garden and dogs.

As they stepped outside the car, there was a man waiting for them with a smile. He looked really old, maybe in his early seventies.

Alex noticed the board that bedded a name.

JACK WASHINGTON

CHAPTER 22

Uncle Jack took a small stagnation as he approached to have a good look at all three of them.

It was not long before Laura recognized him.

"Uncle Jack!" she said as she walked towards him in joy and contentment.

Laura had been trying to get in touch with him ever since the Professor was murdered. Maybe one of the many calls she had made ever since reached him after all.

"I thought I would never see you again, I am so glad you both are all right," Uncle Jack said hugging Laura while looking at Alex.

"And who do we have here?" he continued questioning, turning to look at Ben.

"He is my friend Ben, Uncle," Alex said, moving toward him.

It was a really long time since Alex had seen him when he was still young in his childhood. Back then the Professor took care of him. Laura, on the other hand, had been in touch with him now and then.

"What is this all about, Uncle Jack?" Alex asked looking at the driver who was now standing relaxed. "And how come you never called back?" he said remembering how Laura had made the calls for a few days.

"Let's go inside first, I'll explain everything," he said, turning to walk inside his home along with Laura.

"I think you guys should clean up first. We can talk while we have breakfast. I got it served up knowing it would be almost morning that you all would reach here," Uncle Jack said, walking towards another man as they entered. He looked like his caretaker.

"Freddy here would show you your rooms, be comfortable and please ask if you need anything. We would meet at the table in half an hour," he continued giving them a welcoming smile, feeling happy to see the kids after a long time.

Soon all three of them had freshened up. It really had been a hard night.

Alex noticed the design of the room and the books. They were not different from the duplex. He knew how the Professor and Uncle Jack had been friends for a long time and that they came from the same background.

The aura of the place brought back a few memories but he was soon distracted.

"Sir, the breakfast is ready and your friends are waiting for you," said Freddy, knocking at the door before Alex answered it.

Alex was quick to respond. "I'll be there in a moment," he said giving a friendly smile.

CHAPTER 22

As soon as he made himself comfortable on the table his curiosity got the best of him.

"Uncle Jack, what's happening? Why are these people attacking us? And what are you doing in San Francisco?" questioned Alex recklessly, looking at Uncle Jack.

"Right, after John was attacked, I was next. But whoever was behind this didn't get me and neither did he get what he was looking for," Uncle Jack said looking at him intensely.

"What do you mean?" Alex asked, ignoring what he already understood.

"You tell me, I mean you already know what I'm talking about, don't you, Alex?" he said inquisitively looking at him.

"The letter, you mean!" he replied adding something.

"Right, so it's a letter," Uncle Jack said, thinking something. "Soon after the escape, I moved around a bit to figure out what was happening and then finally, I decided to come here until things are settled."

"But why didn't you call me back?" Laura said confusingly.

"It was too big a risk to take for I didn't have a clue where you guys were. So, after working hard a friend of mine working with the San Diego police department told me about your location. I had to call a few people working for security who I knew back from the old days and they decided to give me a hand to bring you guys safely to me," Uncle Jack said explaining the situation.

"Thank you, Uncle Jack," Laura said, coming over and giving him a hug.

"It was a tragedy 'cause we lost a guy in the process. But I don't understand what you guys were doing in the library," asked Uncle Jack, looking at Alex and Laura.

Alex, Laura and Ben looked at each other briefly before Laura spoke.

"Uncle Jack, father gave me this letter to give to Alex," she said, showing him the letter she had been keeping safely all this while.

Uncle Jack took out his glasses from his top left pocket and paused before taking a sharp look at it.

"With the question of the universal constants, you have broached one of the most interesting questions that may be asked at all. There are two kinds of constants: apparent and real ones. The apparent ones are simply the outcome of the introduction of arbitrary units, but are eliminable. The real [true] ones are genuine numbers which God had to choose arbitrarily, as it were, when He deigned to create this world. In my opinion now is – stated briefly – that constants of the second type do not exist and their apparent existence is caused by the fact that we have not penetrated deeply enough. I therefore believe that such numbers can only be of a basic type, as for instance π or e." "=D-" "ϕ"

$$16.259.72.97.2.7.$$

"I know this letter. John showed it to me a long time back," Uncle Jack said, taking a quick look at it.

"Did you notice something?" Alex said quickly testing him.

"Wait a minute, what is this? It looks like some kind of a symbol," Uncle Jack said noticing the "ϕ" and "=D-". "And what is this number?"

CHAPTER 22

"Yup, what do you think?" asked Alex hoping to hear something new.

"The "ϕ" represents the divine constant, this letter is clearly pointing at the power of the constants most likely the constant for the Unified Field Theory," Uncle Jack said, understanding the meaning of the letter.

"I think you are right," Laura said with a smile. She had known Uncle Jack to be a smart man.

"I think he is trying to relate the constants of all the theories together," Alex said, trying to sound smart.

"Not necessarily, if that were the case, all theories would have to stand true," Uncle Jack said, pointing out the basic flaw in the assumption Alex was making. "But you may be partially right. Maybe not all theories, just the constants in the theories that make the most sense," Uncle Jack said smiling from the corner of his lips.

"What do you mean?" Alex asked.

"Back when John and I were friends, we were trying to work on a way to combine all the constants together to find the ultimate universal constant, that was one way we thought we could make it happen," Uncle Jack started to talk about his days with John. "Yeah, we made a lot of mistakes then, but the basic mistake we made that time was we overlooked the theories we were taking the constants from," continued Uncle Jack.

"You mean theories that were not valid. But why would you do that?" asked Alex curiously.

"For one, we didn't have the exact reason to discard that theory. Technology was changing every day and theories were being proved right and wrong over and over again, there were people working on both sides of the fence," Uncle Jack said, making a point.

"Talk about the grass which is always greener on the other side," interrupted Ben, tired of being quiet all this long.

"Damn right. However, later someone did something similar and came out with the fine structure constant," continued Uncle Jack.

"You mean combining the universal constants? I thought that would lead to the ultimate universal constant," Alex said confidently.

"Only if we are able to find the real values of the constants," Uncle Jack answered.

"The dimensionless values," Alex said, remembering what he had told Ben before.

"Yes, I think I don't have to tell you it is the same reason why even fine structure constant is not the ultimate constant. We know it is a product of the combination of other universal constants but we don't know the real values of the universal constants. So, we don't know how they came together to give the fine structure constant," Uncle Jack said, explaining.

"So, the fine structure constant is just a glimpse of what the ultimate constant should look like," Alex said, questioning.

"It's rather hard to presume that way. The ultimate constant is proof of an ultimate force. The fine structure constant is, of course, an important discovery as it is dimensionless (pure number) and is the combination of other universal constants such as E, and h," Uncle Jack said, arguing.

CHAPTER 22

"So, the point is, we need to know where all of this leads to," Alex said coming to a conclusion looking at Ben, Laura and Uncle Jack.

"Yes, I may say so. If you need me to help you, you have to tell me everything that happened from the beginning," replied Uncle Jack, looking at Alex with curiosity.

"Well, I think I should start first," interrupted Laura, simultaneously looking at Alex and Uncle Jack.

"Alright," Uncle Jack said, settling himself on an easy chair.

"It all began when I came back from New York. It was late, was raining that night and I could not find father anywhere," she started to say, remembering the night the Professor was attacked.

"Go on," Uncle Jack said, his attention completely on her.

"After calling him which didn't help much as there was no answer, I got nervous and was about to register a complaint to the nearest police department. That's when I saw him walking outside the duplex," she said remembering how worried she was back then.

"So, you must have run out to him," Uncle Jack said, listening to her.

"Exactly, that's what I did. I ran out of the duplex and he saw me standing in the rain," Laura said looking at Uncle Jack. "I asked him where he had been and he told me he had gone to the university for some urgent and important work that he had," she continued.

"Did he tell you what work it was?" Uncle Jack asked quickly, realizing there might be something there.

"No, he didn't. He didn't talk much, it was very strange," she said, going back to the moment he kissed her good night.

"Listen, it's all right if you need to take rest," Ben started to say as he thought Laura seemed to get more and more emotional now.

"No, it is OK, I need to do this," she said looking at Ben. "After wishing me good night I went back to my room and I guess he did the same. But then later as I had fallen deep asleep on my bed, they attacked," Laura continued looking at Alex and Uncle Jack.

"What happened?" Uncle Jack said, looking at her with care and trust.

"I heard gunshots, I ran upstairs and found him on the floor and there was blood," she said breaking down in tears.

"Laura, please. Hold yourself together," Uncle Jack said, coming over and trying to console her.

"He gave me this letter and he told me to find Alex," she said looking into Alex's eyes.

"But how did you escape?" Uncle Jack said, confusingly.

"My friend Rachel helped me out. I somehow managed to get out of the duplex and to the highway where she saw me and took me to the railway station," she said explaining.

"So, you got the train and that's how Alex came into the picture," Uncle Jack said, understanding the scenario.

"Yeah," Alex said in confirmation.

"All right, what happened next?" Uncle Jack asked, looking at Laura.

CHAPTER 22

Laura was about to speak when Alex stopped her. "I'll take it from here," he said looking at Uncle Jack to share his bit. "We found out that the letter was given to the Professor by someone named David and we thought the best thing to do would be to find out whether he was there with the Professor during his Caltech years," began Alex, starting to tell his part.

"Then, what did you do?" he said looking at Alex.

"I went to Caltech to inquire about him," Alex said when he was briefly interrupted by Uncle Jack.

"And what did you find out?" questioned Uncle Jack, almost curiously.

"That I was right, he and Professor were good friends and also that David was working on a theory regarding Many Worlds, but nothing beyond that. Later, we found an address on the back of the letter," Alex said, telling him what followed.

"What address?" Uncle Jack said, again sounding a bit confused.

"David's address was written at the back of the letter," Alex said looking into his eyes.

"So, you guys went to London," Uncle Jack said in surprise.

"Well, that's the only clue we had then," Alex said looking at Laura and Ben.

"So, what did you find?" he asked looking at all three of them.

"We found that he and his wife had been killed years back," Alex said looking at Uncle Jack.

"Alex, did you forget the locker?" Ben asked remembering the clue David had left.

"Oh yes, we found that David had left clues for the Professor," Alex said, remembering David's diary and Albert Einstein's desk.

"What clue?" he questioned with his eyes becoming wide.

"The clue that led us to Albert Einstein's residence to find the constants that the letter had been emphasizing. We also tried to link the constant of the speed of light 'c' to the string," Alex said looking at Uncle Jack who was looking keener than ever before.

"To the string theory? But why?" Uncle Jack asked trying to understand the course of events. "Wait a minute, does it mean…" he said, realizing something. "It would only lead to time personalization, the speed of light influences time and in string theory. It would make time personal for all entities and it would be something like super position," Uncle Jack said, finally understanding the idea.

"Yes, a phenomenon that is often talked about in quantum mechanics, especially in *Quantum Interpretation of Many Worlds*. You would know that better than anyone," Alex said, looking at Uncle Jack.

"But what's the point?" Uncle Jack said still wondering.

"That's what we are trying to find out when we came out with another clue," Alex said continuing his story.

"What clue?" Uncle Jack asked a bit puzzled.

"In the letter, we found another series of numbers and we didn't know what they were until Ben suggested that they look like index numbers for books kept in a library. It was not late when

CHAPTER 22

Ben suggested that it must be from the Professor's study," he said looking at Laura with a smile.

"That's when you guys went back to the duplex," Uncle Jack said, looking at all three of them.

"Yes, we did. And I found something that I actually never would have expected," Alex said remembering the book on Chaos.

"What was it?" Uncle Jack asked, sounding eager to hear what Alex was about to say.

This time Alex told him what was on his mind, "*Quantum Interpretation of Many Worlds* is a dynamical system and so is Chaos theory and that's what we found in a book on Chaos theory."

"Yes, I think I'm getting older now," Uncle Jack said with a competitive smile at Alex.

"So, what did you find in the book? You must have found something relating the Chaos to *Quantum Interpretation of Many Worlds*, that should be interesting," continued Uncle Jack in anticipation.

"We found a clue that was trying to relate the Chaos Theory and Richard Feynman and that's where the trail ends. We were trying to figure it out when your guy found us and brought us to you," Alex said, looking at Uncle Jack and the others.

"In between all this we got help from two of Alex's friends who helped us understand the clues, string theory and Chaos Cable (dynamical system)," Laura said looking at Uncle Jack with affection.

"And we have been attacked twice," added Ben, speaking up after a long time.

"So, there were no more clues," Uncle Jack said looking at them.

"No, none. Wait a minute, there is one important thing that I've missed telling you, Uncle Jack," Alex said, suddenly remembering something.

"What is it, Alex?" questioned Uncle Jack inquisitively.

"There was the year 1926!" Alex replied with an enigma.

"Yes, I just remembered that was the year Albert Einstein had written that paragraph," Laura said when suddenly Alex spoke again.

"No, I'm not talking about 1926 in that paragraph, it was also there in David's diary and maybe in the book we found in Professors' s study too," Alex said thinking about all of them.

There was a moment of silence before Uncle Jack spoke. "1926... of course," he said excitedly.

CHAPTER 23

"What? What is it?" Alex questioned in joy and amusement.

"Before I explain to you about 1926, it is important that you know a little more about Richard Feynman," Uncle Jack said with a keen look in his eyes.

"Please," Laura said impatiently.

"There were a lot of developments that took place in the first half of the 19th century as far as physics goes, but I'll come back to it later. For now, let me tell you something about Richard Feynman," Uncle Jack said thinking something, looking at all three of them. "He was a prodigy. To begin with, he started solving and making theorems of his own while most of his counterparts were struggling to find their way out of high school. He was a mathematician of a different kind," Uncle Jack continued.

"Wow!" Alex exclaimed, looking at Uncle Jack.

"Later, in his life, he graduated from Caltech with two PhDs, he also helped in the formation of the basic model for particle physics as we know it today," Uncle Jack said looking at Laura.

"Cool," Alex said, looking at Uncle Jack.

"Yes, but that is only one of the reasons he became famous. The other which is more important for us is his famous Path Integral Formula," Uncle Jack said, looking at Alex with a smile.

"I'm confused because I don't know much about it, just that I feel I've heard about it before. Yes, I have read it, it's in quantum mechanics. That's what we found in the library while going through his works," Alex said, remembering and pointing out when he had read it earlier.

"Do you know what it is?" Uncle Jack questioned ironically.

"Will somebody please tell me what's going on? This Path Integral Formula or whatever it is, it's beyond my understanding," Ben said, again feeling a little left out.

"Calm down, Ben. I'll explain later," Alex said, telling him not to interrupt.

"Why am I always the last one to know? Anyway, please continue, Uncle Jack," Ben said helplessly.

"Quantum mechanics is governed by a very important principle which is known as the uncertainty principle," Uncle Jack began with the explanation looking at all three of them.

"Yeah, I think it was founded by Werner Heisenberg," Alex said, remembering a little what he had read a long time back.

"Yes, it forms the backbone of quantum, stating clearly that one could only get to know the position or velocity of the particle at a time," Uncle Jack said, revising to Alex about quantum mechanics.

"You mean you can't know them both simultaneously, no matter what," Laura said looking at Uncle Jack.

CHAPTER 23

"Absolutely not," replied Uncle Jack. "Now you must understand that the quantum world is very confusing and it is not easy to determine the position of the particle," Uncle Jack started to speak again, feeling happy that everyone was paying attention.

"What about velocity?" Laura asked looking at Alex and Uncle Jack.

"That doesn't concern us. For now, let's concentrate on the position of the particle," replied Uncle Jack, thinking something. "Now where was I?" he asked, feeling a little distant.

"The position of the particle," Alex said reminding him of where he had left the conversation.

"Yeah, all right. Now, this is where Feynman made his mark. He found an easier and much quicker way of finding the position of the particle with the help of his formula," Uncle Jack said coming back from where he left.

"The Path Integral Formula," Alex spoke, realizing what Uncle Jack was getting at.

"Bingo!" Uncle Jack exclaimed.

"But all this still doesn't explain what Feynman has to do with the Chaos theory," Laura said disappointingly.

"It is not Feynman, it is his formula that has something to do with Chaos theory," Uncle Jack said, trying to make everyone feel relaxed with a smile.

Alex quickly turned his head to Uncle Jack. He knew something important was going through his mind. "It's his formula? But how?" he questioned curiously looking at Uncle Jack.

"The position of the particle in quantum mechanics is defined by a wave function," replied Uncle Jack speaking slowly now.

"What is that?" asked Ben, feeling lost from the beginning.

"Well, light sometimes tends to behave like a wave and otherwise as particles which we know by experiments carried out. That said, taking the wave nature of the light we define the position of the particle by a wave function which is given by a mathematical equation," Uncle Jack said looking at Ben trying to explain to him.

"So technically positions of particles are determined by equations," Ben said, understanding things a bit more clearly.

"Yes, then again, there are many such wave functions for each particle and that is where Feynman's Path Integral Formula comes into play. It tracks down the probabilities of these wave functions to reveal their density," Uncle Jack said, speaking ever so carefully making sure everyone understands.

"I don't get you completely," Ben said reluctantly, looking at Uncle Jack.

"Think of it as each particle has several trajectories which tend to land them in different positions. Feynman's formula calculates the probabilities of these trajectories to reveal a set of trajectories which are common to all particles, much like the average of overall trajectories. Only in the following case, the average is not described by one trajectory but by a set of trajectories and that is why we call this set of trajectories 'density'," Uncle Jack said coming to a conclusion, looking at all three of them sharply.

"Is it…" Alex said, thinking something.

"Yes, Alex you are thinking in the right direction, the trajectories, the averages. Richard Feynman's Path Integral Formula brings

CHAPTER 23

out the dynamic nature of quantum mechanics," Uncle Jack said, interrupting Alex knowing what was going through in his mind.

"In a very strange way, if I may say so, this makes quantum mechanics and Chaos both dynamical systems," Alex said, wondering at the impact of such an idea.

Alex went into deep thought; he knew he had stumbled across a powerful idea.

"One more thing, does this mean Feynman's famous formula plays a fundamental role in the theory of *Quantum Interpretation of Many Worlds*?" asked Alex curiously to Uncle Jack.

"Of course, it will play a fundamental role as according to the theory of *Quantum Interpretation of Many Worlds*, each trajectory (position) acts like a choice for a different universe," Uncle Jack said affirmatively.

"Where does this bring us?" inquired Laura, looking at Alex and Uncle Jack.

"Let's link up all the clues that we have come across till now and see what we get," Ben said, coming out with an idea.

"I think, for once, I agree with you," proclaimed Alex telling Ben.

They gathered all the clues and placed them on a small table located on the side of the room where Uncle Jack was sitting contentedly.

"So, we have the letter written by Albert Einstein in 1945, talking about the constants," Laura said.

"It is the one that talks about the ultimate universal constant, remembering the symbol of the divine constant "ϕ"," Alex said, reminding him.

"Yup, all right. I remember the dimensionless constant," Ben said sternly, irritated. "Right, and don't forget it also told us about the constants and pointed us towards the constant of the speed of light 'c' when we found the note in the locker," Ben said remembering. "Then the note from the locker pointed us to the constant of the speed of light, I am talking about the file which happened to be the next clue that we found in the study of Albert Einstein. According to the next clue we found in the file we combined the constant of the speed of light with the string theory and what did we get then?" Ben questioned, becoming a little confused.

"We found that time becomes different for all the bodies irrespective of the distance between them," Laura said remembering.

"Wait, does it include us?" questioned Alex looking at Uncle Ben curiously.

"Well technically and theoretically, if there are other universes, it should," Uncle Jack said confirming.

"That would mean Many Worlds Theory has multiple timelines. According to *Quantum Interpretation of Many Worlds*, there is a different me in a different time existing in another universe," Alex said, looking at Uncle Jack and Laura.

"So, what you guys are saying is there are other worlds. Are you guys serious?" Ben said mockingly.

"Well, the clues and the theory all point toward this fact," Uncle Jack said his voice becoming hard, looking at Ben.

CHAPTER 23

"Let's not get ahead of ourselves. We don't have any practical proof of this," Laura said looking at everyone.

"You mean not yet," Alex said looking into her eyes.

"Are you serious, Alex? You really think there are other worlds or universes?" Laura asked, thinking Alex must be out of his mind.

"We don't have a complete picture yet, there is still more," Uncle Jack said trying to calm them all down.

"Yeah, you are right. We just found out that *Quantum Interpretation of Many Worlds* is a dynamical system," Alex said, acknowledging the irony of the matter.

"So?" questioned Ben, not quite understanding where Alex was going with the connection between Chaos and quantum.

"So, if there is a way to find a pattern in Chaos, there's also a way to find a pattern in *Quantum Interpretation of Many Worlds*," Laura said, understanding what Alex was saying.

"Ideas of finding a pattern in *Quantum Interpretation of Many Worlds* has already been put across," Uncle Jack said, looking at Laura and then turning to Alex. "Yes, you do understand it now, don't you, Alex? Do you want me to tell them or would you do it yourself?" Uncle Jack asked smiling, looking at Alex.

"Richard Feynman's Path Integral Formula plays the same role as genetic algorithms (computer programs) plays in calculating and revealing patterns in the stock market which is a kind of dynamical system just as *Quantum Interpretation Of Many Worlds*," Alex said explaining to Ben and Laura.

"Wait, quantum interpretation of many worlds or other universes include such as ours, that's what you said earlier, right?" Ben said, thinking something.

"Yes, I did, why?" Alex asked, looking at Ben.

"So, you are saying just like stocks in the stock market, the timelines in *Quantum Interpretation of Many Worlds* have patterns too," Ben said, raising his eyebrows, remembering pattern/proportion reveals the constant.

"Yes, that fits the theory but what is more important is we don't know what this pattern/proportion is and more than that we need to find the force that drives this pattern/proportion," Alex said telling him how important this was.

"So, this is the ultimate force that you were talking about earlier when you said the ultimate constant is not just a number, it's the force. I think you said, 'it's not just math it's physics'," Ben said smiling, reminding Alex what he had told him earlier when they had first read the letter written by Albert Einstein.

"Yes, now you understand if we find this force we will find that constant," Alex said feeling excited, realizing now how far they have come together in their quest.

"You are missing a very important point here, Alex," Uncle Jack said, interrupting Alex.

"What is it, Uncle Jack?" asked Laura looking at him inquisitively.

"*Quantum Interpretation of Many Worlds* is a theory yet unproved so if the theory itself doesn't exist everything that we have said would be meaningless," Uncle Jack said, reminding him of a point that had gone unnoticed.

CHAPTER 23

"I am more than sure that the theory exists. All the clues are pointing to this fact and we will prove it by finding that ultimate force," Alex said, looking at Laura and Ben with determination.

"If you do find the ultimate force, Alex, it would indeed prove the existence of many worlds and state the existence of *Quantum Interpretation of Many Worlds* theory correct. But remember, the force you will find would be completely new, unlike gravity or electromagnetism. It would be the next benchmark in physics," said Uncle Jack, giving him courage.

"I think this makes Richard Feynman really special," Ben said, looking at all of them.

"Wait I forgot to ask one thing, how is Richard Feynman's Path Integral Formula the same as a genetic algorithm in the stock market?" Ben asked, looking at Uncle Jack, Laura too nodded along.

"Algorithms, commonly known as programs, work in dynamical systems like the stock market and others by computing data points over a period of time. In dynamical systems, this is known as the 'Geometry of Time Series'. This 'Geometry of Time Series' can be converted to non-linear equations in mathematics. If you remember, I told you, wave functions are also equations and it so happens that they too are non-linear. Now you understand computer programs (genetic algorithm) and Richard Feynman's Path Integral Formula is actually calculating the same thing," explained Uncle Jack slowly, so that Ben understands everything.

"Geometry of Time Series?" Ben asked again reluctantly.

"Statistics, like graphs/bar diagrams/frequencies, etc., reveal the Geometry of Time Series," Uncle Jack said patiently, trying to make him understand.

"There's still a very important clue that we are missing," Alex said, suddenly getting a brainwave. "What's with the year 1926?" Alex asked, remembering how it was marked in the diary and also in the paper they found at Albert Einstein's residence.

"I was coming to that. Remember, how I was about to tell you the developments in the early 19th century and how the set of trajectories was called 'density'?" Uncle Jack said, starting to tell them something.

"Yeah," said all three of them, waiting for Uncle Jack to answer.

"Richard Feynman's Path Integral Formula is also known as 'Probability Density Function' and you would be surprised to know he wasn't the first one to form it," Uncle Jack said, now remembering his Caltech days. "Yes, my friends, it's true. The first person who came out with 'Probability Density Function' in quantum mechanics was Max Born," continued Uncle Jack. "Although Heisenberg's contribution was equally important as it was he who along with Born developed a new kind of mathematics to understand the mechanics of particles on the quantum level with the help of matrices," Uncle Jack explained calmly.

"New mathematics?" he questioned confusingly.

"Yes, the one which famously came to be known as matrix mechanics," answered Uncle Jack. "It was a complicated method but it was the first of its kind that helped us to know the position of the particles," spoke Uncle Jack.

"You mean, the probabilities for the positions of electrons," Alex said, pointing out something.

"Yes, it was later that Feynman developed the Path Integral Formula which is also known as 'Sum Over Histories' 'cause of its approach to finding the solution. It was an improvisation on

CHAPTER 23

Born's Probability Density Function," continued Uncle Jack with confidence.

"So, this means, Feynman's Path Integral Formula is actually a function," proclaimed Alex.

"I would say so," answered Uncle Jack, swiftly understanding that Alex was getting somewhere with this.

"A function gives us a pattern, a proportion and in turn, a constant," Alex said, thinking ever more so quickly now.

"Wait, I think I can help you. I think I have a book that talks about Born's Probability Density Function," Uncle Jack said, leaving the room for a brief moment and returning with a book that had the face of Max Born over it. "Here, look," Uncle Jack showed the article about Born's Probability Density Function pointing it out with a marker.

Just as Alex saw it, he was taken aback by something.

Looking at his reaction Laura asked, surprisingly, "What is it, Alex?"

There was no movement from Alex, his eyes were just fixed on something.

As Laura and Ben bent forward to see what it was, the two had their eyes wide open.

Out there was a symbol for Probability Density Function…

___ "ϕ" ___

After a brief pause, Alex spoke, turning to look at Laura in her eyes, "Laura, your father was a genius…"

CHAPTER 24

"It was staring at our faces since the very beginning and we didn't have a clue," Alex said, wondering how he could have missed something like this.

"The symbol for divine proportion and Probability Density Function are identical!" Laura exclaimed, marveling at how the Professor had linked the clues so precisely.

"That's the John I know," Uncle Jack said, looking at the symbol on the letter amazed at how John had linked them up.

"Of all the people who made their mark in the development of physics by far, Probability Density Function seems to be the most extraordinary as of now," Alex said, wondering what the future was about to offer to them.

"It certainly does but I bet Einstein did see this coming," Uncle Jack said, thinking something.

"Why'd you say that?" questioned Alex.

"Einstein knew about his discovery, Max Born was given a Nobel prize for Probability Density Function," Uncle Jack said, looking at Alex in excitement, trying to state a point when Alex interrupted.

CHAPTER 24

"I agree, at the same time, I think that Werner too had a very big role to play as it was he who come up with a matrix mechanics representation of quantum mechanics along with Born which eventually led Born to discover the Probability Density Function," Alex said, trying to establish a point.

"He did, in fact, even Jordan came along to share the Nobel but what is interesting is Born got his credit almost two decades later. While Werner and Jordan got their Nobel in the 1930s. Born got it in the 1950s," Uncle Jack said confidently.

"In which year did you say he got his Nobel?" Alex asked him curiously.

"I don't know the exact year, but I think it was somewhere in the mid-fifties," Uncle Jack said, with a little embarrassment.

"I thought this was about Albert Einstein," Ben said, thinking about the letter.

"So did I, but I think there is a bigger picture to all of this, I think Einstein played a big role in bringing to notice that the ultimate constant had to be the one which was dimensionless," said Alex, thinking about the letter.

"You mean, just a number without any dimensions of mass, length, temperature or time," Ben said, trying to sound smart.

"Yes, Ben. I know you finally understand. Now, please let me think," Alex said, wanting to concentrate.

"I think we need to look into more information regarding Max Born, but first, I need to know how everything started in the first place," Alex said, looking at Uncle Jack.

"Well, if you must," Uncle Jack said, knowing what Alex was asking. "It was during the Caltech days, I know it's hard for me to explain what happened and how, but I'll try my best," Uncle Jack continued as he looked at each of their faces.

"I know whoever is behind this has a history that goes back to the time you got to know Laura's father," Alex said confidently.

"How are you so sure about this?" questioned Uncle Jack with surprise.

"'Cause I know somebody had been keeping an eye on the Professor ever since he was a student in Caltech," Alex said with confidence.

"I'm afraid you are right but it's not just John who was being attacked. I was with him in every step and I know what troubles we have been through together," explained Uncle Jack, remembering the times they were attacked.

"I want to know who is doing this. Who killed the Professor? Who is behind all of this?" Alex said in a hard voice.

"I will tell you, Alex. Let me explain," replied Uncle Jack, coming closer to him. "But I have a condition," continued Uncle Jack, looking at all three of them as they looked back at him in confusion. "From here on, you have to make me a part of this quest wherever it takes you," Uncle Jack said, smiling.

"Uncle Jack, I have already lost my father I don't want you to…" Laura said, disagreeing.

"Nothing will happen to me, darling. I haven't survived this long for nothing and I have got my security agency to protect us," said Uncle Jack, in a way telling Laura to relax.

CHAPTER 24

"Maybe Uncle Jack is right. At least this way we all will be together and safe," Ben said, contrasting to what Alex and Laura were thinking.

"Ben is right, this way all of us will stay together and can protect each other. Look, Alex. Frankly, I don't care what you say I'm coming along," Uncle Jack said getting support from Ben.

"I don't know," Alex said, looking at Laura and then turning back at Uncle Jack and Ben, helplessly knowing he couldn't tell Uncle Jack to go back on his decision.

"Now, if you let me, I have lots to tell you," Uncle Jack said looking at Alex resuming to tell everyone about his yesteryears.

Alex looked at him curiously.

"It started with four of us, John, I, David and Rudolph. I and Rudolph were younger than John and David," Uncle Jack said, starting to explain everything from the beginning. "It was during our post-graduation days that we four became friends. I was assisting John and Rudolph was assisting David," continued Uncle Jack. "John and David were quite close since the very beginning. I don't know how exactly they became friends but I do remember John telling me he was going for a walk," Uncle Jack continued before pausing for a moment to remember.

"How did the Professor meet David?" asked Alex. wanting to know about their friendship.

"I thought you will ask me that," replied Uncle Jack with a smile. "It was during a football game," Uncle Jack said, looking at all three of them making sure he had their attention.

"Professor, football game? That's hard to believe," Alex said, thinking something.

"Yeah, I know. But back then John was a big fan of football games and he knew all about the teams then," Uncle Jack said explaining and remembering the good old days.

"What happened then?" Alex questioned.

"John and David became best friends. I and Rudolph only got to know David during the later years like I told you before. However, when I did get to meet John before his Ph.D. he did always talk about David and his extraordinary talents in physics," Uncle Jack said, this time looking at Laura.

"Who was he, Uncle Jack? David? Father never spoke of him and yet you say they were very close friends," asked Laura, still confused.

"There was a reason why John never spoke about David, just listen," replied Uncle Jack, looking at Laura with tenderness and sensitivity. "David was like any other person trying to find something new in classical physics but the reason he got so famous among his contemporaries was because he had a way to his vision. He could imagine what others couldn't," Uncle Jack said, remembering the time he spent with him.

"That's what Einstein once said, 'Imagination is more important than knowledge'," recalled Alex, understanding what Uncle Jack was trying to say.

"Exactly, it was not like he was good with numbers but he could virtually perceive theories in a way others could not," answered Uncle Jack smiling at Alex. "During the time John and David became friends David played a big role in influencing John's ideas of understanding classical physics and in a way this made him better," Uncle Jack continued. "Later, David asked John to help him with his Ph.D. and that he would do the same for him. That's

CHAPTER 24

when I and Rudolph came into the picture," Uncle Jack was now coming to the later years.

"What happened then?" asked Ben, who was now equally involved.

"Something none of us had ever expected," Uncle Jack said, deeply remembering the tragic event.

"What?" all three of them questioned simultaneously.

"A few papers got stolen from a lab, papers that belonged to a guy named Cody," Uncle Jack said, recalling the events.

"There was also an interesting thing that happened, something that brought a big turn in David's life," Uncle Jack continued to keep Alex and others interested.

"About his death," Alex said swiftly.

"More than that, you see the papers which got stolen were of *Quantum Interpretation Of Many Worlds*, something that even David was working on then," replied Uncle Jack, giving a break to the thoughts that were going through Alex's mind.

"You mean the same theory the clues are pointing at as of now," Laura said, getting a hunch on what Uncle Jack was thinking.

"That's right, my dear," Uncle Jack said, nodding his head. "All four of us found out that there was someone who was trying to set David up," explained Uncle Jack, remembering the arguments that followed. "We were not able to comprehend the situation when something worse happened," Uncle Jack looked at Alex deeply as he said this.

"You mean," Alex was about to say something when Uncle Jack came back to it.

"Yes, the earthquake that took David's life," Uncle Jack said in a hard voice, looking at Alex.

"But Uncle Jack that can't be," Alex said, trying to tell the truth about David's death.

"I know he didn't die just then," he said, looking at Alex believing what was there on his mind.

"How did you know?" he replied looking at Uncle Jack, feeling hyper.

"John told me just after they attacked Clair," Uncle Jack said, looking at Laura.

"What? Mom? But I thought she died in an accident!" Laura said, feeling hurt in her heart.

"Yes, you were very young, Laura and John never wanted you to know about all this but then I always told him someday he had to tell you the truth. John was attacked, they took him by surprise and Clair happened to lose her life in the middle of all this," explained Uncle Jack, looking with deep affection toward her.

"This happened before they attacked David?" asked Alex, trying to keep Uncle Jack talking.

"Yes, they figured David was close to finding out the ultimate constant," Uncle Jack said, looking at Alex now.

"The ultimate constant, of course," Alex murmured, thinking something.

"But what did all of this have to do with my mother? Why did they kill her?" screamed Laura in rage, with watery eyes.

CHAPTER 24

"It was just bad timing, child. Your mother had nothing to do with any of this, she was just at the wrong place at the wrong time," Uncle Jack said, trying to console her.

"We are sorry, Laura, all of us," Alex said, looking at Ben and Uncle Jack.

"Alex is right. Laura, we will find whoever is behind this and the day we do, he would take his last breath before he goes behind the bars," joined Ben, trying to calm her down.

"Please tell us, Uncle Jack, what happened after the earthquake in Caltech?" Alex questioned, wanting to know the whole story.

"It took John some time to figure out who was behind setting David up and it turned out to be none other than Cody," Uncle Jack said, now bringing some light on the matter.

"How did the Professor come to know about this?" Alex asked, obstinate to know the facts.

"I remember John once telling me how he had spotted Cody with a guy carrying a gun. Later that year, there was a death in Caltech and John found out that it had a connection with David," continued Uncle Jack, bringing more facts into the picture.

"Who died? Who? And what connection?" asked Alex without wasting another moment.

"His name was Jason Clement and I believe David had given him some papers related to his research on *Quantum Interpretation of Many Worlds*. It was the same guy who revealed the truth about Cody and his intentions," explained Uncle Jack patiently.

"So, it is Cody who is behind all these killings," Laura said in rage.

"Not quite, later John found out that there was one more person who was working with Cody," Uncle Jack said, waiting to reveal one more surprise.

"Who was it, Uncle Jack?" asked all three of them.

"It came to both I and John as a surprise but it was the truth. The other person working with Cody was none other than Rudolph. As for Cody, it all made sense as he was the only one working on the same theory as David," Uncle Jack said slowly so that all three of them can listen to him loud and clear.

"Why Rudolph?" asked Alex, furiously.

"Maybe I missed telling you about the fact that when I was assisting John and Rudolph was assisting David, he never really liked David much," Uncle Jack said, remembering how Rudolph used to always be uncomfortable with David.

"You mean to say that he was jealous of David," asked Laura.

"In a way, yes. You see, David had a way with people, something Rudolph always lacked from the beginning," Uncle Jack said, now laying back, feeling kind of tired from all the talking.

"What do you mean, Uncle Jack?" Ben asked in confusion.

"I mean he was always teased by his contemporaries for being a bum sucker and David's popularity made him insecure," explained Uncle Jack, looking at Ben.

"So, you mean to say Cody and Rudolph are the ones who have been behind all these tragedies and now they are after us," Alex said, carefully analyzing things.

CHAPTER 24

"Yes, and the only way we can outrace them is to find out what the clues lead to," concluded Uncle Jack.

"You mean, we need to find that ultimate force before they do," Alex said in determination.

"Exactly, and it turns out as of now we are in the lead," Uncle Jack said, smiling in a way cheering them up.

"Do you have any idea where Cody and Rudolph are as of now?" asked Laura inquiring.

"Guessing from the past they have always been able to track John and me. By that means I believe, they are already here," Uncle Jack said, making them aware that they will have to make a move faster.

"Did they always know what David was up to?" asked Alex inquisitively.

"Nobody knew what David was up to. Not even me or John. The man was master of the bluff, he tricked everyone in Caltech to assume he was dead even though he spent years researching UFT," explained Uncle Jack to Alex.

"What was he researching in *Quantum Interpretation of Many Worlds*?" asked Alex, yet again wondering about the man in question.

"I don't know, but I think he made it pretty clear to John. He was the only one who had the complete picture," Uncle Jack said, thinking about the Professor.

"And now it is up to us to complete what they started and reveal their theory to the world," Alex said, looking at everyone.

"To do that, you will have to get into the mind of the one who made it all possible," Uncle Jack said, looking at Alex.

"You mean David," replied Alex, thinking something.

"But you can't do it alone, you will need help," Uncle Jack said, looking at Laura.

"That is the reason why Professor gave her the letter to get to you. You see, John must have known this was coming and I believe he must have laid a plan, a plan you both were a part of," explained Uncle Jack.

"And you'll need me," Ben joined in. "After all, you need someone to handle the expenses," Ben continued with a smile, looking at Alex and Laura.

"You will need someone with experience," Uncle Jack said.

Alex got the hint that from here they all were together in this.

"If I'm thinking right about David being the man that he was, I believe the man was a visionary," Alex said, wondering about the guy who had the key to their quest.

"He indeed had a vision, he saw what others couldn't," Uncle Jack said, looking at Alex.

"What was it?" Alex asked inquisitively.

"You should know, Alex, you have the clues," replied Uncle Jack, giving him a hint.

"Of course, he saw the string theory coming even two decades before it actually did, the clues all point towards that. He knew how big a role string theory would play if fused with the speed of

CHAPTER 24

light. Uncle Jack, this man was a genius," replied Alex, analyzing the clues in amazement.

"He was more than that, Alex. He was your father," Uncle Jack said reluctantly.

CHAPTER 25

"My father?" Alex said almost whispering, the words barely coming out of his mouth.

"Yes, you see, after John was attacked it was too late for David to react to the threat that he was about to face. By then he was already dead and when John got to know about it, he found that David had left him a note letting him know where you are," Uncle Jack said, explaining to Alex, knowing it was important for Alex to know the truth.

"I was not with them when the attack happened," Alex said, feeling confusion and rage.

"I'm afraid I don't know how the attack happened, what I do know is your father wanted to protect you and he knew that you are not safe around him anymore. That's why he sent you up to a safe place knowing that he could come back to you when his troubles were over," replied Uncle Jack, looking back at him kindly.

"Then why did he leave Professor the note? He could have come back to me himself," asked Alex, almost breaking down, thinking and questioning the circumstances.

"Because David had known by then that it was too late for him to reach out to you. Cody and Rudy were on him and the only

CHAPTER 25

person he could trust then was John. So, he wrote John a note, a note that I found later but it was half burned. All I could make out from what was written was that David had a son. Later John told me he was going to adopt a boy. I knew then that you were David's son, later when I spoke to John about this, he confirmed. He said, a time would come when you will know the truth but before that, you should know nothing about this," Uncle Jack said, finishing the story and looking at Laura and Ben, who now looked even more so astonished.

Alex looked at Laura before asking, "Did you know?"

"No, she didn't have a clue. This was a secret kept between John and me. I felt that time was right for you to know the truth," Uncle Jack said, putting a hand over his left shoulder. This was his way of telling Alex to calm down.

"I need some time on my own," Alex said, running up the stairs.

"We don't have time, Alex," Ben said reminding him of what Uncle Jack told them a few moments ago.

"I need a moment, Ben!" Alex shouted, looking at him and Laura, his pitch going way up.

"Ben, let him go. He will be back," Laura said, looking at Alex; she understood the fact that Alex needed a moment to himself.

As Alex came up the stairs, his mind was split in trying to handle twin feelings, on one hand, he had emotions running, all the memories about the Professor, about Laura and on the other hand, he knew it was not the time for emotions, everybody's life was in danger. He had to be rational.

However, as he entered a room somehow, he wanted to forget everything, everything that was happening around him and try to remember the faces of his mother and father.

He sat on the bed, slowly thinking how all this time he had felt so alone. After so long today he had learned the truth, he remembered how he had longed for their presence and support all his life. From the beginning, Alex had the urge to know more about David, to start with he didn't know what it was but now he knew it was a connection he shared with him. A connection he intuitively knew but couldn't understand. David was his father.

Alex realized that he had to get back to Uncle Jack. He got up restlessly and made his way to others.

"There you are, we had started to wonder if you would do something stupid," Ben said, looking at him.

"Are you all right?" asked Laura with a smile, coming closer and giving him a hug.

"Man, we should do this more often," Ben said as he joined them making it a group hug.

"Get over it, Ben," Alex said moving away while feeling a lot better, knowing his friends needed him the most at this hour.

"I think we should get going," Uncle Jack said, looking at all of them.

"Good idea, but where are we going now?" asked Ben, looking and smiling at Uncle Jack.

"Alex, can you show me the letter John gave Laura once again?" asked Uncle Jack, coming towards them.

CHAPTER 25

"Sure," Alex said, handing over the letter to Uncle Jack.

"You told me about how you guys have come so far, the Chaos theory, the fusion of speed of light and the string leading to a superposition and *Quantum Interpretation of Many Worlds*. Also, now we know both Chaos and *Quantum Interpretation of Many Worlds* are dynamic in nature, which led us to Probability Density Function," Uncle Jack said, looking at the letter.

"Which I think is a function of the ultimate constant," Alex said confidently.

"I think you are right. But even if that's the case, we are only halfway on our quest," Uncle Jack said, bringing something to their notice.

"What do you mean?" asked Laura and Ben.

Alex already knew what Uncle Jack was trying to say.

"Look at the letter, the "ϕ" points to the Probability Density Function. That's what we have found but there is another symbol "=D-" that we know nothing about," Uncle Jack said pointing at the symbol in the letter.

"With the question of the universal constants, you have broached one of the most interesting questions that may be asked at all. There are two kinds of constants: apparent and real ones. The apparent ones are simply the outcome of the introduction of arbitrary units, but are eliminable. The real [true] ones are genuine numbers which God had to choose arbitrarily, as it were, when He deigned to create this world. In my opinion now is – stated briefly – that constants of the second type do not exist and their apparent existence is caused by the fact that we have not penetrated deeply enough. I therefore believe that such numbers can only be of a basic type, as for instance π or e." "=D-" "ϕ"

NUMERICAL ENIGMA

16.259.72.97.2.7.

"So if we understand what "=D-" in the letter means, we will find the ultimate constant," Ben said excitedly.

"I think that would be right, Ben," Laura said looking at Alex and Uncle Jack.

"I think I have seen the symbols somewhere," Ben said, trying to remember something.

"What does it mean?" asked Laura, looking at it and then towards Alex.

"Well, if I knew I would have said it already," Alex said, looking at Laura flamboyantly.

"It can be anything, maybe like one of the constants or function like the one we've found now," Uncle Jack said, thinking something.

"Wait a minute, I am sure that I have seen this symbol somewhere," Ben said, stressing on his memory.

"Well, if you know it, why don't you just tell us already?" Alex said, mocking Ben.

"If you would just let me remember it," he replied amusingly.

"Guys, please stop arguing, and Ben if you have seen it before, please tell us quickly," Laura said politely, looking at Ben.

"Oh yes, I remember now. I saw it at Russel's place when we were discussing Chaos theory," Ben said, swiftly understanding that they had to get moving.

"That's great, let's go," Uncle Jack said happily.

CHAPTER 25

"Wait a minute, are you sure about this, Ben? We don't have time to go on hunches right now," Alex said, questioning Ben.

"Hey, come on, man. I know what I am saying," Ben said, now getting a bit annoyed with his attitude.

"Alex, I think he is right. We should get going," Laura said, looking at Ben and swiftly taking Alex's hand and pulling him away.

"It's going to be a long drive," Alex said, looking at Ben and Laura.

"It doesn't matter how long it takes us if Ben is right. It's gonna be worth it," Uncle Jack said looking at Ben, and giving him a smile.

"I am right, Uncle Jack. But sometimes, it's just frustrating to be underestimated by a good friend," Ben said looking at Alex, who now gave him a friendly grin. "Now, what's that supposed to mean?" exclaimed Ben in confusion.

"It means no matter what he says, he still has faith in you, Ben," Uncle Jack said looking at Ben, giving a pat on his shoulders.

"Yup," said Ben, thinking something.

So they were making their way back to San Diego.

It was a long journey but Russel was happy to see Alex and company again.

"So, what makes you come back to me?" He questioned looking at all of them, telling them to have a seat.

As they entered and made themselves comfortable, Alex didn't waste any time on small talk, he wanted to get to the point as soon as possible.

However, he did formally introduce Russel to Uncle Jack.

Alex had told Uncle Jack how Russel had earlier helped them understand a bit of Chaos theory.

"I'm pretty impressed by what you have to say about the chaos theory, young man," Uncle Jack said, nodding his head.

"Uncle Jack, can we just?" Alex said looking at Uncle Jack and Russel simultaneously.

"Yes, of course. I'm sorry, I forgot we are running out of time," Uncle Jack said, getting what Alex was thinking.

Alex showed Russel the letter and the symbol.

"With the question of the universal constants, you have broached one of the most interesting questions that may be asked at all. There are two kinds of constants: apparent and real ones. The apparent ones are simply the outcome of the introduction of arbitrary units, but are eliminable. The real [true] ones are genuine numbers which God had to choose arbitrarily, as it were, when He deigned to create this world. In my opinion now is – stated briefly – that constants of the second type do not exist and their apparent existence is caused by the fact that we have not penetrated deeply enough. I therefore believe that such numbers can only be of a basic type, as for instance π or e." "=D-" "ϕ"

16.259.72.97.2.7.

"You see this?" Alex said pointing his finger at the "=D-" symbol.

"Yes," answered Russel. It sounded like he was at ease with it.

"Ben saw the symbol at your place and we want to understand its significance," Alex said, looking at Russel.

CHAPTER 25

"Here it is," suddenly Ben exhaled, showing a book in his hand which had a similar symbol on its cover.

"It is a logic gate," Russel said almost using his common sense.

"What?" Ben questioned half-heartedly.

"It's a bloody logic gate, everyone knows this," Russel said, looking at all three of them.

Ben and Laura looked blank while Alex and Uncle Jack were thinking something.

"Look, it is the mother of all circuits, all right? This is the 21st century, it is used in every computer and cell phone," Russel said explaining to Ben.

"You mean most of the gadgets that we use in our daily life," Alex said, looking at him.

"Exactly, look, this is a symbol for 'AND' logic gate and it's used in most of the electronic gadgets to compute data," replied Russel, looking at Alex and then simultaneously at all of them.

"Well, do you have any idea what it has to do with "ϕ"?" asked Alex, showing him the letter again.

"I don't even know what that is to begin with, but if I may say so it looks like the symbol for divine proportion," Russel said, looking at the symbol.

"It is called the Probability Density Function," Alex said, raising his voice, getting impatient. "It's got to do something with quantum mechanics," continued Alex.

"Look, dude, I don't know much about quantum mechanics and to tell you honestly, I don't know much about this logic gate either. I just recognized the symbol. I am into dynamical systems, dude," Russel said, trying to calm Alex down.

"All right, what else can you tell us about it?" asked Uncle Jack stepping forward.

"Well, it has a lot to do with high-tech electronic devices. I won't be surprised if it's a big deal in the field of signal processing as well," Russel said, seriously looking at Uncle Jack.

"Signal processing," muttered Alex.

"Are you deaf? Didn't you hear me say 'cell phones' earlier?" exclaimed Russel, irritated by Alex. "Look, if you want to know more about this you will have to dig deeper because I can't explain to you this in detail, it deals with binary stuff," continued Russel, judging how badly Alex wanted to know about it.

It wasn't his fault. His expressions were saying it all. On the other hand, Laura thought their work here was almost done. Not that they completely found what they were looking for but they knew now what "=D-" stood for.

"Hey Alex, I think Russel is right and we should call it a day," Laura said coming closer to Alex.

"I think you are right. We will just have to dig a little deeper to understand what this 'AND' gate is trying to tell us," replied Alex, understanding Laura's point.

"Hey, Russel, do you mind if we spend the night here?" Ben said looking out, noticing that it was getting dark.

It had been a long drive for all of them and they were all very tired.

CHAPTER 25

"Of course, I don't mind if you guys are comfortable with the place," Russel said cheerfully.

"Thanks, Russel. We really appreciate this," Alex said as Laura smiled at him.

As they all were about to go off to sleep, Laura noticed that Alex was a little restless.

"What is it, Alex? What are you thinking?" she asked coming closer, and sitting beside him.

"It's just that I can't help but notice that how close this "=D-" is to reality," Alex said, looking outside the window toward the night sky.

"What do you mean?" she asked, trying to understand what Alex was getting at.

"I mean when Russel said that "=D-" is used in almost all the electronic devices he really meant it. Today so many of our lives depend upon these devices and technology," Alex said explaining to her.

"All right, but why are you getting so restless about this?" she questioned yet again.

"You don't get it, do you? The "=D-" is going to give us the ultimate constant and if it is so close to reality, it means the ultimate constant must be…" Alex answered, thinking something.

"Must be what?" she asked curiously now.

"It's real, Laura. The ultimate constant is real and all around us," Alex said looking at her and then turning his head back toward the twinkling stars in the night sky. Only this time, Laura joined him.

CHAPTER 26

The next morning Alex woke up and the first thing he saw was Ben who seemed to be in some kind of hurry.

He looked at Ben as he was putting food and other items from the refrigerator into his bag. He turned his head to find Laura still trying to find some way to go back to sleep, struggling to close her eyes unsuccessfully. Before he knew, Ben made his way to Alex, he looked surprised and enthusiastic.

"What happened? Why you are putting all this stuff in your bag and why are we packing?" Alex said perplexed by all the random happenings around him.

"It so happened in the morning that I was talking to Uncle Jack about our visit to your father's apartment, the place he was put up in just before he passed away. Uncle Jack thinks there might be something useful for us to catch up there," Ben said, simultaneously trying to wake up Laura.

"And why is that?" he questioned back, looking at Ben.

"Why don't you go and ask him yourself?" Ben said giving a faded smile.

CHAPTER 26

"What's going on here?" Laura said softly pushing herself up, coming out of her sleep.

"Hurry up, we got to get moving," Ben said, looking at her.

Ben gave a signal to Alex to explain to Laura what was going on.

"Let's go," Alex said, looking at Laura.

"Go where?" asked Laura, barely understanding the situation.

"Just get your stuff, I'll explain later. I'll be back in a moment and could you please take care of my stuff?" Alex asked politely, getting up, and becoming a little hyper.

"All right, but where are you going?" she asked, noticing she was a little late.

"I just want to go see Uncle Jack," Alex said turning his head back, moving away from her.

"What is it, Uncle Jack?" Alex asked as he came closer to him, his eyes still trying to get used to the daylight and his body language, a little curious.

Uncle Jack was busy searching for something when he heard Alex ask him a question.

"Ben and I just happened to get up a bit early and found ourselves discussing about how you guys went to London," Uncle Jack said.

"Yeah, but I didn't get you, what about it?" Alex questioned, looking at Uncle Jack who was still trying to figure out where he had kept some of his belongings.

Uncle Jack didn't answer him for a few seconds. "Where the hell are my glasses?" Uncle Jack murmured amusingly.

Alex picked up the glasses fallen around the couch and gave it to him, easing out his frustration. "You didn't answer my question," he said, passing him the glasses.

"Well, I thought there might be something interesting for us down there in London to find," replied Uncle Jack, wearing his glasses, feeling competent now.

"How are you so sure?" asked Alex yet again, still not clear where Uncle Jack was going with this.

"Your father was an interesting colleague, Alex. He always had something or the other up his sleeves. In the morning when Ben and I were going through the book you found in John's safe in his study, I found the years that you found in the book were not just years, they also combine to give a particular address. The address of the apartment David stayed in during his last years in London and I bet he still has some surprises left for us," Uncle Jack said, explaining to Alex what he was thinking. "Here, have a look at it again."

Newbury House

10-13 Newbury Street London EC1A 7HU

BLOCK 1-9-4 HOUSE 8

BEHIND BLOCK 1-9-7 HOUSE 7

"There is definitely something there. You are right, Uncle. But I thought you knew about my father's whereabouts?" claimed Alex, first thrilled by Uncle Jack's discovery and then questioned him with a grin.

CHAPTER 26

"No, Alex. The only person who knew about David's whereabouts was John," Uncle Jack said smiling.

"I think you told me that before," Alex said, thinking something.

"Yes, I think I did, in fact, I was pretty impressed by how you guys were able to figure out where David was when Ben told me the story," continued Uncle Jack, patting his shoulder and moving away.

"You bet," answered Alex as Uncle Jack left the room. "All right then," Alex said to himself before making his way back to Laura.

As soon as he got to her he was pretty surprised that Laura had already finished, taking care of most of his stuff including hers too.

"Wow, I didn't think you would be finished packing already. That was quick," exclaimed Alex as he stared at Laura who gave him a smile.

"Alex, give me a hand with this," she said picking up one of the bags. They knew it would still take them some time to reach their destination. It was going to be a long journey.

"C'mon, guys. We have a plane to catch," Ben said, almost shouting.

Soon, they bid goodbye to Russel and were making their way to the airport when Alex explained to Laura what Uncle Jack had found recently in the book of Chaos.

It didn't take them long to go through the formal procedures and were sitting on the flight, making their way to London before they knew it. As they were on their way, Ben came up to Alex.

"Hey, listen. I hope we didn't forget anything because we were in such a hurry. I packed up a lot of stuff to eat if we are going to stay in a hotel for a few days," Ben said, asking Alex if he had forgotten anything.

"Thank you, Ben, but no, I don't forget anything," Alex said, looking at him.

"All right, man. Why are you getting worked up? I was just trying to cover your back," Ben said, thinking Alex got offended. He quietly made his way back to his seat.

Soon all of them were in London.

"Here we are," Ben said, looking at Uncle Jack.

"So, this is where David had been all those years while he had been writing to John," Uncle Jack said as he stepped on the ground.

"Yeah," said Alex as all of them made their way through the lobby.

"How long before we get there?" Uncle Jack asked, looking at Alex and Laura.

"A couple of hours may be," Alex said, looking at Laura trying to confirm.

"I'll be back, I have to make a phone call," Laura said, moving away from all of them.

"Phone call? Who are you calling?" Alex and Uncle Jack inquired simultaneously.

"Relax, I just want to talk to Rachel. She had been such a great help to me and I had not been able to say a proper thank you to her till now," Laura said, provokingly looking at both of them.

CHAPTER 26

"All right, we will see you outside the entrance. Don't make us wait too long," Ben said, leaving her.

"I won't, you guys, take my luggage," Laura said as she looked around for a phone.

As they moved out of the airport Ben was about to call in a cab. That is when Uncle Jack couldn't help himself asking, "Hey, you didn't happen to see something unusual when you were here the last time, did you?"

"Something unusual in what sense, Uncle Jack?" Alex and Ben asked in confusion.

"Some kind of a secret drawer," Uncle Jack said looking at the two of them.

"No, no, why are you asking?" said Alex and Ben looking at each other and turning toward Uncle Jack.

"Well, all right, anyway," Uncle Jack said, turning his face away from them.

"Why you think we should have?" Alex asked suspiciously.

"Probably," answered Uncle Jack turning toward Alex, and giving him a wink.

"Back in Caltech, I remember John would often tell me how David had secretly made spaces for stuff he didn't want anybody to get their hands on," Uncle Jack said, remembering his conversation with the Professor.

"Really, we never thought of something like that," Ben said excitedly.

"I wouldn't expect you to," replied Uncle Jack.

"So, if there is something of this kind why didn't he inform the Professor about it in the letter?" Alex asked, looking at Uncle Jack in a way questioning him.

"It's not that simple, Alex. Since John already knew about this stuff and maybe he wanted to tell Laura but he didn't have time. So, in the end, he did leave us a clue in the book," Uncle Jack said, explaining to him.

"Right," exclaimed Alex, thinking Uncle Jack could be right after all. The Professor never had time to tell Laura. Everything happened so quickly.

"Well, are we making a move or what?" Ben said impatiently.

"Could you relax for a bit? We are waiting for Laura," Alex said sharply.

"Why have you been coming onto me these last couple of days? Everything I say seems to offend you," Ben said, trying to resolve what was going on with him and Alex.

"Well, forgive me, but I didn't know I had a dad before these last couple of days when running around for my life. There's something called being emotionally vulnerable and stressed," Alex said, trying to make his point.

"You guys got to calm yourself down. Ben, you got to stop asking him too many questions and Alex, you need to be stronger," Uncle Jack said looking at both of them.

"Yeah, all right," said both of them looking at each other.

"Where the hell is Laura, anyway?" Ben said looking behind.

CHAPTER 26

"Here I am, did you miss me? What's going on?" she said looking at Alex who seemed to be thinking something.

"What is it, Alex?" Laura said looking at him.

"I think we've to call a taxi before I say anything," Alex said raising his hand, calling for a cab.

"Alex is right," Uncle Jack said, agreeing.

As they stepped into the cab, Alex started explaining to Laura what Uncle Jack had on his mind about how David used to keep hidden draws and shelves to keep important things. "Uncle Jack believes we might have missed something back at my father's apartment the last time we visited, like a secret lock or vault of some kind," Alex said, telling her about the conversation that he had had with Uncle Jack in her absence.

"Well, I think this can be helpful, but I hope we don't get into any trouble again," she said thinking about all the horrifying attacks that had followed them.

"For what's on stakes here, it might just be worth it," Ben said, looking at Laura.

"Don't worry. I have informed my security agents about our location," Uncle Jack said trying to make everybody feel safe.

As they reached their destination they kept their baggage in the cab, telling the driver to wait.

They made their way up to Mrs. Mc Adams the second time and she was more than happy to see them again with another visitor.

"Mrs. Mc Adams, we would like to take a look at the apartment one more time, if you wouldn't mind," Alex said looking at her.

"Oh please, you all are welcome. It is not every day that I have the pleasure of such good company," she said, delighted to see Alex again. "But I'm curious what has brought you back," she continued to ask him, slowly coming forward.

"Mrs. Mc Adams, actually, I am his son," Alex said explaining everything except for the secret lock or vault that they had come looking for.

"Oh my, no wonder, you know you are so much like him," she said with a warm smile before handing the keys to Alex.

Alex thought of not wasting any more time as he had the keys to the apartment.

Mrs. Mc Adams tried to offer them some homemade cookies but all of them refused politely telling her that they were in a hurry, but Alex promised her that they would return.

As Alex unlocked the door, all of them made their way into the apartment.

It was the same, nothing had changed. Everything was rested, unmoved and untouched or so it seemed. There was a lot of dust on the furniture. They looked around carefully trying to notice if somebody had been there before them.

Suddenly, Laura noticed something, there was a slight change in the placement of an old table and she could make out by the slight difference in the change of the placing of one of its legs.

"Somebody has been here before us," she said grabbing everybody's attention.

As everyone came over, she pointed toward the table leg. It was clear that somebody had been here before them.

CHAPTER 26

"Does this mean we are late to find whatever we came looking for?" she said looking at Alex and Uncle Jack.

"Maybe, maybe not, we still have to search," Uncle Jack said looking at her.

"That right, let's split," Alex said, beginning to move.

As they began their search, Alex and Uncle Jack remained in the main room. Ben made his way to another corner of the house.

Laura followed Ben's trail.

They all were busy trying hard to find something reasonable.

After looking around for some time Ben got tired, "There is nothing here," he said giving up.

Alex and Uncle Jack too seemed to be out of luck.

Laura made herself comfortable sitting on the chair near a mirror when she noticed something strange.

As she went closer to the mirror, which was more like an old dressing table, broken yet somehow standing, she noticed something that she had noticed earlier but didn't think of it much when she came to the apartment the last time.

There was a small sparkle, shining thing that was reflecting light.

Before she thought it was the mirror but now as she came closer, she found that the reflection was indefinite, it was coming through a small crack in the mirror.

She quickly grabbed the chair to break the mirror.

NUMERICAL ENIGMA

She shattered the mirror with one heavy blow.

There it was, staring at her face.

Laura shouted in excitement, "I found it!"

CHAPTER 27

"I found it!" exclaimed Laura making sure the rest of them heard her.

Within a few moments, Alex, Ben and Uncle Jack come jogging around the corner. Soon, they too saw the piece of shining metal that was visible through the crack of the mirror.

"What is that?" Ben said, trying to guess while looking at the shining metal.

"We will soon find out," Alex said, moving closer to the mirror.

"It looks like silver," Uncle Jack said as Alex removed the broken pieces around it.

"I think you are right," Alex said, taking out a small symbol box.

"Does it have a lock?" Laura said as Alex kept it on an old piece of furniture that looked like a study table.

"It does, it seems like a combination lock," Alex said looking at Laura and the others.

"Alex, do you think it has the same combination as the locker that we opened earlier?" Ben said offering help.

"I don't know, let me try," Alex said turning to move his fingers on the combination.

As he did, Laura, Uncle Jack and Ben awaited restlessly to see what happens. To everyone's disappointment, it didn't work.

"This is not working," Alex said, trying to think of some other combination.

Uncle Jack himself was a little perturbed by the combination. Suddenly, thinking something he spoke, "Alex, by what you have told me the locks you guys encountered in your journey opened by a combination of numbers of a constant, isn't it?" Uncle Jack said, remembering what Alex had told him earlier.

"Yeah," Alex said, looking at Uncle Jack getting his point.

"Are you suggesting that like all the other combination keys, even this has a combination of numbers like that of a certain constant?" Alex said grinning, looking at Laura, Ben and Uncle Jack.

"Well, it's worth a try," Ben said, looking back at Alex.

"All right, so let me see, we have tried the "phi"- divine proportion 1.618," Alex said thinking of a constant.

"The combination here suggests three numbers, try the fine structure constant," Uncle Jack said, analyzing the combination lock.

"And that is?" Alex asked looking back at Uncle Jack.

"137," Uncle Jack said, confidently looking at him.

As Alex moved the combinations to the set of numbers all of them heard a click. Yes, it opened! Their patience had paid off.

CHAPTER 27

Alex looked at them, noticing everybody had the familiar smile on their faces just as he did.

As he took out the piece of paper and opened it, Laura and Uncle Jack came closer to read what was written.

It was strange; the paper had only two words written on it.

1930 —Bruno Rosie

"What does this mean?" Ben and Laura exclaimed in confusion.

"It means David and John already knew that they were in a fix with Cody and Rudy following them and they left clues everywhere so that their theory does not fall in the wrong hands," explained Uncle Jack.

"So, this is just another clue like the ones we found earlier?" Ben said getting the picture.

"Yes, I'm afraid so," said Uncle Jack, looking at the piece of paper.

"What is it pointing at? I mean does it relate to the 'AND' gate which the Professor was hinting at through his letter?" Ben said in a little confusion about where their quest was heading. "I thought we had to know more about the "–D=" that they found in the Professor's letter in order to find the ultimate constant," asked Ben looking at all of them.

"That is our goal, but we can't ignore other clues. Who knows, maybe this clue has a connection with the "-D=" the Professor mentioned," assured Alex, looking at Ben.

"Does it?" Ben asked, looking at Laura in a way asking her.

"Let's find out," Uncle Jack said looking at all of them; everybody knew he had something on his mind. "All I know about Bruno Rosie is that he was a brilliant electrical engineer who once headed the post of Institute Professor at MIT. But I know someone who might be able to help us know a few more things about him," explained Uncle Jack letting the others know what he was thinking before.

"Who is that, Uncle Jack?" Ben questioned in his familiar tone.

"Robert, Robert Shaw. The guy has been working on some of his subjects and I bet he would be able to tell us everything we want to know about Bruno Rosie," replied Uncle Jack, sounding sure about his friend.

"So, the sooner we get to him the better it would be," Alex said, thinking about not getting into any trouble.

"Alex is right. That is why we must act swiftly before they get to know, we don't want Cody and his guys to get a hunch about what we are after," Uncle Jack said, agreeing with Alex.

"So, where is your friend, Uncle Jack?" asked Laura, looking at him.

"We will have to catch a flight and by the looks of it, we are already a little behind," answered Uncle Jack looking at his wristwatch.

"A couple of minutes won't kill us," Alex said, moving out.

There was no time to waste.

"But where are you going?" asked Ben, following Laura and Uncle Jack's lead.

"To New York," Uncle Jack said, turning back and looking at Ben.

CHAPTER 27

Alex noticed that Uncle Jack's security was still keeping their presence felt, although discreetly. It was a relief for him to know that he and others were in safe company.

"Let's go, everyone," Alex said, climbing inside the cab.

Others followed him swiftly. As they were making their way to the flight, Ben looked at Alex in amusement.

"What is it?" Alex asked, looking at him sternly.

"Nothing. I'm just trying to get the pieces right in my head," Ben said shrugging, pulling his shoulders together carelessly.

"What pieces?" he questioned, looking at Ben.

"You know from the beginning, the constants, the constant of the speed of light, the string, Chaos, quantum interpretation of many worlds and the function we found, hmm… I'm forgetting the name, what was it?" Ben said, trying to ask him something.

"Probability Density Function," Alex said, reminding him.

"Yup, you told me it had something to do with the "=D-" symbol that we found in the letter earlier," asked Ben thinking something.

"Yup, we know that "ϕ" is the Probability Density Function. I think that it is this ultimate function and the other symbol in the letter "=D-" might lead us to the ultimate constant," Alex said in a way going through all the findings, telling it to Ben.

"You mean the 'AND' gate that we know, the "=D-" is the symbol for 'AND' gate," said Ben, remembering their last meeting with Russel.

"Yes, but there has to be something more to it," Alex said, trying to analyze the facts.

"So, you think the clues your father left us would help us to know more about "=D-," asked Ben looking at Alex, this time he grabbed Laura's attention too.

"I don't know, Ben. I am just as lost as you are right now," Alex said looking at him in confusion.

"I have a feeling it can," Laura said looking at Alex.

Alex saw that there was a comforting look in her eyes.

"I think your father knew that someday you would know the truth, something he shared with the Professor. That is why this quest was entrusted to us, Alex," murmured Laura, trying to encourage Alex.

"Have faith, son. Things would work out just fine," Uncle Jack said with a smile, looking at Laura and Alex.

"So, this Probability Density Function," Ben started to ask something yet again.

"What about that?" Uncle Jack asked, turning his face towards Ben.

"Well, you said it was a mathematical expression for wave functions and it showed the state of the electron by tracking down the probabilities of 'states of electron' that are common to all electrons and the same thing is done by Feynman's Path Integral Formula," asked Ben refreshing his memory.

Uncle Jack noticed that they were still a few minutes away from the airport, so he decided to explain to Ben a thing or two again.

CHAPTER 27

"You are right, let me elaborate a little on the subject. Every electron has probable trajectories which represent the different states of the electron simply meaning their positions. Also, there is a set of trajectories which are common to all electrons thereby representing the most probable 'state of electron' meaning a position which is common to all electrons. This position common to all electrons explained by a particular set of trajectories is called density, and that is why it's called Born's Probability DENSITY Function," Uncle Jack said, beginning with the explanation.

"But you said that Feynman's Path Integral Formula does the same thing?" Alex questioned.

"It does, in fact, it's the same thing. Both Born's Probability Density Function and Feynman's Path Integral Formula have identical outcome, both give results of the same problem. However, there is a slight difference in the method of Feynman's Path Integral Formula," Uncle Jack started to state his point. "Feynman's Path Integral Formula collapses the wave function after representing a series of states of the electron in the end coming to the 'final state of the electron'. Meaning the position which is common to all electrons. This is the reason why Feynman's formula gives a faster result. However, Born's formula gives a more detailed result," Uncle Jack said, thinking back on his studying years.

"So, that is the reason why Feynman's formula is preferred to Born's, 'cause it is way lot simpler and less complex," Alex muttered to himself.

"But Uncle Jack, we have missed an important detail. According to Pauli Exclusion Principle, no two identical electrons can share the same state," said Alex, making an important point.

"You mean in the same universe. Alex, you must understand your father by now," said Uncle Jack, giving Alex a hint.

"Of course, if there were multiple universes, electrons could in fact share the same state. David had found a way to get around Pauli Exclusion Principle without violating it. My father was always one step ahead," Alex said to himself and smiled.

"I hope you understand now, Ben," Uncle Jack said with a smile, looking at Ben.

"Yes, so the series of the states of electron Feynman's formula goes through will resemble the different trajectories of electrons in Born's Probability Density Function," answered Ben confidently letting Uncle Jack know that he understood everything he said.

"Very good, Ben. Feynman's formula is also known as the 'sum over histories'," replied Uncle Jack looking at him proudly.

"The sum over histories," Ben said to himself.

"I am impressed," Alex said looking at Ben, this time avoiding mocking him.

"Charming," Laura said looking at Ben, joining in lifting his spirits.

"It's here," Alex said abruptly looking outside through the window letting everyone know they had reached the airport.

Everybody got down swiftly without wasting much time.

"All right, here is what we got to do. We are a little short of time, so Alex, you take Laura along with you and buy the tickets to New York for all of us, me and Ben will follow you," Uncle Jack said, looking at all of them.

"Why aren't you coming along? We will go together," Laura said almost grabbing Uncle Jack's arm.

CHAPTER 27

"No, my dear. I must inform Robert that we are coming. He usually doesn't like surprises," Uncle Jack said, telling Alex to move along.

Soon Alex and Laura were making their way up ahead.

Suddenly one of the men from Uncle Jack's security made his way up to Ben and gave him a small case. Ben felt confused as if the man had appeared out of thin air.

"There is medication and a few other important items that belonged to sir, please take good care," said the man passing the case to Ben pointing at Uncle Jack.

"Sure, thanks," Ben said noticing he had already started walking away from him.

"All right, Ben. Let's go," Uncle Jack said putting the cell phone back in his right trouser pocket. "Did you get my stuff?" continued Uncle Jack, looking at the keys in Ben's hand.

"Yup," Ben said making a move realizing Uncle Jack was a bit slow for them.

"Hurry, Uncle Jack, we don't want to be late," Ben said taking his hand.

Soon they were with Alex and Laura who were glad to see that they had made it in time.

"Did you inform your friend, Uncle Jack?" Laura asked looking at him.

"Yes, he would be sending us a pickup at the airport," Uncle Jack said looking at them.

That is really helpful, thought Ben. It was time for all of them to board the flight.

"So, Uncle Jack, what does this friend of yours do?" Alex asked as their flights took off and they made themselves comfortable in their seats.

"He is a professor of electronics at New York University," answered Uncle Jack confidently.

Chatting with Uncle Jack Alex lost the track of time and soon they were in New York before they knew it.

There was a pickup for them just as Uncle Jack had expected. Within no time they were at the residence of Robert Shaw.

Upon entering Robert gave them a warm welcome.

Uncle Jack didn't want to waste any time, so he got straight to the point.

When he questioned him about Bruno Rosie, Robert paused before replying, "The man you're talking about founded the bases for 99% of the technology we use today. *Bruno Rosie, was a revolution.*"

CHAPTER 28

Alex looked at everyone before asking, "What do you mean, he was a revolution?"

"The man was a brilliant engineer and invented a number of electronic systems for the understanding of today's modern technology," Robert said with a calm look in his old yet seemingly sharp eyes. "What have you got for me, Jack?" he continued to question Uncle Jack.

"These boys might just be on their way to discover the future of physics and a new theory," Uncle Jack said, knowing that he knew Robert very well and that he could trust him.

"And how might that be?" Robert questioned looking at Alex and others.

"This girl here, she is John's daughter. You remember I told you about my friend John?" Uncle Jack said getting up and walking toward Robert.

"Yes, of course, your friend from Caltech. I suppose the guy who was into particle physics if I'm not wrong," Robert said, looking at him.

"Also, this is David's son," Uncle Jack said pointing toward Alex.

"Is that right?" Robert said now looking at Alex. "But I thought you told me David died with his pregnant wife a long time ago," Robert said, looking back at Uncle Jack.

"Yeah, well, it turns out I was wrong. John told me the truth and took a promise never to share it with anyone," Uncle Jack said, remembering the Professor.

Robert got up and made his way to Alex making sure that he got a good look at them.

"Your father was a brilliant man I had a chance to meet him briefly, but he left a lasting impression," Robert said, coming closer to Alex, putting his hand over his left shoulder. "So, what is it that you want to know about Bruno Rosie and what has led you to come to me, Jack?" Robert said looking at Uncle Jack.

"Well, there are a couple of reasons but the important ones being, you know better about this stuff other than anyone that I know," Uncle Jack said looking at Robert. "John and David were working on a new theory, one that could eventually lead them to find the Unified Field Theory," Uncle Jack said explaining things to Robert.

"How are you so sure of all this? Do you have any confirmation?" Robert said looking at all of them simultaneously.

"They left me and Laura clues," interrupted Alex, letting Robert know what they had in mind.

"That's right and the last one led us to come to you," Uncle Jack said, now looking at Alex, asking for the piece of paper he found at David's apartment before.

As Uncle Jack took the paper from Alex, he turned towards Robert to show him the year and the name.

CHAPTER 28

Robert took out his glasses and look at the paper. It was right there.

1930 – Bruno Rosie

"Were there other clues as well?" Robert asked, looking at Uncle Jack and turning toward Alex, to look into his eyes.

"Yes, it all started with this letter," Alex said now passing the letter to Robert making sure he didn't miss anything.

"With the question of the universal constants, you have broached one of the most interesting questions that may be asked at all. There are two kinds of constants: apparent and real ones. The apparent ones are simply the outcome of the introduction of arbitrary units, but are eliminable. The real [true] ones are genuine numbers which God had to choose arbitrarily, as it were, when He deigned to create this world. In my opinion now is – stated briefly – that constants of the second type do not exist and their apparent existence is caused by the fact that we have not penetrated deeply enough. I therefore believe that such numbers can only be of a basic type, as for instance π or e." "=D-" "ϕ"

16.259.72.97.2.7.

"This is definitely going to tell you about the ultimate constant," Robert said sharply looking at the letter. He was quick to analyze the symbols at the end of the paragraph. "So, did you find where the symbols were leading you?" questioned Robert, looking at all of them.

"We were able to figure out the first one with the help of Uncle Jack. However, we were working on the second one. That's when we found the note at my father's residence," Alex said, pointing at "=D-" and coming closer to Uncle Jack and Robert.

"Where did it lead you?" asked Robert reflecting on "ϕ"

"We believe the first symbol "ϕ" is pointing toward Probability Density Function and it's pointing toward the many worlds interpretation of quantum mechanics," Alex said, looking at Uncle Jack and then toward Robert.

"Is that right, Jack?" asked Robert, introspectively looking at Uncle Jack.

"I'm afraid so," Uncle Jack said, agreeing with Alex.

"There is one more thing I think we are missing," Alex said, thinking something.

"What?" Uncle Jack asked waiting patiently for him to answer.

"Well, yes, we also have reason to believe that many worlds theory of quantum mechanics is deterministic and have patterns, since we found clues that were trying to connect the many worlds interpretation of quantum mechanics with the Chaos theory," Alex said, remembering the connection between genetic algorithm, Born's Probability Density Function and Richard Feynman's Formula.

"You mean to say it's dynamical?" Robert said in certainty.

"Well, yes, deterministic, dynamical. You got the point," Alex said, looking at Robert.

"That fact has been the talk of the town lately," replied Robert when Alex told him about the dynamic nature of the theory of 'Many Worlds'.

"Is it?" Alex muttered thinking something.

"Yeah, but what patterns are you talking about?" Robert questioned.

CHAPTER 28

"We don't know yet, that's what we want to find out," Alex said, swiftly looking at Robert.

"Robert, like we told you, we were led toward the Probability Density Function by the first symbol. I think that combined with the second symbol "=D-" will lead us to the ultimate constant," Uncle Jack said, trying to get to a point.

"Yeah, but it is essential to understand the pattern to understand the constant," Robert said trying to correct them.

"Whatever that you find first, the constant or the pattern, it does not matter as long as you find it – one would eventually lead us to another," Laura said, stepping up.

"Laura is right, Uncle Jack, Mr. Shaw. However, we are missing the main point," Alex said looking at both Uncle Jack and Robert.

They looked at each other in confusion.

"Did you forget, Uncle Jack, why are we here in the first place?" Alex said trying to remind him of something.

"Yes, of course, Bruno Rosie!" Uncle Jack exclaimed, looking at Alex. Robert himself felt amused, the conversation and letter had made him completely forget about the reason why they were all gathered up in the first place.

"Yes, about Rosie. He was a man of extraordinary talent, the physicist had a talent for particle physics," Robert started to explain.

"Go on," Uncle Jack said making his way to his seat and making himself comfortable.

"He conducted a number of particle experiments on electronics and studied cosmic rays extensively," Robert too now started to walk towards a chair kept opposite Uncle Jack.

As Robert was explaining Ben couldn't help noticing the interiors and the huge house he lived in.

The man is well accomplished, Ben thought to himself bringing his attention back to Mr. Shaw.

"He was from Italy, Venice, completed his degree from there and later in life taught at MIT (Massachusetts Institute of Technology). Among his peers there he was known to have a paramount knowledge of cosmic rays due to his extensive research on the subject, which he did earlier in his life," stated Robert, picking up an old, expensive pipe.

"Why did you say the man was a revolution?" Alex asked, remembering his earlier statement.

"Well, that is because he is actually the father of modern circuits," Robert said, now placing tobacco in his pipe.

"What do you mean?" Alex asked yet again.

"Like I said the man conducted many practical experiments with electronics, that led him to develop the first electronic circuit," Robert said, trying to reestablish his point. "The circuits within the modern devices that we use today in our daily life are just improvisation of his first electronic circuit," continued Robert.

"What is the difference?" Ben asked reluctantly.

"It's the semiconductors which are used today," Robert said, looking at Ben.

CHAPTER 28

"Of course, the invention of transistors," exclaimed Alex, noticing that Uncle Jack had a smile on his face now.

"Yes, it began in the 1950s and by the 1960s they were ruling the world of electronics," Robert proceeded to talk about the semiconductors.

"But what do transistors have to do with Bruno Rosie?" questioned Laura, in little confusion so as to read where the conversation was going.

"It has everything to do with Rosie," Robert said looking at Laura, giving her a smile.

"Can you please explain?" Laura started to say.

Robert couldn't help but blush by looking at Laura's incompetency to understand what he was saying.

"All right, let me explain to you the basics. Before transistors, there was something called Geiger tubes," Robert started to explain as Alex and Uncle Jack patiently listened to him.

"What are Geiger tubes?" Laura asked yet again in confusion.

"Originally, they were vacuum tubes, I won't get into much detail but it would be important to understand that Geiger tubes were essentially composed of vacuum tubes which helped in the understanding of electric signals," Robert said now keeping his attention on Laura.

"So you mean, transistors were a step evolution to these Geiger tubes," Laura said, now understanding a little bit.

"Exactly, they both helped in the understanding of electrical signals, to be precise, they helped in amplifying the signal so that they could be measured accurately," Robert continued to explain, puffing smoke from his pipe now and then.

"Why are they so important?" Laura questioned beginning to understand the notion.

"It would be important to think how most of the electronic devices today run on the principle such as theirs," Robert looked at Alex and Uncle Jack who in turn looked at Laura, giving her a nod.

"You mean everything?" Laura questioned raising her eyebrows, looking at Mr. Shaw.

"Laura, the chip of the modern day computer comprises of one million transistors," Robert said giving Laura a wide smile.

"So, you are saying that transistors are an improvisation on Bruno Rosie's Geiger tubes," Laura said, now getting the point.

"I would say that is correct," Robert said, now looking at Ben.

Ben was keenly listening to Mr. Shaw trying not to ask any questions this time and let Laura do the talking.

"So, now we know a little about Bruno Rosie. Robert, can you tell us if there is something important that Rosie did in the year 1930," Uncle Jack said, observing that Laura was now quite satisfied with Robert's explanation.

"You know, I'm more into Rosie's cosmic rays research than his electronic experiments," Robert said, a bit agitated.

"This is important, so, I mean, I hope you understand," Alex said politely coming to Mr. Shaw.

CHAPTER 28

"You know, we have come a long way, Robert. You don't want to disappoint the children, do you?" Uncle Jack said almost mocking him.

Mr. Shaw took a brief look at everyone before replying, "All right, follow me, everyone," he said getting up from the chair still holding the pipe in his hands steadily. As everybody was following him Ben had an increasingly persistent question that was disturbing him.

He thought for a second and then decided to ask Mr. Shaw. "So, I know this sounds stupid but previously you told Laura that there are about one million transistors on our modern day computer chip. How is that possible?" Ben asked reluctantly.

"Transistor is an electronic component like many other electronic components. It is diffused on the silicon chip which is a semiconductor," Robert said, feeling tired.

"What is a silicon chip?" Ben muttered trying not to amuse Mr. Shaw anymore.

"He means microprocessors like I5, Pentium, and ones used in computers," Laura said softly, trying not to embarrass Ben in front of the Professors.

"Yes, all right," he replied smartly, looking at Laura.

"Here we are," proclaimed Mr. Shaw. After taking a few turns, they entered his library.

"This might take me some time. I hope if that's all right with you," he said, trying not to offend his guests.

"That's alright, Robert," Uncle Jack said, looking at him.

"Yes, sir, please. We will be right here," assured Alex, warmly telling Mr. Shaw to carry on.

"I would have to search but I'll get back to you as soon as I find something," Mr. Shaw said, looking at Alex and Uncle Jack and then moving on.

Uncle Jack, Alex and others waited for a while going through Mr. Shaw's collection of books. Alex noticed that he was an avid reader and had books on all kinds of stuff.

Uncle Jack, on the other hand, took a moment to see what Robert was up to and found him delving in and going through certain books.

In a short while, Mr. Shaw returned looking rather perplexed and astonished.

When asked by all of them why he looked so disturbing, he replied, *"I am sorry. Bruno Rosie was not the first to develop the electronic circuit."*

CHAPTER 29

"What? What do you mean by he wasn't the first person to discover the electronic circuit," asked Alex, thinking what Robert would say next.

"It says here that Rosie was researching the subject of electronic signals for a very long time. However, there was another guy who did work on a similar thesis and discovered an analogy quite parallel to his," Mr. Shaw said, explaining.

"What analogy are you talking about?" asked Alex, guessing what was coming next.

"By analogy, I mean the same ideas. His ideas were very much the same as the one used by the other guy that I was talking about, the only difference was the equipment being used during their experiments. The important thing to notice is this that, like Rosie, he too ended up discovering the same phenomenon of electrical signals," Mr. Shaw said, looking back into the book.

"Who was this man?" Laura asked inquisitively looking at Alex, expecting an answer.

"It says here his name was Werner Kolhörster," Mr. Shaw said, carefully reading it from the book he held in his hand.

"So, what was his thesis all about?" Uncle Jack asked, coming closer.

"Like I told you about the Geiger tubes before, unlike Rosie who used multiple Geiger counters as apparatus in his experiment, Werner Kolhörster used only one," Mr. Shaw said, explaining.

"And still it was enough for him to grasp the new understanding of the electrical signals," Uncle Jack said, getting the point.

"Not completely, but to a certain extent, yes, it did," answered Mr. Shaw not intimidated by Uncle Jack whatsoever.

"Mr. Shaw, I know you told us about Geiger tubes earlier but I still fail to understand them completely. Would you please tell us about them once again?" Alex said trying to bring clarity to the subject at hand.

"I think the boy is right, Robert. It seems the Geiger counters are an essential part of it. Why don't you help us understand something more, please?" Uncle Jack said requesting.

"Like I told you before, Geiger counters are vacuum tubes, let me elaborate on them a little bit," began Mr. Shaw.

"Please, I hope this will not be too technical," pleaded Ben.

"You don't have to worry about it, I promise," Mr. Shaw said, confirming.

"Please, sir," Alex proceeded.

"All right, now the thing about Geiger tubes is that it helps in amplifying the signal," Mr. Shaw began to reconnect his studies and explained. "I think I had told you before about that and now I want to go on in detail explaining to you how it works."

CHAPTER 29

"You mean its function?" asked Alex understanding his view.

"Correct, the reason I did not want to go on much in detail was because I thought it would become too complex for you to understand but I believe you leave me with no option now. However, in light of the matters, I'll try my best to make it as simple as I can for you to understand," Mr. Shaw said, thinking deeply now.

"Go on, Robert," Uncle Jack said, listening carefully.

"The basic principle of vacuum tubes as in G (Geiger) counters is to detect ionized particles," Mr. Shaw said, making a gesture with his hand, leaning forward and looking at all of them simultaneously.

"What is an ionized particle?" asked Ben.

"You see, when ionized rays are passed through the vacuum tube (Geiger tube) the tube ionizes a single particle and detects the signal," Mr. Shaw said, proceeding.

"What is an ionized ray?" Ben asked, further confused.

"Ionized rays are radiated beams or electromagnetic waves that carry high energy, the best example would be Gamma rays," Mr. Shaw said, easing his curiosity a bit.

"Another good example for them can be X-rays," Alex said confidently.

"That would be true," Mr. Shaw said. "It is important to note that on a common definition, they are known as transverse waves," continued Mr. Shaw.

"Right, transverse waves and longitudinal waves I know about them, like you mean to say sound waves are not transverse. They are longitudinal, I know," Ben said, now understanding giving a wide smile.

"Very good, Ben," Mr. Shaw said.

"It seems you remember more from your school days than I thought you did," Alex said, mocking him.

"Yes, I think you are right," Ben said still having a wide smile on his face.

"Oh, stop it, you two. Please, Mr. Shaw," Laura said in a way telling him to proceed with his explanation.

"So, yeah, when a radiation, say a Gamma beam is passed through the tube, it is made to interact with inert gases like neon," Mr. Shaw said thinking something simultaneously.

"Why is that?" Ben asked yet again.

"This is because there's always a reaction between the inert gases and radiation," Mr. Shaw answered, looking at him.

"And this leads to ionization of the particle," Laura said, understanding it quite a bit.

"Yes, that's the idea," Mr. Shaw said, now turning towards her.

"So, what happens next?" asked Alex going along.

"Well, the ionized particle gets separated from the rest and is registered by the counter," Mr. Shaw said, getting the crux of it.

"So, that is why it is called Geiger counters," Alex said thinking about the word counter coming into being.

CHAPTER 29

"Well, technically yes, but also 'cause Hans Geiger invented it," Mr. Shaw said improvising.

"How long this whole process takes?" asked Jack.

"Not long, it's quite simple when the particle is registered, a sound of a click is heard," Mr. Shaw said with precision, looking toward Uncle Jack.

"And this process is absolute?" asked Alex.

"During an age when there were no transistors, you can assume it got a lot of recognition. Of course, as scientific history proceeds, we realize that today we have come a long way from where we left off," Mr. Shaw said with a smile.

"So, you mean the coming of superconductors," Alex said, getting the hint.

"That and many others. The level of sophisticated gadgets that we use today was beyond the imagination of the people then," Mr. Shaw said, looking at Alex.

"Some people," Uncle Jack said, looking at Mr. Shaw.

"Right," Mr. Shaw said, turning towards Uncle Jack and giving him a smile.

"Yes, there are always exceptions," Alex joined in, agreeing with Uncle Jack looking at both of them.

"So, this story, where does it bring us now?" asked Laura looking at all of them.

All the talking and explanation had made Laura pretty confused about where Mr. Shaw was heading with his explanation about Geiger counters.

She looked at Ben only to find him much in awe of Mr. Shaw's intellectual speech. Although Laura was sure that Ben would be quite amused if this went on for another few minutes.

Mr. Shaw turned towards Laura and said enthusiastically, "There is more."

"What?" Laura asked curiously.

"The Geiger counters were the first benchmark invention which helped in the understanding of the electrical signals and there is more to them than what meets the eye," Mr. Shaw began to delve into the subject one more time.

"What do you mean?" asked Alex, getting excited that there was more to know.

Mr. Shaw turned towards Alex and gave him a wide smile noticing the curiosity on his face.

"Go on, Robert. Don't spoil it now," Uncle Jack said, encouraging Mr. Shaw as he too began to get excited.

"I will if would let me speak," Mr. Shaw said with a smile that was still visible across his face. "The major reason that made them so popular among their users was the fact that they were accurate, quick and easy to work on," continued Mr. Shaw looking at Uncle Jack who was now smiling, in a way understanding what he was getting at. "The thing that made them stand out was the fact that they could be used in parallel and could register multiple impulses," Mr. Shaw said highlighting their uniqueness.

CHAPTER 29

"That's what Rosie did, isn't it?" Alex said thinking back to what he got to know from Mr. Shaw before.

"Yes, that was the major reason Rosie is remembered for. He understood the important property of the Geiger counters and made full use of the opportunity."

"But this is just a year later," Alex said in a way not getting impressed.

"Even though it made a lot of difference in the scientific community one can make it sound as if it was not so much of a big deal, but it is the fact," Mr. Shaw said stressing his point.

"You still don't get it, Alex, do you?" Uncle Jack said looking at him, coming closer.

"Get what?" asked Alex in confusion.

"There were few, who had a creative insight into the particle experiments of electronics. Rosie's contribution was not by any means a small one," said Uncle Jack, trying to make him understand.

Alex took a moment for that thought to sink in.

He soon realized what Uncle Jack and Mr. Shaw were trying to say.

What they really meant was there were a few who contributed their creative insights to the subjects such as that of signal processing. He understood in a way he always had a similar feeling about his father. Perhaps Bruno Rosie was not very different from his father, there were few who would acknowledge his contribution to electronics and particle physics.

However, he thought of knowing the essentials of the Geiger counters more and turned towards Mr. Shaw.

"So, what more can you tell us about the origin of Geiger counters in the year 1926? I mean, a year earlier before Rosie went on to work on it," asked Alex, going back to question Mr. Shaw.

"Nothing much, son. At least not if you're asking me about the particle experiments in the year before. In any case, you were asking me something about it theoretically then it's a different story," Mr. Shaw said, taking his attention from the particle experiments now to theory.

"Why? What about the theory, sir?" asked Alex, wanting to know as much as he could about Geiger counters now.

"The theory of experiments of the Geiger counters is something that people still work on today. It's complicated but some believe it has much to offer to the world of electronics," answered Mr. Shaw knowing the complications of the subject that they were discussing.

"Do you know if there is something substantial to offer in the theory?" asked Laura.

"Not yet. But if you want, I'll look into it, but I'll need more time," Mr. Shaw said, looking at Uncle Jack and the others.

"Please, we would be much obliged," Alex said, getting a hunch that there might be something important they have missed.

"The pleasure is all mine, son. After all, it is as interesting for me to pursue this quest just like all of you. Let me know if there is anything else I can help you with," Mr. Shaw said, kind enough to give them all the help they needed.

"Thank you," said all of them.

CHAPTER 29

Alex's mind was on a trip. He was eager to grasp the understanding of the Geiger counters with the help of Mr. Shaw and somehow, he knew instinctively that it had some connection to what they were looking for.

Laura, on the other hand, was quite convinced that Mr. Shaw would be able to successfully tell them more about the Geiger counters in the future.

Ben looked at Uncle Jack in a way that was quite lethargic. Although he had enjoyed his time with Mr. Shaw, he was mentally exhausted from all the talking about the type of waves and the Geiger counters.

Alex had a question on his mind that he wanted to put across to Mr. Shaw for quite some time now.

"Sir, before you started explaining to us about the Geiger counters you told us that Bruno Rosie was not the first person who discovered the electronic circuit, do you know who discovered it first?" questioned Alex remembering the beginning.

"Oh, yes, of course. I'm sorry I don't have that knowledge, but I do think I would let you know the next time I tell you about the Geiger counters," Mr. Shaw said, winking at Alex.

There was a moment of pause before Alex's cell started to ring.

"Unknown number," Alex said and answered it swiftly.

"What? Is this? But…" Alex muttered, as all of them looked at him attentively.

They heard a gunshot. Panicking, they looked at each other as Alex spoke, "They're coming."

CHAPTER 30

"Quick, follow me," Mr. Shaw said, understanding the gravity of the situation.

All of them knew they didn't have a moment to waste.

Unlike Alex and Ben, this time Laura was a little more overtaken and agitated. The violence she had encountered along this journey had now started to get on her nerves and her willpower was slowly trying to give up on her.

Alex saw the look in her eyes and made her first go ahead and told her that Ben and others are just behind her and not to worry.

"We are going to get through this together," Alex said looking into her eyes, giving her confidence that she was not alone.

Uncle Jack, however, was struggling to be quick. His age was taking a toll on him.

Mr. Shaw made some swift turns to enter an underground chamber. He opened a small but comfortable passage for them to reach out.

"This will get you out of here in no time," he said as he told others to make a go at it.

CHAPTER 30

Quickly all of them made their way without looking back or thinking what they might face when they get out.

"Laura, you go ahead with Ben. I'll bring along Uncle Jack," Alex noticed that it was important for him to help Uncle Jack.

Ben took the lead without showing any reluctance. He knew they were running out of time.

"No, I'll help you too," Laura said looking at Alex and farther back toward Uncle Jack who was behind them, falling back on their trail.

"There is no time to argue, just go," Alex said, looking at her and then toward Ben who in turn quickly got hold of her and made his way out ahead.

Alex quickly made his way to Uncle Jack who in turn was quite relieved to see him.

"You should be running along with Laura and Ben. There is no time," Uncle Jack said telling Alex to carry on, thinking otherwise.

"No way, Uncle Jack. I am not leaving you behind," Alex said, denying him.

Alex turned to Uncle Jack. He quickly understood that at the speed that Uncle Jack was going he will not be able to make it. He told Uncle Jack to stick tight.

"I'm going to have to carry you," Alex said, coming closer.

"Are you sure?" responded Uncle Jack in amazement at Alex's determination.

"It'll be all right. Just do what I tell you to do," Alex said.

Uncle Jack nodded his head in confirmation.

Alex got hold of him and with all the power in his shoulders, picked him up and made his way quickly to the other end of the passage.

"What about Robert?" Uncle Jack asked knowing that they had left him back there.

"Uncle Jack, Mr. Shaw is a smart man. I am sure he will figure a way out, after all, it's his home and I bet he is out of trouble," Alex said telling Uncle Jack that there is no need for him to worry and they had other things to think about other than Mr. Shaw.

"Where are we going? Do you have a plan?" asked Uncle Jack as Alex almost reached the end of the passage.

He could suddenly see two figures. It almost seemed like he knew who that was. As he came closer, he knew it was Laura and Ben. Coming out, he put Uncle Jack back on the ground.

A man quickly came running; it was almost as if he appeared from nowhere.

"Ricky, how come you are here?" questioned Uncle Jack as he quickly recognized the face.

"There's no time to talk. They're already at the back of the passage where you came from and they are speeding toward you. We have no time, we must hurry," said the man looking at Alex and Uncle Jack.

"It is one of my security guards," Uncle Jack said, looking at Alex and his confused expression.

CHAPTER 30

That was the first thought that Alex had when he saw the man. It so turned out he was right.

"All right, let's go," Alex said swiftly.

"So, we had this parameter all checked before you went in, in case something happened."

"That was really clever of you, Ricky," Uncle Jack said looking at him and feeling proud of selecting him as a part of his security.

Laura gave a sigh of relief and looked toward Alex and Ben. They, in turn, were now smiling at each other.

"What next?" Alex asked looking at Ricky and Uncle Jack.

"Quick, follow me," said Ricky and started to make his way toward a certain direction.

The urgency could be seen in everyone as they made their way walking behind Ricky.

In a moment they were on another road where Ricky made a redial call from his cell.

A car almost crashed on them as they stood numb.

"That was fast," exclaimed Ben, still reviving from the breathless run from Mr. Shaw's residence.

All of them climbed in without saying another word and Uncle Jack told the driver, "Take us to a safe destination."

The car drove through the location and finally, they took the worried look off their faces.

Once again, they had beaten the odds to come out safe and sound, not to mention unharmed from another disastrous situation.

Alex was the first one to speak up. "I think it would be better for us to relax at an unknown place before things get messier," he said thinking and looking at Uncle Jack.

"I think Alex is right. Robert said that he would look into a few more books and get back to us. As of now we can't leave the city," Uncle Jack said in agreement with Alex and looked toward Ben and Laura in confirmation.

Ben and Laura responded with weak smiles.

Running around in different parts of the city searching for a way to settle in had got Ben thinking something. He was sure that nobody had been following them anymore, yet there were moments when he felt restless.

Realizing Ben felt uncomfortable, Laura decided to speak up. "What's wrong, Ben? Why are you so restless?" she asked allowing herself to adjust on the seat, to give him some comfort as he was sitting behind her.

"That's alright, Laura. I am comfortable like this," he said with a blurry smile.

"What are you so worked up about?" Alex asked, knowing there was something wrong.

Alex had known Ben a long time and there was no way Ben could go about hiding things from Alex.

"I was just thinking about our escapes from these guys in Geneva and before that," Ben said, looking at Alex.

CHAPTER 30

"What about that? What are you trying to say?" asked Alex, now seeking his attention.

"Before these guys have always tried to follow us but lately they have stopped doing it. I'm just wondering why," Ben said, trying to make Laura and Alex understand.

"It didn't cross my mind before but you are right, Ben. He is right, Alex. How come they always know where we are heading, even though we ourselves have no idea where we would be heading next," Laura said now looking at Alex and Uncle Jack.

"This is bad," Uncle Jack said feeling a little scared and overwhelmed by the situation.

"Don't worry, Uncle Jack. We will think of something," Laura said, trying to calm him down.

It was not hard for all of them to know deep inside how scared they all were. Even Uncle Jack had been feeling low for quite some time and yet none of them wanted him to know that they all were worried.

Alex now knew that the responsibility was more than what he had imagined at the beginning of all the running around that he and the others had to do.

He knew it would come to this, yet Uncle Jack decided to accompany them in their quest for the truth. In the beginning, he had warned Uncle Jack that things could get nasty and still he wanted to be with them. It was his choice.

Alex knew that bringing Uncle Jack along with them had its pros and cons. Of course, he was also the reason that they were still alive. If it weren't for his bodyguards, they'll be dead already.

Soon they arrived at a luxurious hotel, the driver stepped out first and after a brief interval of time, returned to them.

"Sir, I have made the reservations and I think it would be best if we just stay here until Mr. Shaw contacts us," Ricky said, coming over toward the window where Uncle Jack was sitting.

"Thank you, Ricky," Uncle Jack said and told them to get out of the car.

Since there were two rooms that were booked Alex and Laura decided to stay put in one of them and Ben and Uncle Jack took the other.

All of them relaxed as they realized how tired they were. After a few moments, Ben came over to the door where Alex and Laura were putting up.

"What happened?" Alex said and opened the door.

"Nothing, we were going to sleep and I thought I should inform you, in case something happens," Ben said looking over at Laura over his shoulders.

"That's really thoughtful of you, Ben," exclaimed Laura with a warm smile.

"If you guys were going to sleep as well I just thought one of us should stay awake, in case, you know," Ben said, thinking something.

Alex was tired but he knew he couldn't sleep even if he wanted to. There was too much going on in his head. He still remembered the call he received at Mr. Shaw's place. He didn't tell anyone but it was still on his mind, the confusion was obvious but he was careful not to show it.

CHAPTER 30

"No, Ben. I don't think so, I will be going to sleep. You must be tired, you should get some rest," Alex said, telling him to carry on.

"All right, you take care, if that's what you want but I do think you should get some sleep," Ben said knowing for sure that Alex was tired as hell. "Take care," continued Ben, looking at Laura, she responded to the same.

As soon as Alex closed the door Laura was the first person to notice his anxiety.

"What's wrong, Alex?" she asked as he turned around.

"Nothing, I have just been thinking about the man who called me earlier," Alex said, knowing it was hard for him to hide anything from Laura. It was also that Alex thought that this was the right time to share this with Laura now that they were all by themselves.

"Right, the call that told us that they were coming for us," Laura said, remembering correctly.

"Yeah."

"Well, whatever it was, one thing is for sure. Whoever called you, he's not our enemy. Otherwise, he wouldn't have warned us," she said thinking something, making a point.

"I hope you are right, I'm just curious who could it be," Alex said as he took Laura's palms in his own.

Laura reacted by gripping his palms affectionately before speaking, "It's going to be alright, Alex," saying, she laid her head on his shoulders.

Alex couldn't help but notice how the unwanted turn of events had allowed him to come close to Laura. It allowed him to feel differently for her. Time since he had waited for a moment like this, yet here they were, running for their lives, comforting and encouraging each other.

It had been a long time since they were this close, however, this was different. Trying to stay alive, looking out for each other's backs somehow this journey had become an emotional rollercoaster for him.

At the same time, Alex feared that it wasn't the same with Laura. He wasn't really sure if she was going through the same feelings, even though there were moments that were truly intense.

Alex decided to speak to her about his feelings, waiting for the right moment. Maybe when all this was over, he would tell Laura about his true feelings after all. In the midst of his thoughts, he felt excited and scared at the same time.

Perhaps I am falling in love, he thought to himself, just as Laura wrapped her arms around him.

Her face was now closer to his chest. His heartbeat had suddenly picked up pace.

Alex once again looked at her. She had fallen asleep, and he observed and caressed her, realizing she could hear his heartbeat going faster.

With her eyes closed, Laura had a faded smile across her face.

CHAPTER 31

In the other room, Ben had a question on his mind as well.

As Uncle Jack became comfortable and took a few steps toward the bed for a nap he turned to look at Ben. "What are you thinking, Ben?" he asked as he took off his glasses and kept them on the side table next to him.

"Nothing. I was just thinking about the "=D-" symbol we spoke about when we met Russel."

"Yeah, I've been thinking about that as well," Uncle Jack said, thinking something, looking away from him. "Aren't you feeling sleepy?" continued Uncle Jack feeling too tired to talk about anything at that point.

For a moment, Ben had failed to understand that Uncle Jack was an old man and the day had made him tired and exhausted.

"I don't know I just think we all are stripping away from the main objectives," Ben said, sounding worried.

Ben so wanted his thoughts to clear up and felt Uncle Jack could help. Then, on second thought, he felt it was better to call the day off. So, he joined Uncle Jack, climbing onto the other side of the bed.

"There is nothing to get so worked up about, Ben," Uncle Jack said relaxing.

"Why do you say that? I mean I don't even know why we are trying to look for more information regarding this Bruno Rosie guy," Ben said trying to understand where all of their efforts were heading.

"I can't say much, Ben. But it seems to be our primary concern as of now. Moreover, you are missing an important point here," Uncle Jack said, looking at Ben who was now looking back at Uncle Jack.

"What is that?" he asked blankly sounding confused.

"What if everything that we are doing now has something to do with the second symbol "=D-"?" Uncle Jack said, trying to make him understand.

"I don't understand how that can be possible," Ben said in a perplexed tone.

"Look at everything that has happened with you, Alex and Laura up till now. Hasn't it turned out to be for some reason or another? Although initially, it didn't make sense to you or the others, eventually you all got what you were looking for in the end. What I am saying is that let things move at their own pace and slowly the pieces will fall into their places and you will get to see the full picture," Uncle Jack said, trying to ease him out.

"I hope you are right, Uncle Jack. But this time all of this somehow seems to be too random," Ben said, trying to look back on the past few days.

"What do you mean by too random?" asked Uncle Jack seriously.

CHAPTER 31

"I mean you remember when you told us about the Probability Density Function?" Ben said, trying to clarify.

"Yes, of course, I do," added Uncle Jack, remembering back when he was explaining to them about Max Born.

"I mean, everything seemed very clear to me up till then but somehow we got into this Geiger counters and Bruno Rosie and since then I am all confused about where and what we are looking for," Ben said, explaining.

"That's right. I told you about the Probability Density Function but have you forgotten what happened after that? We now understand the meaning of the first symbol in the letter that Professor gave Laura," Uncle Jack said, trying to make Ben understand the course of events.

"Yes, I remember it according to the letter we went to Russel to find more about "=D-" and that made sense until we got that note from the house of Professor David," Ben said, telling Uncle Jack what was in his head.

"So, what about that?" questioned the Professor, in a way telling Ben to speak freely now.

Uncle Jack collected what Ben was saying, it was only later that they found the note in David's apartment and on the face of it, it all seemed as if the note had no relation with the second symbol. Jack thought that this was the reason behind Ben's confusion.

Now Ben spoke freely.

"I mean, suddenly we forget all about the second symbol in the letter "=D-" and are now on a totally different search," Ben said making his point.

"You mean the search for more information regarding Rosie," Uncle Jack said, understanding his point.

"All right, now I can see what's troubling you. You are scared about the fact that what if Rosie has nothing to do with the second symbol "=D-" in the letter," Uncle Jack said, looking at him and pausing for a moment.

"Exactly," Ben said, feeling he was rightly understood.

"Well, that is not possible, Ben," Uncle Jack said with a smile, still looking at him.

"Explain," Ben said curiously.

"You see, every clue or the fact you have encountered in your quest until now has something to do with the letter and the ultimate constant we are all searching for. Therefore, it would be foolish to assume that the note which we found in David's apartment is random and has no connection to the letter or the ultimate constant," explained Uncle Jack carefully so that Ben understands.

"So, you mean, for instance, the paragraph that we found in Albert Einstein's residence and the book on chaos theory at the Professor's library had something to do with the letter. So will be the case with the note that we found at Professor David's home," Ben said, understanding.

"Yes, I am glad that you get the point. Now, let's just revise where we stand maybe that will clear things up in your head," Uncle Jack said trying to show him the complete picture.

"That sounds like a good idea," Ben said agreeing to go along.

CHAPTER 31

Ben noticed that suddenly Uncle Jack was not feeling sleepy anymore. In fact, he was more than happy to make Ben understand the small and little details that they had come across up until now.

"Okay, so where shall I begin?" muttered Uncle Jack to himself thinking something.

"From the beginning," Ben said, eagerly encouraging.

"Ok, Ben. Let's start from the beginning. First, you got the hint about the constants, right, that was from the content of the letter?" Uncle Jack said, going back and remembering everything that had happened with them from the beginning.

"Yes, I remember Alex explaining to me the essence of the constants and then of course the first symbol for divine proportion," Ben said, recollecting.

"It was the constant of divine proportion that helped you to open the locker," continued Uncle Jack as he caught up with what Alex had told him.

"Right," Ben said, nodding. "Yes, the one in which we found the clue to the file kept in Albert Einstein's residence," continued Ben, adding his bit.

"Yes, what was that all about? Tell me again," Uncle Jack said, trying to remember unsuccessfully.

"In the file, we found the paper. An article of the special theory of relativity – projecting the property of constant of the speed of light," Ben said, remembering accurately.

"Yes, the one that told you time is different for different bodies in space and then you linked that property to the string theory as suggested in the same paper that you guys found at Albert Einstein's residence," Uncle Jack said, now remembering fairly.

"Yeah, which showed us that time can be different for all bodies taking the multi-dimensional aspect of the string theory, a unique yet interesting quality. I mean that's what Alex said if I remember correctly," Ben said, going back in his mind thinking about the events of that day.

"Yes, I believe that could be theoretically shown. The idea was very close to the concept of superposition and that was why you looked into *Quantum Interpretation Of Many Worlds*, am I right?" Uncle Jack said, remembering what Alex had told him back then.

"All right, which then led us to know more about the dynamical systems and its other properties," Ben said, continuing.

"Correct, what comes next?" Uncle Jack said, thinking hard.

"The chaos theory and Richard Feynman's Path Integral Formula," Ben said, reminding Uncle Jack.

"Of course, that was when I told you the connection between the genetic algorithm and Richard Feynman's Path Integral Formula, also, about *Quantum Interpretation Of Many Worlds* and Chaos both being dynamical systems," Uncle Jack said, now recalling it well.

"Yes, that's how we found the Probability Density Function and that's when Alex told me that it was the function that we had been looking for. I remember him telling me that every constant has a function and even the ultimate constant would have one such function," Ben said, getting excited now.

Ben remembered the conversation that he had with Alex about all patterns revealing a constant and patterns can be represented

CHAPTER 31

by functions, thus a function will always point towards a constant and vice versa.

"Correct, so, for instance, if we take the Probability Density Function to be the function of the ultimate constant and then if we consider the nature of the Probability Density Function, which is to reveal a pattern in Chaos or otherwise to show that order exists in randomness than that, in turn, gives us a property of the ultimate constant and should help us to know a little more about it," Uncle Jack said, revising his memory.

"If indeed our assumption about the Probability Density Function to be the function of the ultimate constant is correct. I mean all the clues point towards that single fact, I hope we were right. If this is right, there should be a pattern in reality in our life," Ben said in confusion.

"Absolutely, that's what I meant. However, as I said the limitations of the Probability Density Function exist in the quantum world. In short, the clues that we found linked the ultimate constant to the *Quantum Interpretation of Many Worlds*. So, if the theory of *Quantum Interpretation of Many Worlds* is true and we prove it, it will directly lead us to the ultimate constant," Uncle Jack said, explaining to him again.

"Does this mean that we would be able to safely say that Probability Density Function really shows a property of the ultimate constant if we are able to prove that *Quantum Interpretation of Many Worlds* is true?" Ben questioned, thinking hard.

"There is no reason to disapprove that Probability Density Function is an important part of *Quantum Interpretation Of Many Worlds*. Once *Quantum Interpretation Of Many Worlds* theory is proved correct, it would definitely show us the way to the ultimate constant," Uncle Jack said, coming to a conclusion.

"But if that were true then the second symbol in the letter should also have something or the other to do with *Quantum Interpretation Of Many Worlds* which is not seeming to be the case right now," Ben said, looking at Uncle Jack with a bit of concern.

"That should be the appropriate way to look at it. That is why we need to be patient and let things move along in their own way," Uncle Jack said, now making Ben feel relaxed.

Finally, Ben's mind became clear as to what was happening around him. You have to wait for some things to make sense.

"Alex once told me that the ultimate constant is not just a number, it's a force," Ben said, remembering what Alex told him back when he spoke about the contents of the letter.

"Of course, it's the same force I am talking about which drives the Probability Density Function, the force that revealed to us the pattern in Chaos and such a force will be the mother of all forces," Uncle Jack said, agreeing with Ben.

"So, the first symbol in the letter told us about the function of the ultimate constant and next we decided to find out more about the second symbol," Ben said, coming back to the point.

"Yes, and I think it will lead us to the ultimate constant and to that ultimate force or it will help us to understand *Quantum Interpretation Of Many Worlds* and further perhaps help us prove it," Uncle Jack said with a smile.

"So, if it does, one way or another we would find the ultimate constant cause *Quantum Interpretation of Many Worlds* and the ultimate constant are related," Ben said now accepting the facts.

"True, and there is another thing I notice that just now, Rosie has nothing to do with Probability Density Function. That's why

CHAPTER 31

I strongly have a feeling he is in some way related to the second symbol," Uncle Jack said with a glow on his face.

"You are right, that is the only possible connection now that we can think of," Ben said with a spark in his eyes.

There was no way that Uncle Jack could be wrong about this. They both had considered hard facts, after all.

"I think I should tell this to Alex and Laura," Ben said, suddenly getting up from the bed, feeling energetic and enthusiastic.

"I think you should," Uncle Jack said, encouraging him.

Ben could no longer wait to share this new idea with Alex and Laura as he took a pause before he got up and made his way to the door.

Just as Ben opened it a familiar face grabbed his attention.

Yes, he was sure it was him.

He quickly closed the door upon himself praying that the man had not noticed him. Perhaps it was because he was facing the other side.

As soon as Uncle Jack saw the look on his face he knew there was something wrong. He was there staring at Ben.

However, Ben's thoughts were elsewhere, the man he saw was the same one who was chasing him back in Geneva.

Soon he realized Alex and Laura were in trouble.

He picked up his cell and called Alex without wasting a moment. As the phone rang Ben told Uncle Jack to call his security swiftly.

NUMERICAL ENIGMA

Alex picked up the phone. He looked at Laura; she was awake now.

She gazed motionless as she saw Alex's eyes turned wide, he turned the cell on loudspeaker.

Before they knew it, panic hit both their bloodstreams.

Ben was shouting, "Get out of there, they are coming for you!"

CHAPTER 32

There was a quick knock on the door. Alex grabbed a chair and told Laura to open the door. They knew before any one of them said anything, Cody's men were here to take them away again.

Laura walked slowly towards the door giving a sign to Alex. She opened it.

A man who came in was dressed like a waiter but the gun he was hiding in his hand underneath the napkin told a different story altogether.

In a deep, scary voice, he said, "Move back, where is the boy?" he questioned holding her back. Alex was holding his breath waiting for the right moment to attack.

Slowly, Laura stepped back and the man entered the room.

As soon as he was inside, Laura shouted, "Alex, now!"

The man had a brief look at Alex before he blacked out.

Alex took the gun from his hand and grabbed Laura's hands, moving out of the room.

He stood there for a moment looking at both ends of the corridor briefly still hiding his face. There was no one. It was time for them to move out.

Laura felt a strange surge. She felt different. Something was different from the way Alex was holding her this time. She noticed a little bit of fear in his gesture, nonetheless, she liked it.

Making sure that no one was around, Alex turned towards Laura before she could say anything more. Alex looked at her intensely.

Laura could now see clearly in his eyes, it was fear, maybe the fear of losing her, she thought to herself. Right at that moment, she couldn't think about anything but Alex.

Alex's voice broke her chain of thoughts. He moved the gun tucking it between the jeans under his shirt and told her to grab their belongings and moved out.

Laura already knew there was not much time. She took a quick look at the room to see what was necessary for them to take along. She found a few things and started to put them in her bag along with both of their clothes. Suddenly, her cell started to ring again.

It was Ben.

"What's going on, are you guys all right?" he said almost grasping for his breath.

"Yeah, we are just making our way out," Alex said, sounding firm.

"All right, I and Uncle Jack are doing the same. Now, look, I have an idea," Ben said, trying to help.

CHAPTER 32

There was too much that was going down in both Ben and Alex's minds at that moment, yet they were trying to stay calm and figure out a way to fool Cody's men.

Alex still held on to Laura with her palm in his grasp.

"What is it?" asked Alex, quickly realizing anything would help them as of now.

"You have a window near the kitchen, right?" Ben asked him urgently.

"What's on your mind?" Alex asked making his way back to the room and going toward the kitchen, noticing the window Ben told him about.

"You are not telling me this is the way out," Alex said answering Ben, trying to ask him for another way out.

Alex knew that it could be really risky and dangerous with Laura by his side.

"It's all right, let's do this," Laura said looking at Alex confirming that it was all right for her to go on.

"There are going to be Cody's men in every corner of this building and the only way out for us is to move out of the building. You will find stairs that will lead you down toward the back end of the hotel. We will meet you there," answered Ben's voice on the receiver.

"Good one, Ben. It sounds nice," Laura said with a smile which felt quite amusing to Alex as he wondered how she could smile at this very situation.

"All right, Ben. I'll see you there, are you and Uncle Jack leaving now?" asked Alex, opening the window and looking toward the stairs.

"Yeah, we are," Ben said in a hurry.

"All right, Ben," Alex said, disconnecting while closing the window.

Laura once again checked her bag for their belongings.

"Are you done?" asked Alex as she saw her looking at some stuff in the bag.

"Almost," she said her hands swiftly and finely grabbing what looked like an identity card kept on the top of the fridge in the kitchen and slipped it inside her right pocket.

"What was that?" questioned Alex in confusion.

"Oh that, it's nothing, just something we lawyers have to carry along with us," Laura said quickly, urging him to carry on.

"Let's go," she said swinging the bag on her shoulders.

"Give me that, I'll take care of it," Alex said taking the bag off her shoulders.

They made their way out of the window and onto the stairs.

Laura paused for a moment looking down; she got a sudden rush of horror from the altitude.

This was not so surprising to Alex. He knew that Laura had always been afraid of heights.

CHAPTER 32

"Be careful, don't look down," Alex said, holding her slowly and stepping forward.

He did that in a way showing her how to do it. Laura held on to him closely looking for comfort and encouragement. Alex, on the other hand, gave her all the support she needed.

Slowly as they made their way down, Alex noticed that Laura was getting the hang of it. Moreover, he was surprised to see that Laura was no longer feeling scared and nervous that was quite unlike her.

He smiled faintly and started to mummer a song.

Laura's face suddenly lit up. It was a music that Alex used to play when they were young. Laura was surprised that Alex still remembered it.

The feelings of fear started to get replaced by her state of mind which now was absorbed in a childhood memory. She could imagine her childhood so clearly even as the circumstances were so drastic.

Walking down the stairs, with railings so weak and dangerous, she could see Alex playing that music on the piano and how much she loved him playing the music like he did when he was so young. Often the Professor would make him play the piano in the afternoon while he took a good nap.

Laura could sit there for hours listening to him. That's how good he was, of course, she didn't know that though years had passed, he could play the piano equally well today. What Laura didn't know was that Alex used to play it just for her.

Alex was still trying to shift her attention; he knew Laura always got scared from altitudes.

They were now looking at each other continuously. It was like Laura was in a completely different place.

As soon as they reached down and stepped on the rough cement, Laura realized where she was. It was like she woke up from a dream.

As Alex turned his head on the side ends of the block, hoping they were all alone, Laura looked away.

She was hoping that Alex would not be able to guess that she was in a completely different zone that belonged to her childhood just a second back.

But it was already too late. Alex had already noticed it. That look she gave when she ignored him when he used to play the piano for her many years back.

Sounds coming from upstairs suddenly grabbed his attention and he became cautious of who it was.

She took a moment to get her thoughts back to reality. Then, standing there she looked around to see if it was safe or not.

By the time she turned to Alex to say something, Alex was trying to call Ben and Uncle Jack.

He didn't get a response.

"What's wrong? Whom were you calling?" asked Laura.

"It's Ben, but he is not picking up the call," Alex said, looking into her eyes.

"Maybe, it's 'cause of Uncle Jack. He is really old, you know, to walk down the stairs like that, it's not easy," she said politely.

CHAPTER 32

"Yeah, you are right," Alex said suddenly getting a worried look on his face.

"What's wrong?" questioned Laura yet again.

She knew that Alex was thinking about Uncle Jack and wanted to comfort him.

This time Alex took a moment before replying, "How come these guys always get to know, where we are?" Alex said, thinking strongly.

Laura kept silent, she started thinking and then after a moment of pause she said, "This is not the time to think about them. I think we should try to look for Uncle Jack and Ben."

Suddenly Alex's cell started to ring again.

It was Ben.

"Where have you been, Ben? What's wrong? I have been trying to reach you for so long," Alex said in a hurry, moving away from Laura.

"Alex, me and Uncle Jack are in a little trouble here. We have reached the ground but there are a couple of men here who seem to be very suspicious, it's like they are looking for us," Ben said in a whispering voice.

"Shit!" explained Alex in disappointment; Laura could see the reaction from a distance.

"I have a gun, I can come to you and get you out of there if you want," Alex said with his hand reaching down to the gun.

"No, that is too risky," Ben said, trying to hold him back noticing that could become life-threatening.

"Ben, what should we do?" asked Alex, thinking fast.

He knew it was a confusing situation, but they had to find a solution.

"It would be best if I and Uncle Jack would stay here for a couple of more minutes until these guys scatter elsewhere and then we can meet at a commonplace," Ben said, getting an idea.

"OK, but what about Uncle Jack's security," asked Alex, waiting for Ben to answer.

Alex thought Uncle Jack's security could come for their help in a needy situation like this. They would surely be glad to get a helping hand. He wanted to ask Uncle Jack about his security men. Suddenly, Ben spoke again, his voice becoming softer.

"I don't think so, Uncle Jack has been trying to call his guards, but no one is responding. These guys must have taken them out but there is a backup guard, if I'm not wrong, toward your end. You can take the car along with Laura."

"What about you guys?" asked Alex, thinking about Uncle Jack and Ben.

"We can meet you guys later as soon as we get out of this trouble," Ben said again, reminding Alex of the car.

"What about the keys?" Alex asked not noticing how far he had walked away from Laura.

"It's in the car, you go now. Don't waste any time," Ben said, almost disconnecting.

CHAPTER 32

"OK," Alex said disconnecting and turned around.

He looked blank and motionless.

He ran and looked around the block everywhere but couldn't comprehend what had happened.

Where is Laura? He questioned himself.

CHAPTER 33

Alex looked around blankly, still trying to comprehend the situation. The awkwardness in his walk was apparent as there were Cody's men all around. *Did by any chance one of them found her? Could it be that she had fallen into some kind of trap?* Alex thought rapidly coming up to a number of conclusions each time hoping and praying to himself that he is wrong.

He walked along both ends behind the hotel. He was trying to make his movements concealed because he wanted to stay hidden from the men around him. He could hear voices coming from the people talking to each other living in the building on the other side of him. He could see people chatting, eating, laughing and doing all kinds of stuff.

His mind again focused on Laura. Even after searching the whole block, he couldn't find her. Suddenly his cell phone rang.

It was an unknown number.

"Hello," he answered in anticipation hoping it would be Laura.

"North, South, East, West, 34.1382360000 -118.1253430000, remember the constants, you have the key. You'll find what you're looking for there," a voice said.

CHAPTER 33

Before Alex could ask anything the call had disconnected.

The man had disconnected the call on purpose and the conversation was weak and brief but it was enough for Alex to know who it was.

Things were not making sense. Laura had disappeared and someone had called him and given him some kind of numbers. However, he was sure that someone was the same person who had informed him about Cody's men when they attacked him at Mr. Shaw's residence.

Alex's mind was now quickly trying to analyze what was going on and where had Laura suddenly disappeared. More than that he had to tell Laura about this call. Maybe she could help him make sense of it all.

Alex knew there was not much time and he had to go back to the car Ben had told him about. But Laura was nowhere in sight.

He thought she might have made a move to the car. But why she will do that without him? It was absurd. *No, that was not it,* thought Alex to himself. Laura would never go anywhere without him.

He thought of calling Ben and Uncle Jack but chucked the idea on second thoughts thinking they had enough problems on their own hands to worry about in the first place.

His mind was in two places at once.

In a split second, his mind was trying to make sense of the numbers he had just heard from an unknown person and then he was thinking about Laura again.

I have to calm down, Alex thought to himself.

Nonetheless, if Laura was safe, she couldn't have gone too far. He asked and spoke to no one but himself thinking how he could be so careless, he should have never let Laura get out of his sight.

On the other side, Ben and Uncle Jack had now found a window for escape. Waiting for as long as they had, now they saw the men slowly making their way back to the other side of the hotel. They waited till the last moment for the coast to get clear. Soon they were able to get to the streets.

Ben called for the cab as soon as possible.

"Wait, what about Alex and Laura?" Uncle Jack asked, looking at Ben. He was now worried about Laura and Alex and he looked forward thinking how it would be better for him to see all of them together.

Ben looked at Uncle Jack. He knew what he was thinking.

"Don't worry, we'll call them once we are away from this mess," Ben said, looking at Uncle Jack.

For Alex, things were getting out of hand.

Suddenly, he heard some footsteps and got a little shaken up thinking it was Laura and looked eagerly.

Soon that little smile on his face disappeared as he saw what looked like a shadow of a man with a pistol advancing toward him.

He quickly dived behind the garbage dump. He stayed still, making no movement at all and slowly he pulled himself up, holding his legs towards himself to sit tight.

He looked to take a peek at the man with a pistol, still feeling a little afraid. He saw the man advancing towards him, coming

CHAPTER 33

closer with every step while looking around. Soon he heard a few more footsteps. They were the same men which Ben and Uncle Jack had seen earlier.

With each passing moment, he came closer and soon Alex knew the man now was standing next to the garbage dump, one more step and Alex could be in trouble.

Suddenly, the man stopped just when he was about to step forward. Alex heard a voice.

"Let's go, they are not here," said a guy standing maybe a few feet away from him.

The man stepped back prepared to leave the place.

Alex now let go of the breath that he had deliberately stopped before.

After a few moments, he got up and thought of leaving himself. There was nothing much he could do just moving around here.

As he started to walk, a pair of hands grabbed him from behind.

Without turning he knew who it was, he could realize a feeling of those soft hands anytime anywhere.

It was Laura.

Alex turned around half serious and half happy and a memory came flashing back belonging to his childhood.

They were too young then and playing hide and seek. Young Alex was restless; he was trying to seek Laura out. The smell of the Professor's residence was still fresh in his heart and mind. After looking around in almost all the rooms Alex went to the garden, young Alex searched and searched until he was dead tired. It was then that Laura came and grabbed him from behind.

It was a similar kind of feeling Alex felt today. Perhaps Laura was thinking the same thing.

"Did you miss me?" she said sounding hyper.

Alex turned back to look at her face. He noticed her eyes were shining bright. He held her face gently and said, "Where the hell have you been I have trying to find you everywhere."

"I had to give a call to Rachel, it was important. I had promised her that I will be in touch," Laura said enjoying the attention she was getting.

"You could have gotten killed out there," exclaimed Alex holding her, coming closer. "We have to be careful," continued Alex still looking at her.

Laura looked at him a little taken aback at first but then smiled and replied, "Relax, I'm all right, see, I'm in front of you," she said before giving him a hug.

"You are," Alex said taking her in his arms.

It had been a while since Laura gave him a hug like that and for what it was worth he was pretty relieved to get one finally.

They stood there for a moment before Alex's phone rang. Alex took the cell out of his pocket with Laura still in his arms.

It was Ben.

"Ben, I was about to call you, are you guys safe?" asked Alex taking his attention back from Laura.

CHAPTER 33

"Yeah, listen, is Laura with you?" asked Ben confusingly.

"Yeah, why are you asking?" Alex said, a little surprised by his question.

"Nothing, me and Uncle Jack were just making our way back to see Mr. Shaw once more when I saw someone talking to a guy near the hotel. To me, it looked like Laura," Ben said clarifying.

"No, Ben, Laura is with me, you might have seen someone else," Alex said looking at Laura.

"All right, then, so I'll call Mr. Shaw letting him know to meet up at a common destination," Ben said, thinking something.

"Yeah, it's about the time we meet him," Laura said overhearing the conversation.

"I don't think that will be possible, Ben. Something has come up," Alex said, remembering the call he had received earlier.

"What is it?" asked Ben inquisitively.

"I'll tell you later. Meanwhile, you go meet Mr. Shaw and try to find something more about Bruno Rosie," Alex said, explaining to him.

"Even Uncle Jack is saying the same thing and he thinks the second symbol we found in the letter is related to Bruno Rosie in some way," Ben said, happy to tell Alex and Laura this new idea.

"That's brilliant. Let me know how it goes, we'll see you guys later," Alex said as Laura watched him getting a little excited.

"You guys take care," Ben said lastly.

"You too, Ben," Alex said before disconnecting the call.

"What was that all about?" asked Laura just as Alex put the cell back in his pocket trying to get a confirmation from him about what she had in her heart.

"Nothing. Ben thinks he saw you talking to some guy," Alex said letting her know.

"That must be the guy I was asking for the change when I called Rachel, but why didn't he stop?" asked Laura, looking at Alex.

"Maybe he was in a hurry," Alex said, looking at Laura with a smile. He was now really happy to have Laura back at his side.

"So, what now?" Laura asked while looking into his eye.

"There is something I need to tell you," Alex said, looking back at her with curiosity getting the best of him. He wanted to tell Laura about the call he had received earlier while he was still searching for her.

"What is it?" Laura said, hoping Alex was not going to propose her. Of course, if he did, she would have said yes but the time was not right. *It would be best for them first to get out of this mess,* thought Laura.

"What is it?" she asked yet again eagerly.

"There is someone who is helping us," Alex said, beginning to tell Laura about the call.

Alex knew that Laura had Ben right about the person who had made the call to Alex earlier back at Mr. Shaw's residence. It was the same guy who had helped them out then.

CHAPTER 33

"What do you mean?" she asked in confusion.

"Back at Mr. Shaw's place, I got a call that helped us to escape out of there and just a few moments ago the same man called me and told me a bunch of numbers. I don't know what to make of it," Alex said, trying to tell Laura everything.

"There was someone who knew beforehand that Cody's men were coming for us? And what numbers?" asked Laura now feeling excited herself.

"Yeah, the numbers 34.1382360000 -118.1253430000," Alex said remembering.

"Alex, I can't tell you much about this man except for the fact that he likes geography a lot," Laura said with a smile.

Alex suddenly remembered about the north, east, south and west the voice had muttered on the receiver but he was too much in jeopardy to get the point. But now Laura was right.

Laura had understood the meaning of the numbers even without Alex telling her the rest that had followed.

"These are coordinates, you jackass! latitude 34.1382360000, longitude 18.1253430000."

CHAPTER 34

The new revelation had made both Laura and Alex hyper. Alex looked forward to reaching his new destination. From the perspective of the situation, there were two obstructions they faced.

Alex needed a map to pinpoint where exactly they were going and the second thing they needed was a car.

"Let's get a taxi and get out of here," Laura said, beginning to get impatient.

"We need a map, Laura," Alex said taking her hand and making his way to the open street across them.

"You think I don't know that," Laura said, mocking him intentionally, and looking ahead toward the traffic and people walking by.

"What's your point?" Alex said looking at her and raising his eyebrows.

"When will this cell come in hand?" Laura said, taking out a cell phone.

CHAPTER 34

Alex grasped her point immediately. Laura was talking about using the cell phone to find out the location where the co-ordinates were pointing at.

She quickly moved her fingers on the keypad of her cell while Alex called for a cab for them to get in.

As soon as Laura and Alex got into the cab, Laura spoke out loud as if she was taken aback by something. "Alex, look at this," she said, showing Alex the screen of her Nokia N97.

Alex looked at the screen confused at first and then looked at Laura in bewilderment and thrill.

"Is this what I think it is?" he asked, staring at Laura.

"Yes, I think it's Caltech," Laura said, pretty amazed herself.

Although Alex looked forward to this new advancement, his mind was thinking about something else.

"What is it? You look blank," she said curiously.

"Nothing, I was thinking how we will get there," Alex said letting her know what was going on in his mind.

"I think I have a solution for that too," Laura said, thinking something and then smiling.

"What is it?" asked Alex sounding a little off.

"Rachel wanted to meet me when I spoke with her a while back. I think this will be a good time for me to go and see her," Laura said, telling Alex about the idea.

"You mean Rachel is in Pasadena?" Alex asked in joy, thinking how things were falling into place.

"Yeah, I think she'll make all the arrangements for our stay," Laura said, knowing she won't be able to refuse her. After all, they were best friends.

"That's great! Well, give her a call," Alex said, pointing Laura toward her cell impatiently.

Laura wasted no time in reacting and called Rachel.

Laura told her that she was with Alex and they needed to come and see her. She also told her that they have some work in Pasadena leaving the details for later. She knew it was evident that Rachel would eventually find out the truth. Rachel was more than happy to help her.

"It's done," Laura said, smiling and giving Alex a hug.

"What did she say?" Alex said, now feeling a little relaxed.

"She said she will book our flight tickets. We'll just have to take out the printouts of the tickets," Laura said, explaining her conversation to Alex.

"That I think we can do at the airport," Alex said, suggesting they don't waste any more time.

"I think that's a good idea," Laura said, nodding her head.

"Take us to New York Airport," Alex said loud enough for the cab driver to hear them.

As they reached, the first thing Alex did was to take out the printout of their tickets as Laura waited a long for him to come back.

CHAPTER 34

This time Alex decided to keep an eye out for her just in case she decided to disappear again.

As he collected their printouts and made his way back to Laura, she asked, "Listen, you said the man on the call said something about the key and to remember the constants. What do you think that means?" she said remembering what Alex had told her earlier.

"I don't know yet. Maybe we'll get to know more of it when we reach there," Alex said, not thinking much. "However, I do think whatever that we'll find out there is extremely important," Alex, taking the tickets, moved toward the boarding holding Laura's hand gently as they made their way to their flight.

"What do you think he was referring to?" Laura questioned again.

"I don't know Laura, I don't know," Alex said climbing into the flight.

Laura, occasionally noticing expressions on his face, felt that somehow it was unintentionally unusual. Maybe there was something Alex was not telling her.

Alex himself had a hint of what he may find in Caltech. Something related to Caltech had to be in the context with the Professor or his father, David. He preferred to keep Laura in dark till the time came.

However, observing Laura sitting quietly, Alex thought to himself perhaps she was thinking the same thing. Gradually, as minutes passed by Laura fell asleep on his shoulders.

In a few hours, they arrived at their destination. Laura was greeted with a big hug from her best friend. Alex felt good coming back to the place where he grew up.

"I was so worried about you that night. I'm so glad you are alright," Rachel said pulling herself away from her. "Who is he?" Rachel continued now turning her attention toward Alex.

"This is Alex, the one I was telling you about," Laura said with a smile looking at Alex and Rachel simultaneously.

"All right, I am glad to meet Laura's second best friend," she said, shaking his hand.

"I hope you're not jealous," Alex said with a friendly tone.

"Till now I'm not but you never know," Rachel said, getting friendly.

"I'm glad to meet you too, Rachel," Alex said shaking her hand and noticing her brown eyes and long, golden hair. Rachel looked much younger than a girl of her age.

"So what are you guys doing here?" she said coming close sounding excited.

"You remember, I told you about my father's letter and all the scientific tit bits of it?" asked Laura, looking at Rachel.

"I remember you telling me about his research, a new theory and all the clues that you guys have been getting," Rachel said, confirming confidently.

"Well, there is this man who has been helping us lately and he helped us locate a clue here in Pasadena."

"All right, go on," Rachel said, hearing every word of Laura carefully, now getting serious.

CHAPTER 34

"This time he is helping us to find another clue and we believe it's somewhere in Caltech," Laura said, telling Rachel her purpose for coming to Pasadena in the first place now.

"But Caltech is a huge place, do you even know where to look? I mean you have to have something to begin with," Rachel said, joining some facts from her end.

"She is right," Laura said looking at Alex in disappointment.

"If I remember correctly, he said, 'you have the key'. That would suppose he's talking about some kind of a locker," Alex said, remembering what he had heard earlier on the phone.

"But there are so many lockers in Caltech. How would we know which one is he talking about?" Rachel asked, looking at both worriedly.

"I think I know which locker he is pointing towards," Laura said, looking at Alex.

It was not long before Alex knew that Laura was thinking the same thing that he was. As both of them looked at each other Rachel was left clueless.

After a moment Rachel spoke impatiently, "What are you guys staring at each other for? Tell me alrcady, guys."

"I think the locker he is pointing towards belongs to my father," Laura said, looking at Alex.

"The Professor was working at Caltech for a long time. It is obvious what we are looking for in his locker," Alex said, looking at Laura and coming closer to her.

Laura too thought it make a lot of sense since the last time she met her father he told her that he had gone to the university to make a call. Yes, there was definitely something inside his locker. Something that they had to find out before anyone else does.

"All right, I'll take you guys there," Rachel said, without giving away another moment, understanding the gravity of the situation.

"Let's go," Alex said as they followed Rachel to her car.

It wasn't long before they reached Caltech.

Laura was asked for identification in order to see her father's locker. She showed it and both were standing in front of the Professor's locker in no time.

Rachel wanted to come but Alex told her to stay put for this time. She understood and decided to stay back in case they needed a backup.

"What about the key?" Laura asked Alex in confusion.

Alex looked at his neck. He had been carrying the key with him all this while. At the same time, Alex knew why the Professor had given him the key to keep it safe all his life. It was for this very moment that he had been carrying this key, for it was a responsibility that was given to him by destiny.

As he took it out and placed it in the locker, it was a perfect fit. As he turned it over, he realized there was also a combination lock.

"Remember the constants," that's what the voice said. Alex remembered the constants he was told about earlier on the call he had received.

It was a seven-digit combination.

CHAPTER 34

"Let me try the speed of light," Alex said, thinking something.

The seven-digit combination could only have one sound constant as a password and only the speed of light had a seven digit number.

He knew he had only one chance to crack it. This was it and he was confident there was no other constant that would fit the criteria.

As he pushed in the numbers, the locker opened with a buzzing sound.

Laura and Alex could wait no longer to see what was inside the locker. Was it another clue left by the Professor or by his father?

Alex could no longer comprehend what he would encounter. He felt his heartbeat getting faster with each passing moment. He reached into the locker without thinking.

There were the letters sent to the Professor by his father. Suddenly, for Alex, everything stopped for a moment. The power of a single thought had made him numb.

"What's wrong, Alex? What are you thinking?" Laura asked, beleaguered by his reaction.

There is only but one person who would have known about the locker and its content.

"My father is still alive…" Alex spoke.

CHAPTER 35

Laura took a pause for a moment trying to digest what Alex said about his father. "Are you sure?" she asked unnervingly, her words coming slowly out of her mouth.

"This is what it looks like," Alex said, simultaneously looking at her and back to the locker. "We have to find him, he might try to contact us again," Alex said, thinking something.

Laura noticed the bunch of papers inside it. "What is that?" she asked inquisitively.

Alex looked back into the contents of the locker, looking at what seemed to be piles of paper or letters of some sort.

"Check these out. These are letters that were written by my father to the Professor," Alex said, showing the letters to Laura.

"Oh my god, look at the date. They were written after the earthquake happened, that is, after David was supposed to be dead," Laura said, noticing the date on the letters. All were dated after 1980.

"So, my father must have written them to the Professor in order to inform him about his escape," Alex said, wondering.

CHAPTER 35

"It means we were right, your father had been set up in some conspiracy. That's what Uncle Jack told us, right?" Laura said remembering what Uncle Jack had told him about David and the stolen papers.

"Let's see what we have here," Alex said taking out some files.

Laura on the other hand started reading the letters.

"This is unbelievable! Alex, look at this!" Laura said, realizing something as she unfolded the contents of the letter.

She forwarded a letter to his hands as Alex lean towards her.

Hey, David. It was good to see your reply. Yes, after you left, things have been a little bumpy for me and Jack. There are a few important things that I need to tell you. First, Clement is dead, and second, I think I know who is behind all these evil happenings. I and Jack seem to think it is Rudy and Cody who tried to set you up.

"These other letters prove that the Professor and your father worked with each other. This was during the time that he was considered dead in Caltech," Alex said, turning the letter and noticing the address.

Laura already knew it; she had already seen the date on the top of the letter before Alex started reading it.

"Look, there is more," she said pushing her hands into the locker.

Alex and Laura started to unravel the contents of the locker. Soon, both of them sat on the ground and started to arrange the letters by their date. Alex told Laura to keep an eye out for, in case she finds something interesting.

It was not long before Laura spoke, "Alex, look at this. This is your father's writing," Laura said showing him a letter.

All this is bad news, John. Clement was the only person who could lead us to the culprit, I'm sorry for him. What you said in context with Rudy and Cody was shocking. Keep a close watch, John; I have a bad feeling about this. Make sure you move out of Caltech as soon as possible and try to take Jack with you. John, the papers you found in Clement's pocket are very important although they are just a part of my major thesis which I'm working on right now, they are still important. What I'm working on right now is in accordance with the search for U.F.T.

"All right, according to this letter, there were two guys as Uncle Jack had suggested. I suppose his theory was right," Alex said, looking at Laura.

"Yeah and you see, here it seems there was this guy Clement who knew the truth but he died before he could tell anyone anything," Laura said, pointing out about Clement.

"I don't think he just died, Laura. I think he was murdered by Cody and Rudy," Alex said thinking something.

"So that no one could ever know about the attack on David," continued Laura adding a bit. "Alex, look here," Laura said going through another letter.

The quantum theory thus alternatively suggests ideas that there exist multiple universes for each corresponding outcome.

Though without any proof, this concept of quantum has become of great interest to me. I'll keep updating you about my findings. Please do tell me how things are going in Caltech from time to time. It's been a while since I left that place. I miss it, John, more than anything else. At the same time, I need to tell you a few important things on a more personal note, will do that in my next letter. Take care, John.

"Yes, of course, quantum mechanics and multiple options, my father was working on *Quantum Interpretation of Many Worlds*," Alex said smiling.

CHAPTER 35

He was sure now that they were on the right track in their quest for the ultimate theory.

"Here is another one," Laura said, giving Alex another letter.

John, I have had a change of heart, I have started to believe that the string might just be real. However, there is something more interesting that has grabbed my mind. I'm somehow convinced that the string theory is not the key to UFT.

I am convinced even after finding the proof of the string, it will not reveal the ultimate constant. And I had a vision that the ultimate constant lies on the boundaries of the frontiers of science but it's a reflection which reaches far beyond science itself. Therefore, the string, even though able to fuse relativity and quantum, will not yet reveal the UFT.

"This is great," Alex said going on with the subject of the letter, smiling to himself.

"What? What is it?" asked Laura, feeling excited.

"All right, you see, my father gave a part of his research to Clement and later Clement turns out dead. That means someone was after my dad's research. Moreover, the research paper that Clement had was of *Quantum Interpretation of Many Worlds*," Alex said excitedly.

"And we have been working on the same theory lately, it is just as we had thought," Laura said, smiling.

"Going on, the second letter suggests that the string theory is not the Unified field theory according to my dad," Alex said, simultaneously looking at the letter and Laura.

"Why? I am a bit confused," Laura said, looking back at Alex.

"Well, according to this letter, my dad points out that the elementary particle of the string theory, that is, the one-dimensional string can be manipulated and made to support many theories in astrophysics due to its one-dimensional nature," continued Alex.

"So?" asked Laura blankly.

"So, the UFT is a definite theory. It does not have multiple forms," Alex said, raising his arms amusingly, wondering how Laura is not able to understand what he was getting to.

"Alright, I get it. This would mean the string theory is not the UFT," Laura said, looking at Alex.

"Correct!" exclaimed Alex.

"What this means is we have been going in the right direction following the clues," responded Laura.

They both again started to take a look at the letters.

"Alex, look at this," Laura said putting across another letter from his father.

John, there are at present four important constants; c (speed of light), G (constant of gravitation, h (Planck's constant, the constant of action) and e (electric charge). It is now believed that the future of cosmology might reveal a few more, but there exists one ultimate constant. This constant would only be found by intimately combining all the Universal constants as I mentioned. There would be a few others that could be found later in the future. I, though, seldom agree that this combination would possibly point toward the string being the ultimate constant.

As for what I think it would be something more than physical.

"Of course, this is how it started, with the constants," Alex said, looking at the letter.

CHAPTER 35

"Alex, we have to find that ultimate constant," Laura said in a way encouraging him.

"I know, let's just keep looking," Alex said getting back to reading some papers.

When Laura was busy looking over and arranging some letters, Alex came across something.

It wasn't exactly about the UFT, it was about his father congratulating the Professor for getting married.

Congratulations, John. I got the news of your marriage, you'll be happy to know that I too have decided to propose my lady love soon. Her name is Julia. She's the daughter of one of my father's friends. She is a lawyer and a good one too. After she is done with this one particular case we plan to get engaged. We wanted to get married now but, I don't want to risk her life. You know, John, how things have been after I left Caltech.

Laura smiled as she carefully read each word.

Toward the end, however, David did say something important.

"Look, Alex. Your father, he is talking about Unified Field Theory. I don't understand what he means by this?" Laura said, pointing something out in the letter.

Anything that we can understand, anything that we can predict has a uniform pattern. Things that are in order become easy to comprehend. On the other hand, random events seem complicated and difficult to understand. What I'm trying to say here is all patterns are proportions.

Therefore, I'm concluding that since the quest of UFT is to find that ultimate pattern that would help us to understand the mechanics of this reality, it would also be an ultimate proportion. Thus, my search now for UFT has shifted to find that ultimate pattern or proportion.

"He was looking for a pattern that could lead him to the ultimate constant," Alex said, looking at Laura.

"Well, did he find it?" asked Laura looking back at him.

"I think he did. That is why he left all the clues for us, the Professor and David, both of them," Alex said, looking confident. "Here, there is another," Alex said as he worked himself back into the locker.

John, I'm sure by now you too would have been trying to find a theory with an ultimate constant. It has been five years since I last wrote to you about the UFT having the ultimate proportion (pattern). I am sure you might have got my hint about the constants, as these are the constants which balance and preserve the proportions and the proportion in turn reveal to us the patterns. I am now convinced that such a constant or proportion (pattern) will have a universal quality like its counterparts G and h.

Thus, I believe under all the complex theories of our universe, lies this simple yet mystical ultimate proportion (pattern) or constant.

"My god, this letter is written five years after the last one. Look at the year," Laura said, noticing the date.

"That's not what particularly grabbed my attention," Alex said going through something.

"What?" asked Laura, coming closer and trying to see what Alex was reading.

"Laura, this is great! My father is talking about simplicity under surface complexity," Alex said.

"Chaos theory, dynamical systems," Laura said, pausing for a moment.

CHAPTER 36

"Yes, we are on the right track. This is a good confirmation and if I'm not wrong the next thing we will see in these letters will be the mention of Probability Density Function," Alex said, quickly moving his eyes through the letters.

"Wait a minute, Alex, look at this," Laura said.

However, by my study of the ultimate constant, I believe that this uniform string theory will not lead to the UFT because it would lack the knack for proportionality, as I had told you before in my previous letters. John, I have found that the function of the ultimate constant has to stand for all of the universes if there exist any other than the one that we are in, for the same reason that it (the ultimate constant) has to be pure. It has to be beyond the realms of human measure. Just like in the case of a fine structure constant, which is a pure value formed by the combination of other universal constants h, c and e.

Also, I have a feeling that it does not stop just there. It will also have something more to offer.

For now, I fail to understand what it would be. To tell you the truth I don't even know what it is. However, I do know it can prove the existence of other universes. Thus, my search for now is shifted to Quantum Interpretation of Many Worlds ever more so powerfully.

"You were right, this is the one," Laura said, showing it to Alex.

"Yes, of course. The Probability Density Function is the ultimate function. The real question is what this function represents other than the states of particles in quantum mechanics. I mean it should direct us to a constant, I don't get it," Alex said, helplessly.

"Wait a minute, Alex, calm down. You said all constants have patterns, right?" Laura said, holding a letter and remembering what Alex and had said about proportions and patterns being one and the same thing. "And the function shows us the way to find that pattern," continued Laura.

"Yes, what is your point?" Alex said wondering, looking at her.

"Take a look at this," Laura said giving him another letter.

John, I have had a change of heart, I have started to believe that the string might just be real. However, there is something more interesting that has grabbed my mind. I'm somehow convinced that the string theory is not the key to UFT.

I am convinced even after finding the proof of the string, it will not reveal the ultimate constant. And I had a vision that the ultimate constant lies on the boundaries of the frontiers of science but it's a reflection which reaches far beyond science itself. Therefore, the string, even though able to fuse relativity and quantum, will not yet reveal the UFT.

"Do you see what I see?" Laura said, reading the expressions on his face carefully.

"Yes, but what does he mean by frontiers of science?" asked Alex in a way questioning himself.

"Let's just keep looking," Laura said as she turned to read the next letter.

John, I see that you have misunderstood my intentions. My aim is to search for the ultimate constant within the limitations of scientific knowledge and data available to me. All I am saying is that since we have been unsuccessful in that, over and over, it might be that we have missed something. Most people in our field try to rely on everything scientific. I believe, for once, we should look at life, for science has now become part of it.

CHAPTER 36

"Alex, I found the concluding letter," Laura said, passing it to him.

"Of course, you were right, Laura. There is a pattern the Probability Density Function is pointing toward but it's not just in quantum mechanics," Alex said, suddenly realizing something.

"What do you mean?" asked Laura, unable to understand the expression on the face of her childhood friend.

"It's in life, Laura. The pattern Probability Density Function is pointing at is in the reality of each of our lives. But on a more practical note, I think it's related to some other scientific notion," Alex said, understanding the idea now.

"What do you mean? Life? I don't get it," Laura said, still unable to comprehend.

"I mean take a good look at all the constants—gravity, electromagnetism, speed of light, and the Planck's constant, all of them play a very big role in our lives. In fact, they are the reason that we exist and most importantly all of them have patterns," Alex said, trying to make Laura understand.

Finally, it dawned upon her. "You mean like planets revolving around the sun, electric current, yes, I get that they all do have a pattern," replied Laura.

"Of course, they have. Planets have a definite orbit, that's a pattern. The flow of electricity which helps us to get things done in our day-to-day life - positive charges and negative charges, that's a pattern," Alex said, amused to see the obvious.

"Right, so you think the ultimate function that is in this case the probability function is pointing toward a pattern in reality as well. But Alex, we notice such things, these are all things we see and feel every day," Laura said, a bit conclusively.

"What if there is a pattern we have not yet noticed? What if we have ignored the obvious? Don't you remember the ultimate constant goes beyond measurement?"

"It's a force," the words coming instantly out of their mouths at the same time.

"Come on, we have to search for more clues and for now, these letters are coming in very handy," Alex said, going back to the contents of the locker.

In the midst of all the letters, Laura found something that made her a bit emotional.

It was a letter from her father to David.

David, I am here to inform you with a broken heart that Clair is no more. I was attacked in my apartment. I must also tell you that this wasn't the first time it happened. I tried to protect her with all I had, but I failed.

It is also my concern that you and Julia should take another residence anywhere else where it would be the best for you and her.

I don't want what happened with me to happen with you, David. Therefore I plead, please listen to me. Go away as soon as you can. I know that you are very close in your study to finding the ultimate constant. This study should not go into the wrong hands, whatsoever. For all my life, I have listened to you. For once, please listen to me.

Alex comforted her calmly. He knew how it felt to know someone you were supposed to be a part of, to know someone who would have made a family. He knew as long as the Professor was there, Laura always had someone to share her thoughts and feelings with. However, now that the Professor was dead, this letter brought back the memories of her father along with the sadness of her mother's death.

CHAPTER 36

Alex always knew this pain, but he never even in his dreams wanted Laura to feel the way he did and yet here she was in his arms, the only place that could now give her a pinch of peace.

Alex knew they didn't have much time.

"Laura, we have to keep looking," Alex said unpleasantly.

"Yeah, I know," Laura said, understanding the situation.

As they both got back to reading the letters and papers, Alex picked up a file. "What is this?" he said, as opened it.

In the file, there was an article which followed as such,

PROBABILITY

A consequence of removing wave function collapse from the quantum formalism is that the Born rule requires derivation, since many-worlds claims to derive its interpretation from the formalism. Attempts have been made, by many-world advocates and others, over the years to derive the Born rule, rather than just conventionally assume it, so as to reproduce all the required statistical behavior associated with quantum mechanics. There is no consensus on whether this has been successful.

EVERETT

Everett (1957) briefly derived the Born rule by showing that the Born rule was the only possible rule, and that its derivation was as justified as the procedure for defining probability in classical mechanics. Everett stopped doing research in theoretical physics shortly after obtaining his Ph.D., but his work on probability has been extended by a number of people. Andrew Gleason (1957) and James Hartle (1965) independently reproduced Everett's work, known as Gleason's theorem which was later extended.

"It says here that this guy had found the existence of 'Many worlds'," Laura said, reading it and trying not to make a mistake.

"That's not important, however, this is. Look at this. He did so with the help of Born rule," Alex said with a faded smile.

"What is Born Rule?" asked Laura, not remembering.

"Did you forget what Uncle Jack said earlier? The Born rule is otherwise known as the Probability Density Function," Alex said, explaining with joy in his eyes.

"This means we were right all along, this is good news, Alex," she said, smiling back at him.

She turned back toward the contents of the file and something grabbed her attention.

"Alex, take a look at this, what are these?" Laura said looking at something.

In front of Alex, there were a bunch of numbers and an address.

"$10^{80}, 10^{40}, 10^{120}$

Oakland, San Francisco Bay Area, California,

Before Laura knew Alex smiled, looked at her and said, "You're not going to believe this, this is our next clue."

CHAPTER 37

"So, do you know what this is?" asked Laura, finally as they came out of Caltech.

"If I'm not wrong, we need to follow the address and there are some large numbers but I don't know what they imply," Alex said reluctantly.

"I guess that's what we got to find out," Laura said.

"All right, let's go," Alex said without wasting much time.

Before they knew it, they were making their way to Oakland, San Francisco Bay Area, California.

Rachel, of course, had been of great help as she gave Laura a handful of finances including flight tickets for Oakland and a couple of contacts that could help her along the way.

As they were traveling, Alex noticed that all this running around had made Laura all worked up and deep inside he thought it would have been better if she was out somewhere safe, although he knew she was not gonna let that happen. She was hell-bent on finding out who killed her mother. Even Alex knew better than that. However, he wanted to make her as comfortable as possible.

He rolled a blanket over her as they made themselves easy on the flight. Laura was half asleep but she opened her eyes gently hesitating to look into his eyes. For Alex too, it had been hard to control his feelings for her. He knew for a long time he had kept his feelings to himself but now that she was with him, slowly it had started to show.

As soon as they arrived at their destination and their plane landed, Laura showed Alex something.

She had brought along a few letters from the locker and there was the one she wanted to show to Alex.

John, I have had a change of heart, I have started to believe that the string might just be real. However, there is something more interesting that has grabbed my mind. I'm somehow convinced that the string theory is not the key to UFT.

I am convinced even after finding the proof of the string, it will not reveal the ultimate constant. And I had a vision that the ultimate constant lies on the boundaries of the frontiers of science but it's a reflection which reaches far beyond science itself. Therefore, the string, even though able to fuse relativity and quantum, will not yet reveal the UFT.

"Like I said, the string theory is not the Unified Field Theory. This letter here brings out the same fact, my dad felt it is an important contribution to particle physics but as he suggests in his last few lines in this letter, even the proof of the string will not make it a Unified Field Theory," Alex said, looking at Laura guiding her about the contents on the letter.

"Why was your father so sure?" asked Laura as she turned over to take care of the single baggage.

"Here, give me that," Alex said as he took the suitcase from her.

CHAPTER 37

Laura smiled as she watched him act like a gentleman which, as far as she knew, was not his thing. Silently, she let herself pass her bag to him and said, "You were saying?"

"Yeah, that string theory is not the UFT because it lacks practical application and it does not have a pure representation. The string constant keeps changing according to the theories it is introduced in."

"Here is another one," Laura said about to bring another letter in front of him.

"Show me the Everett file, I am more interested in that right now," Alex said before Laura could bring the letter in front of his eyes.

"All right, here it is," Laura said giving him the file.

As Alex went through the file he started getting more interested.

"What are you reading?" Laura said as she joined him.

"This is something, look here," Alex said taking her attention to a few lines.

"PROBABILITY

A consequence of removing <u>wave function collapse</u> from the quantum formalism is that the <u>Born rule</u> requires derivation, since many-worlds claims to derive Its interpretation from the formalism. Attempts have been made, by many-world advocates and others, over the years to derive the Born rule, rather than just conventinnally assume it, so as to reproduce all the required statistical behavior associated with quantum mechanics. There is no consensus on whether this has been successful.

"It seems that all the functions stand true, there is no wave function collapse," Laura said looking at Alex and the contents of the file simultaneously.

"Yes, that means all states of electrons represented by the Probability Density Function stand true. Otherwise, meaning that each state of electron exists in a different universe," explained Alex.

"That is how it proves the theory of *Quantum Interpretation of Many Worlds*," Laura said, understanding.

"Yes, but there is one more problem," Alex said, now looking at her.

"And what is that?" she replied.

"There is no way to prove all states of electrons represented by the Probability Density Function are true," Alex said in disappointment, thinking something at the same time. "Oh my god, if we find out a way to prove that all the states of electron represented by the Probability Density Function is true, we will be able to prove that *Quantum Interpretation Of Many Worlds* is real and that might lead us to the ultimate constant as well," Alex said, suddenly getting a brain wave.

"It's like what Uncle Jack said. Find the ultimate constant and prove *Quantum Interpretation Of Many Worlds* or prove *Quantum Interpretation Of Many Worlds* theory and find the ultimate constant," Laura said remembering what Uncle Jack had said previously while they were discussing about Born rule.

"God, Uncle Jack is good," exclaimed Alex with a smile.

"He sure is!" Laura said as they made their way out of the airport to the cab.

CHAPTER 37

It had been a while now that nobody had been on their trail. Laura was careful to see all around before she climbed into the cab. She was just making sure that no one was following them.

In a short while, they arrived at their destination. To which Alex seemed amused and Laura a bit taken aback.

"Of course, I should have known," spoke Alex, raising his eyebrows and taking out the piece of paper Laura had given him in Caltech.

The one, which had large numbers written on them.

$10^{80}, 10^{40}, 10^{120}$

"Know what?" Laura asked, looking at him and then looking toward the huge gate at the entrance.

"These numbers, this address and this place, there is no mistake," Alex said, going over what was going on in his mind once again.

"There is no mistake to what, Alex? Will you just come out with it?" Laura said, getting a little impatient.

"This place belongs to Sir Arthur Stanley Eddington," Alex said, looking down to face Laura.

"Eddington, you mean the famous scientist Eddington?" exclaimed Laura, looking at Alex and the gate with no clue as to what to do next.

"So, what's next?" she said looking at Alex.

"I guess, let's just move out of this cab first and see what we can do," Alex said, grabbing his belongings and opening the door.

He was swift to give the driver his money.

"Now that we have come this far, what you think we should do?" asked Laura said sarcastically.

"Well, for one, let's start by ringing the bell," Alex said and made his way up to the gate.

As he was about to ring the bell, he heard a rough, hard voice.

"What do you want? Why are you here?" Alex and Laura heard this sinister tone.

"My name is Alex and this is my friend Laura, she is the daughter of Professor Gable," Alex said.

"John Gable. I'm afraid we need your help," Laura said, joining in.

They waited for a minute to see if the man on the other side of the speaker heard them.

"Come in," the man said after a brief silence.

As the gates opened, both Alex and Laura were relieved that their journey had not been just for nothing.

As they entered Laura noticed a huge bungalow with gardens on right, left and in front of them. There was a clear path meant to lead them to the entrance. There was security but up to the minimum, from what it looked.

As they walked through the entrance Laura noticed the gardens and the flowers. She was a little enchanted by the natural beauty that surrounded this place.

Alex noticed the number of cars parked at the far end of the pavement. They were far but he could make out the latest Audi

CHAPTER 37

and McLaren. This place seemed like somewhat of a royalty. To Alex, this brought familiarity.

Even Ben had a similar residence, but Alex could make out this was much more lavish.

"Somebody is going to be jealous if he gets a look at this place," Alex said looking at Laura.

Laura smiled as she got the hint of what Alex was trying to say. "You are lucky, he is not here," she said looking at him.

As they passed the entrance a man was already waiting for their arrival.

"Welcome, please follow me," he said pointing out that direction.

As Laura and Alex followed him, they noticed the interiors were equally mesmerizing as the beauty of the gardens that rested outside. The whole mansion looked old and had supposedly an English look to it.

As they followed, the man came to a stop. "They are here, sir," said the man as he told them to come in.

"Thank you very much, Griffin. Now, you can go," said a man, sitting next to the fireplace, and reading what looked like an old newspaper.

He got up and told Alex and Laura to take a seat.

As he stood there, Laura noticed that he indeed was old, perhaps the same age as Uncle Jack was.

"Thank you for letting us in," Alex said as he and Laura became comfortable on their respective chairs.

"So, tell me young man, what's *your* father's name?" asked the old man in his rough, old voice.

"His name is David, sir," Alex said looking at the old guy who was now grabbing his inhaler kept on the side table next to his chair on which also stood a charming lamp.

"David, hmm…, I should have known, you have his eyes," said the man, correcting his glasses a little.

"You knew my father," Alex said almost in surprise.

"I met David briefly but we clicked," said the old man, now replying.

"Who are you?" asked Laura standing up to him.

"My name is Mitch Mauldin, my father and Eddington were close friends. Enough about me, what brings you here?" The man asked looking at Alex and then turning his attention towards Laura.

"It's this," Laura said handing a piece of paper that had the large numbers written on it to Mr. Mauldin.

He leaned forward as Laura got up and passed the paper into his hands.

The light seemed a little dim, so he leaned towards the lamp kept on his side table to get a good look at the piece of paper.

"These are series of large number coincidences which Eddington proposed," said Mitch, looking at Alex and Laura.

"I don't understand," Alex said looking at him curiously.

CHAPTER 37

"Eddington believed that there was some mystical reason behind the number 10^{120} and 10^{80} being the cube and square of 10^{40} respectively. These numbers were important as they signified certain basic properties of our universe. For example, the number of protons and electrons in the observable universe which Eddington calculated to a great level of precision and accuracy," Mr. Mauldin said, trying to explain.

"So, you mean he thought there was some force that led to this magical coincidence by these numbers appearing to be a square and cube of the first number 10^{40}," Alex said, getting the point.

"Yes, but he never got to know the reason behind this coincidence. These numbers happened to appear in certain ideas and theories of physics that scientists worked on time and again. Unsuccessful he was, yet he believed in the importance of these numbers. In his work, several of his equations can be found in accordance with these numbers," continued Mr. Mauldin, trying to tell them about Eddington and his work.

Alex had not heard what Mr. Mauldin said, as he was thinking of something else.

"Alex, what are you thinking?" Laura said, shifting her attention to Alex.

Before Laura could speak anything more, Alex spoke. *"Laura, don't you get it?"*

"Get what?" she exclaimed loudly.

"Eddington was searching for the same ultimate force that we are in quest of right now."

CHAPTER 38

"What are you implying?" asked Laura, trying to get the point Alex was making.

"Look, all these numbers are dimensionless, look at them," Alex said, showing the numbers to Laura, almost whispering. "Maybe Eddington was trying to find the same ultimate constant as we are right now," continued Alex.

Laura looked at him. "That's right," she said to herself. "Maybe we should ask Mr. Mauldin, maybe he knows a thing or two about the ultimate constant," replied Laura softly.

"I knew David and John and when I said that, you should have guessed why I would know about the ultimate constant. Moreover, let me elaborate, that's the reason you are here," continued Mr. Mauldin, still looking at them.

"So, you know what this ultimate constant is," said Alex, surprisingly.

"I don't know what it is, but like other people, I have been trying to find it ever since the dawn of the 1950s," answered Mr. Mauldin.

"Well, what can you tell us?" asked Laura, believing she was in the right place and that she could get any help that was offered.

CHAPTER 38

"Wait here, I have to show you guys something," Mr. Mauldin said and walked off.

He soon returned, holding a book by the cover of it. Alex could guess it was about the works of Eddington. Mr. Mauldin had heard their conversation clearly earlier.

"You know, I may be an old man but that doesn't mean I don't hear right," he said with a smile.

Curiously opening the book he started to search for something.

"What is it, Mr. Mauldin?" asked Alex.

"Hold on, you'll see soon," Mr. Mauldin said and continued to turn the pages of the book.

Alex looked at Laura in confusion.

"Here it is, take it, have a look," Mr. Mauldin said, offering the book to Alex and pointing toward a certain page.

"You too, come closer," Mr. Mauldin said, telling Laura to come closer so that she could see as well.

"OUR PRESENT RECOGNITION OF FOUR CONSTANTS INSTEAD OF ONE MERELY INDICATES THE AMOUNT OF UNIFICATION OF THEORY WHICH STILL REMAINS TO BE ACCOMPLISHED. IT MAY BE THAT THE ONE REMAINING CONSTANT IS NOT ARBITRARY BUT OF THAT, I HAVE NO KNOWLEDGE."

"This is great. Like I said before, Eddington was searching for the ultimate constant as well," Alex said, happy to know that he was right.

"The ultimate constant cannot be measured, it has to be a pure number," Mr. Mauldin said, looking at Alex and Laura.

"Yeah, I've heard that before," Alex said, trying to ask something. "Mr. Mauldin, do you believe that the force ultimate constant represents will be confined to only our universe?" asked Alex reluctantly.

"What you mean by only our universe?" asked Mr. Mauldin, a little taken aback.

"I mean, what if there are other universes? Will the ultimate constant influence them as well?" asked Alex, making sure Mr. Mauldin was getting what he was suggesting.

"Not that I believe in that theory of many worlds or parallel universes, but I do believe the force that the ultimate constant represents is the force that takes into account all of space and time that belongs to our universe or any other," Mr. Mauldin said, stating his point. "Also, I do believe that such a force would in one way or another influence other universal forces," continued Mr. Mauldin.

"Well, thank you, Mr. Mauldin. Is there anything else you would like to tell us about Eddington?" Alex said, preparing to make a move.

"There are not a lot of things that I would like to share at this point, but there is one thing that you should know. Eddington was a man who was influenced by pure numbers. He was much in awe of pure numbers popping up in equations, it didn't matter whether it was in mathematics or physics. It was something he thought that must have an explanation to, not to mention his beliefs were shared by the likes of Albert Einstein," proceeded Mr. Mauldin, to tell more about Eddington.

CHAPTER 38

"Albert Einstein?" Alex said to himself.

"Yes, it is evident in the letter written by Albert Einstein. The one in 1945, the letter that started it. The letter talks about the pure number or otherwise a constant he never found," Laura answered, remembering the letter her father gave her.

"There are certain equations and formulas in mathematics which are quite peculiar and when you encounter them at first, it makes one feel quite mystical about this subject we call mathematics and it is the same feeling that every physicist who has encountered them faced, including Einstein himself. For example, take a look at this," Mr. Mauldin now moved toward Alex to open a page from the book, again showing him something.

$$666 + 6 + 6 + 6 = (6 - 6/6)^{(6+6+6)/6} + 6^{(6+6+6)/6} + (6+6/6)^{(6+6+6)/6}$$

Alex and Laura turned to look at it when Mr. Mauldin spoke again. "Why numbers sometimes combine to form such equations is something nobody knows. Is it just a coincidence? Is it something more? We are yet to find answers to these questions. There is one more thing about the numbers you showed to me, it is not the first time I am looking at these numbers from someone else," Mr. Mauldin said, now talking about the huge numbers Alex and Laura brought to his attention earlier.

"What you mean this is not the first time?" questioned Alex looking at Mr. Mauldin astoundingly.

"Your father came up to me with these numbers years ago," Mr. Mauldin said, getting up and going towards a couch situated in a corner of the room.

"Excuse me! My father, what did he want to know?" asked Alex. The mention of his father suddenly made him hyper.

"About the same thing you want to know, the ultimate constant and stuff like that but, what I told him then is what I just told you now. My answer has not changed, perhaps because I haven't found one, but I thought—" suddenly Mr. Mauldin paused for a moment thinking something.

"Thought what?" asked Alex judging by his expression.

"I thought your father would find the answer to that one day," Mr. Mauldin said looking at Alex. "He was a fine man, you know," continued Mr. Mauldin.

"I know," Alex said getting up.

Just then the phone in his pocket started to ring. It was Ben.

Alex was too late to pick it up and it was disconnected.

Laura looked at him as he spoke to Mr. Mauldin swiftly. "All right, we will meet you later, you take care, Mr. Mauldin," Alex said and looked back at Laura.

"Thank you, for your time, Mr. Mauldin, it's been a pleasure to meet you," Laura said, looking at Alex and giving him a hint that it was time for them to make a move.

Alex understood and they said goodbye to Mr. Mauldin and made their way out of the mansion.

"Who was on the phone?" asked Laura just as she made her way out of the gate.

"It was Ben, but it got disconnected before I could talk to him," Alex said.

CHAPTER 38

Just then his phone rang again. It was Ben calling him again. This time, Alex picked it up in a hurry.

"Yeah, what's going on? Why you disconnected the call before?" Alex said just as he answered.

"I did not. Maybe because of the network, it got disconnected. Where the hell are you and Laura? We haven't heard from you for a long time now. I and Uncle Jack had started to get a bit worried about you both," Ben said, in a way glad to hear his voice after a long time.

"Yeah, we are in Oakland," Alex said, letting Ben know of their location. He had one hand on his ears so that he could hear everything what Ben was saying clearly.

"What? What the hell are you guys doing in Oakland?" asked Ben, baffled to hear about the location.

"I'll tell you when you meet us," Alex said when his cell phone decided to give up. "All right, listen. I am losing battery, I'll call you soon, you take care of Uncle Jack and give me a call later. Do you hear me?" Alex said with the last bit of the battery left in a cell phone.

"Yeah, I'll get back to you soon, also just to let you know, we are at Mr. Shaw's place. You get your cell charged. I'll call you later and take care of Laura," that's all Alex could hear before Ben got disconnected.

"What did he say?" asked Laura as Alex looked back to face her.

"Well, to start with, he was a little scared and asked about our location, but that's alright, I guess," Alex said with a smile.

"Where is Uncle Jack?" asked Laura yet again.

"Uncle Jack is with him and they are right now with Mr. Shaw," Alex said.

"Well, that's a relief," Laura said happy to know that they were out of danger.

Meanwhile, Ben and Uncle Jack were about to discover something for themselves as well.

"Mr. Shaw, what is it that you wanted to tell us?" asked Ben, once again standing in front of Mr. Shaw.

"Well, as you would remember, I told you about Bruno Rosie and his 'AND' logic gate," Mr. Shaw said, looking at both in confirmation.

"Yes, of course, we understood that. But then you told us that something more was there and you needed more time to study," responded Ben, looking at Mr. Shaw.

"I have been doing just that, Ben, and I have found something that I would like to share," Mr. Shaw said enthusiastically.

"Go on, Mr. Shaw. We are with you," Uncle Jack said, giving his old friend some company.

"As I told you before, Bruno Rosie invented his first electronic circuit that is the 'AND' logic gate in the 1930s. But later, as I was digging for more data, I found that his experiment was just an improvisation of an experiment conducted in 1929," Mr. Shaw said, explaining his new findings to both Uncle Jack and Ben.

"What experiment?" asked Ben, a little confused like always.

CHAPTER 38

"If you remember, Ben, I told you about the Geiger counters that Bruno Rosie used," asked Mr. Shaw looking at Ben, clarifying if he remembered or not.

"Yes, of course, I remember them. The vacuum tubes, multiple impulses, right?" Ben said, remembering the conversation he had with Mr. Shaw earlier.

"Very good, Ben. You see, the first use of Geiger tubes for such an experiment was not done by Bruno Rosie, but was actually conducted by two other scientists named William Bothe and Werner Kolhörster," explained Mr. Shaw. "You see, what they did was similar to Rosie's. However, due to their method, they lacked accuracy," Mr. Shaw explained further.

"What was their method, anyway?" asked Ben, who was now listing to Mr. Shaw carefully.

"Their method, let me see," Mr. Shaw said as he looked back into some notes and pages in his lap. "Oh yes, their method was somehow more mechanical rather than Rosie's method who used most essentially electronics," Mr. Shaw said, keeping the details aside and letting him know the difference in the language that he could understand. "However, I should proceed to say that the major difference between both experiments was that in the case of Bruno Rosie one could collect multiple, simultaneous, registered impulses," Mr. Shaw went on to explain when suddenly Ben interrupted.

"Whereas in the case of Walter Bothe and Werner Kolhörster, there was a single, simultaneous impulse," Ben said adding and understanding the notion quite well.

"Beautiful, Ben. I never thought you could understand this just fine," Mr. Shaw said, in a way feeling proud of him.

"That's right, Mr. Shaw, you have a nice way of explaining things, if you know what I mean," Ben said, in a way thanking Mr. Shaw.

"Well, thanks, Ben," Mr. Shaw said with a smile.

"All right, let's get moving, Ben," Uncle Jack said, preparing to meet up with Alex and Laura.

Ben agreed and decided to give Alex a call.

"Hey, Alex, we are making a way to you. Just tell us about your location, like where you'll meet us," Ben said, getting on the call and asking Alex to meet up real soon.

"Hey, I just happened to charge my cell," Alex looked at Laura in order to tell her that Uncle Jack and Ben wanted to come to them.

"We wanted to discuss something with you guys as well. You know, Uncle Jack, me and Mr. Shaw have been doing a little talk here about Bruno Rosie and it turns out he wasn't the first person to invent the electronic circuit," Ben said, trying to explain to Alex what he and Mr. Shaw had been talking about.

"What are you talking about? All right, I have some news for you as well, Ben," Alex said in order to tell him about the locker and the letters.

"We—" just as Alex was about to reveal their side of the story, Laura stopped him. "What's wrong with you?" Alex said, surprised by Laura's behavior.

"Not now, Alex. I just feel this is not the right time to say anything," Laura said looking straight at Alex.

"All right, if you say so," Alex said, turning back to talk to Ben.

CHAPTER 38

Just then Ben was interrupted by Mr. Shaw.

"Wait a minute, I think I found something," Mr. Shaw said, looking at Uncle Jack and Ben.

Ben spoke on phone looking at Mr. Shaw impatiently. "Look, Alex, I'll get back to you later. Looks like Mr. Shaw has something more to say," Ben said disconnecting in a hurry and turning his attention to Mr. Shaw.

"What is it, Mr. Shaw?" Ben said.

"Look at it yourself," Mr. Robert said and turned to look toward Uncle Jack and Ben.

As they saw it, Uncle Jack and Ben had their mouths opened. Uncle Jack thought of how he could have missed something like this and Ben was just stunned.

There it was in front of him.

Max Born and Walter Bothe shared the Nobel in 1954...

CHAPTER 39

Ben instantly gave a call back to Alex and told him about what Mr. Shaw had just shown him and Uncle Jack. "Alex, I want you to catch the first flight back to New York along with Laura. This is important and we need your help to figure this out."

"I'll be there as soon as I can, Ben," Alex said, understanding it was important for him as well to have a talk with Mr. Shaw.

Laura was taken aback by the entire happening. Meanwhile, Alex had something else running on his mind as well.

"Why didn't you want me to tell about the locker to Ben?" asked Alex demanding an answer.

"I just think it is best if we keep this to ourselves as of now," Laura said strongly.

"I don't understand," Alex said, feeling a little perplexed by Laura's behavior.

"Just trust me, Alex," Laura said, trying to convince him.

"All right, if you say so. But this better be for the good," Alex said, looking straight into her eyes.

CHAPTER 39

"It is, I promise. Anyway, what was Ben saying on the phone? I could practically hear him screaming," Laura said.

"Well, it's like Mr. Shaw found out that Bruno Rosie wasn't the first person to invent the electronic circuit and then the trail lead to the famous Walter Bothe and Werner Kolhörster," Alex said, informing her.

"Yeah," nodded Laura, in a way listening to him.

"I guess we are running out of time. I'll explain to you the details on our way. Let's just make a move for now," Alex said, looking at his watch realizing they were losing time.

While they were on their way back to New York, Alex got back to what he was explaining to Laura earlier.

"You were saying," Laura said, beginning to hear what Alex was talking to her about before.

"Yes, the trail lead to Walter Bothe and Werner Kolhörster who had both devised a similar experiment like Rosie, just a year before," Alex said, telling her what Ben told him.

"So, what's the point?" asked Laura in a kind of unsteady tone.

"The point is, Mr. Shaw now has somehow found a link between Walter Bothe and Max Born," Alex said, explaining what the excitement was all about.

"You mean, we were right to think about the logic gates' symbol on the letter the Professor gave me," Laura was interrupted as Alex spoke.

"You mean… the letter Professor gave *us*," Alex said trying to correct her with a smile.

"Yes, of course, I mean the letter that the Professor gave us with the logic gate symbol on it. We were right to think that the symbol would lead us to the ultimate constant," Laura said with a smile, feeling they were getting closer to their goal.

Alex felt the same way that it was now not long before their quest for the ultimate constant would come to an end. The link between Max Born and Walter Bothe was an evident truth of this.

"It's just like you had said, the first symbol led us to the ultimate function and now the second symbol is about to reveal something more, perhaps the ultimate constant," exclaimed Laura.

"Yes, but right now, it is important for us to meet Mr. Shaw," Alex said, bringing Laura's attention to the present situation.

As soon as they landed, they made their way to Ben and Uncle Jack. Uncle Jack had told them about their safe location.

Alex and Laura soon arrived.

"Hello, Mr. Shaw. Uncle Jack and Ben, of course, it's great to see you too," Laura said, coming over toward them.

"It was a nasty escape you guys had the last time. We have to be more careful," Ben said, looking at Laura and then at Alex.

"Yeah, you are right. We were lucky that day," Alex said, agreeing.

"All right, let's not waste time and just get right to it," Alex said, looking at Mr. Shaw.

"What do you have for us, Mr. Shaw?" asked Alex walking toward Mr. Shaw, coming closer.

CHAPTER 39

"I was just digging up some more stuff regarding Walter Bothe when I found this," Mr. Shaw said, showing Alex the article mentioning the Nobel shared between Max Born and Walter Bothe.

"WALTHER WILHELM GEORG BOTHE (8 JANUARY 1891 IN ORANIENBURG – 8 FEBRUARY 1957 IN HEIDELBERG) WAS A GERMAN NUCLEAR PHYSICIST, WHO SHARED THE NOBEL PRIZE IN PHYSICS IN 1954 WITH MAX BORN."

"It seems we have to divert all our attention to Walter Bothe now. Mr. Shaw, is there anything that you found interesting about Walter Bothe?" asked Alex, hoping to hear something new.

"While you guys were on your way here, I found something I am sure you guys would like to hear," Mr. Shaw said, enjoying the attention.

"What is it?" asked everyone.

"It's called the Compton Effect," Mr. Shaw said.

"What is Compton Effect?" everyone looked at each other assuming someone knew what it was.

"I'm sorry, Mr. Shaw, would you care to elaborate?" Laura said, wishing to know more.

"Well, of course, my child. As you remember, Ben must have told you earlier that in 1929 Walter Bothe and Werner Kolhörster carried out experiments that inspired Rosie," Mr. Shaw said beginning to explain.

"Yes, the ones you told us that it was in 1929 the first circuit was introduced," Ben said, pointing out what Mr. Shaw had mentioned to him earlier.

"Yes, Ben. But as it turns out, that too wasn't the first electronic circuit that was created," Mr. Shaw said, now surprising everyone.

"Of course, that is the reason Walter Bothe shared the Nobel of 1954 with Max Born," Alex said, getting what Mr. Shaw was coming to.

"Yes, Alex, you are right. The first person to create the first circuit was none other than Walter Bothe," Mr. Shaw said, making his point.

"What about the Compton Effect?" asked Ben, going back to what Mr. Shaw had mentioned earlier.

"I was coming to that, Ben. Just hold your horses," Mr. Shaw said, looking toward Ben sternly.

"So, if Walter Bothe was the first person to invent the circuit, why didn't he get the credit for it?" asked Laura with persuasion.

"For the simple reason that his experiment was limited and slower than Rosie's," Mr. Shaw said, looking at Laura.

"What do you mean?" asked Laura still unable to understand the point Mr. Shaw was making.

"Rosie's experiment led to multiple, simultaneous impulses getting registered. He made use of Geiger tubes. On the other hand, Bothe's method led to only a single simultaneous impulse getting registered. Moreover, his model was mechanical and much slower compared to Rosie's G-tubes. Nonetheless, Walter Bothe is still given the credit, for he discovered the idea and Rosie improvised on his model," Mr. Shaw said, looking at Laura and explaining the idea.

CHAPTER 39

"All right, so all that you told us about G-tubes and everything, Bothe never really had all that," Laura said, listening to Mr. Shaw calmly.

"It was only later when he conducted his experiments with Werner Kolhörster that he made use of the G-tubes," answered Mr. Shaw.

All this while, everyone was listening to Mr. Shaw. That's when Ben spoke. "Mr. Shaw, you still haven't told us anything about the Compton Effect," Ben said, bringing the topic to the attention of Mr. Shaw back again.

"Yes, the solo experiment carried out by Bothe used the application known as Compton Effect, that's what I was about to tell you guys before," Mr. Shaw said, remembering.

"What about its application?" Laura and Alex asked together.

"Well, I've tried to avoid the complex details, if you must wanna know," Mr. Shaw said a little uncomfortably.

"Please," Laura said with a smile, she knew Mr. Shaw could manage.

"Unlike the experiment carried out in 1929 and 1930, the 1924 experiment carried out by Walther Bothe, there were no G-tubes. There were simply old-time electrometers," began Mr. Shaw.

"Electrometers are the same as Geiger tubes?" questioned Ben hesitatingly.

"Correct, they serve the same purpose but are less accurate than the G-tubes," answered Robert.

"He used inert gases as well, like in the experiments of 1929 and 1930, I guess," Ben said thinking something.

"Your guess would be correct, Ben. The same thing happens, a part of the energy of the radiation gets transferred to a scattering electron," Mr. Shaw said explaining the idea. "Also, in the above case, X-rays or Gamma rays are used," he proceeded.

"Like in later experiments of 1929 and 1930 ionized rays (X-rays and Gamma rays) were applied, the same was used here too," Alex said, trying to grasp what Mr. Shaw was saying.

"Yes, you must understand the idea is the same. It is to measure the charged electron which in turn would create an impulse or a sound," Mr. Shaw said, speaking slowly so that everyone got the idea of what he was implying. "In science, when X-rays or Gamma rays undergo in the matter, they produce a scattering known as Compton scattering which in turn makes the electron gain energy, recoil and then get ejected from its atom. This is the same method that was used by Bothe in his solo experiment," Mr. Shaw said, explaining and looking at all of them time and again.

"Wait, I don't get that recoil and ejecting part of the electron," Ben said feeling a little confused.

"That's alright, Ben. It's not important, what is important is that the ejected electron is then measured by the electrometer," Mr. Shaw said, letting them know the crust of it.

"All right, so unlike the experiments which happened later, Bothe was still the only one who came up with the original idea," Ben said, thinking something.

"That's right, Ben. That's why he was awarded the 1954 Nobel," Alex said, looking at Mr. Shaw who now agreed with him.

"Walter Bothe was a clever man. Even though he didn't have enough level of sophisticated equipment he still made one hell of

CHAPTER 39

an achievement with the following experiment," Mr. Shaw said, implying the greatness of the man.

"So, the Compton Effect was one of a kind experiment which gave inspiration to Kolhörster and Rosie who later improvised on it and changed the world and yet the basic analogy behind all these experiments remained the same and Walter Bothe was credited for it with the Nobel Prize he shared with Born," Alex said, thinking something.

"Exactly, Rosie won't have gotten far if he didn't know about Bothe's experiment," Mr. Shaw said, looking at Alex with a smile.

"Mr. Shaw, is there anything else we should know about Walter Bothe? Because this just seems like a dead end," Laura said, unable to see where this was going.

Alex too was a little confused. He had earlier thought that Walter Bothe's experiment will somehow give him a clue or at least point toward the ultimate constant but there was nothing of that sort. The more Alex and Laura thought about it the less interesting it seemed.

Ben, on the other hand, wanted to know more about Bothe, therefore he insisted to Mr. Shaw to tell him more about him.

To this, Alex and Laura said nothing. They thought maybe just there was still something more to know about Walter Bothe and Bruno Rosie.

Uncle Jack seemed to be amused by the whole thing.

"Robert, isn't it interesting to know that Walter Bothe conducted his experiment almost five years before Bruno Rosie?" Uncle Jack said, noticing the time gap between the two experiments.

"That is exactly what is ironic about Walter Bothe," Mr. Shaw said with a smile. He went back to studying more notes and articles about Walter Bothe.

Alex was hoping he didn't make a mistake in following the clues. Everything was as it should have been.

Just then, Mr. Shaw found something and spoke. "Hey, listen to this. Walter Bothe's method used in this old experiment which is also known as the coincidence method and the result of his experiment the first 'AND' circuit is also known as the Coincidence Circuit," proclaimed Mr. Shaw.

Just as Mr. Shaw said that, both Alex and Laura looked at each other. They did not have to say anything to each other. Both were thinking the same thing in their mind.

To be more precise, they were thinking the same words.

"Did Eddington's 'Huge Number Coincidence' and 'Coincidence Circuit' have something in common?" The thought passed both their minds at the same time.

It was a single word that grabbed their attention.

"Coincidence…"

CHAPTER 40

Just as Alex was about to say something to Laura, his cell phone began to ring.

It was the same unknown number. Alex picked it up hurriedly. It was the voice of the man he was desperate to hear.

"Come to the following address. Come alone. The address will be messaged to you within a few minutes."

The call disconnected before Alex could ask his bit of questions.

Laura looked at him wanting to ask who it was but somehow she controlled herself and told Alex to follow up.

"Alex, I want to talk to you about something important," she said, taking him along.

To this, Ben questioned, "Hey, what's going on? Where are you two going?" he asked as he watched Laura take Alex away before he could ask any questions.

"It'll be just a minute before we are back," Laura said as she left the company of Ben and Uncle Jack.

As soon as they were alone she asked curiously, "Alex, who was it on the phone just a minute back?"

"It was the same man, he said he'll be messaging me an address and he wants me to come alone," Alex said.

"What if you are wrong? What if this man is not your father and our lives get into danger just by following his orders?" Laura said, sounding worried about him.

"It's alright, Laura. I will be OK, don't worry about me," Alex said, looking back at her.

"I want to come with you," Laura said not in the mood to listen to anything Alex had to say in order to testify that it was important for him to go alone.

Alex, on the other hand, knew that there was no way that Laura was going to listen to him. He would just have to drag her along.

Just as he was thinking all this his phone gave a beeping noise – *the address.*

The man had been looking forward to meeting Alex.

"Listen, Alex. You know it's not going to be easy for you to go alone. I am coming along with you, like it or not," Laura said, leaving no space for argument.

"But what about Ben and Uncle Jack?" Alex said, thinking something.

"Don't worry about them, they are grown-ups. They can take care of themselves. Right now, we just have to think about reaching to our destination safely."

CHAPTER 40

"We don't have a ride, what should we do?" Alex said, remembering they still needed a car to travel.

"Wait a minute, I have an idea. Let me ask Mr. Shaw, maybe he can help," Laura said and quickly made her way to Mr. Shaw.

"Mr. Shaw, I need to ask you a favor, if you don't mind," Laura said, softly coming closer to him so that Ben would not hear what she was talking about.

"Of course, my child, anything. What do you want?" asked Mr. Shaw in a caring tone.

"If you don't mind, can I take your car just for a few minutes? It's really important," Laura said in a pleading tone.

"Go ahead, but make sure you don't lose your way," Mr. Shaw said, taking out the key from his pocket and handing it to Laura.

"Don't worry, Mr. Shaw. We will be back before you know it," Laura said as she started to make a move back toward Alex.

It was then that Ben stopped her.

"What's going on? Why you guys aren't telling me anything?" he asked softly, trying to question Laura.

"Ben, don't stop me now. I'll come back and tell you everything, it won't take long," Laura said, convincing him to let her go.

"Where is Alex?" asked Ben yet again turning back to find Uncle Jack busy reading some notes.

"I'm going with him and we'll be back soon and tell you everything," Laura said, moving on as she saw Alex was now standing at the entrance.

Soon both of them made their way toward the parking.

"We need to make this quick," Alex said, looking at Laura as they made their way toward Mr. Shaw's car.

"I think I already know that, thank you very much," Laura said before she made her footsteps quicker.

As they were on their way a bunch of questions engrossed Alex.

Laura knew that there was something Alex was thinking about and she had less patience than Alex anticipated.

"What's wrong, Alex? Is it about your father?" she asked impulsively.

After a long time, Alex felt he had a friend who knew how he felt even before he could say anything.

"Yeah, you really do know me, don't you?" Alex said, looking at her.

Laura just thought about how she felt for him inside, she didn't want him to know yet.

She wanted him to stay by her side but at the same time, she was afraid that if she ever told Alex about her feelings, he would end up taking it hard. Even if that feeling could last for a minute between them, she would still take a chance, knowing that he might end up breaking her heart. Yet, when the time comes, she will tell him. Laura thought to herself.

Seldom that she knew that Alex too felt the same way about her as she did.

It was funny, in their hearts, they were pretty sure that they had feelings for each other, but they preferred not to speak out loud.

CHAPTER 40

"It's going to be OK, Alex. You don't have to beat yourself up about that," she said, telling him to relax.

"I don't know if it is really my father. I don't understand why he never told me that he was alive, moreover, why leave us all these clues and put our lives at risk?" Alex said, sounding all nervous and confused.

On one hand, he was overwhelmed to know that his father might just be alive and at the same time he was angry about the fact that if he indeed was alive why he never tried to get in touch with him.

"Maybe the men who were behind us were also after him and it could also be that he never wanted you to fall into any kind of danger or get exposed," Laura said, trying to give Alex consolation.

"He could still at least get in touch with Uncle Jack. That couldn't have been difficult," Alex said, thinking something.

"There could be many reasons, Alex. Maybe he was just waiting for the right time," Laura said trying to calm him down.

Alex was quiet. He was trying to analyze what could all these years his father had been doing if he was alive. The more he thought about it the more his mind started to get diverted to the clues and ideas that he had left behind. This is when he turned to Laura, willing to shift the topic.

"Laura, you remember when we were with Ben and Uncle Jack and Mr. Shaw spoke about the coincidence circuit?" Alex said now talking about Mr. Shaw.

"Yeah," Laura said, blinking her eyes, she too wanted to speak to Alex about it back then. But she thought it was best to talk about it when they were alone. "You mean, you had the same idea cross your mind?" she said almost hiding her small smile, knowing the tension Alex was going through.

Alex was quick to see through her question and the smile that she was hiding.

"We have a lead, that's what I think," Alex said, almost with a half-smile flashing over his face at the same time not feeling like talking about it. Alex had his father on his mind.

"So, you do think it has something to do with the Huge Numbers Coincidence which Eddington found. What was it called again?" asked Laura inquisitively.

"I believe, his large number hypothesis," Alex said, taking a turn on the road.

Laura noticed, he was driving the car rashly and the darkness of the night sky was not really comforting.

"Alex, do you mind slowing down a bit?" she asked, turning her face toward him.

Alex looked at her almost disapprovingly, but then changed the gears to slow the car down.

"I don't think we need to," Alex said, stressing on his voice.

"What do you mean?" asked Laura, roughly unable to understand what Alex was trying to say.

"We would know our answers in a short while, just hang on tight," Alex said looking at her.

As he looked ahead, the road was all empty and he shifted the gears once again to bring the car back to speed. After driving for

CHAPTER 40

a few minutes Alex looked at Laura. Apart from his father, there was something else about Laura that was bothering him for quite a while. This was a time he thought he could tighten some of the loose ends that were keeping him perturbed.

"What is it? Is there something you want to ask me?" Laura said, judging by the look on his face, wondering what it was now that Alex was thinking about.

"Nothing, it's just, about you," Alex said with something in his mind and doubted whether he should go ahead and question Laura.

"What about me?" asked Laura raising her eyebrows and in a way becoming more curious. "Enough already, what are you talking about, Alex?" she said a bit more loudly, bringing her face close to Alex.

"It's just that you have been acting really strange and mysterious lately," Alex said, looking at her in confusion.

"Huh, what does that supposed to mean?" she questioned looking ahead, shaking up her head.

"You know, you refuse to talk about the letters in the locker in front of Ben and Uncle Jack. I mean, what was that?" Alex said sounding all confused and perplexed with his emotions.

He waited for an answer but there was none. Laura just kept quiet; her lips moved a little as if she was trying to say something but then she controlled herself avoiding the topic.

"What is it? You can tell me, we are in this together," Alex said trying to make her talk.

"Do you trust me, Alex?" Laura asked, this time quickly turning her head toward him.

"Yeah, of course, I do," Alex said, simultaneously looking at her and the road ahead.

"Then please don't ask any more questions, just keep going," Laura said, assuring him.

Alex was a little amused by Laura's behavior, but he did as she told him.

"You know, I hope you know what you are doing, but I don't understand how not saying anything to Ben or Uncle Jack is going to help, that's all," Alex said lastly.

For as long as he knew Laura, he could never really force her to do anything even as children. He remembered she would always get her way with him. That was a part of her nature. The other part of her nature was she could never hurt anyone. Alex knew this and that is why he decided to trust her. Alex turned now again to look at her only to see her tense.

Suddenly, he said something that Laura couldn't think of in a million years, considering the situation they were in.

"Do you have a boyfriend?" asked Alex, looking at her.

"Ha-ha… Boyfriend! What?" she said letting out a short laugh, surprised by his question.

"You heard me," Alex said, nodding a little still looking into her shiny, blue eyes.

"No, do I have a boyfriend? No, I don't, why?" she said looking back at him.

CHAPTER 40

"Nothing, it's been a while, so, I just felt like asking," Alex said, trying to sound casual.

"What about you? And don't you lie, Ben told me about your girlfriend," Laura said with a smile.

It was her turn to ask now.

"I *had* a girlfriend. I broke up, it's been some time now," Alex said, looking at the road.

"Broke up? I feel sad for you, poor Alex," Laura said in a way teasing and comforting him at the same time as she rubbed his shoulder in comfort.

"What about you? New York can't be that bad," Alex said mockingly.

"All I know is it's not New York, it's me. I don't think I have what it takes for a woman to make a guy go weak in his knees," she said thinking something, moving her hands through her hair while looking in the mirror.

"Well, I don't know, if you ask me you are pretty hot," Alex said complimenting her, looking at her with feelings.

"Yeah," Laura said as she now directly looked at him.

Staring at each other they were lost when a car horn behind them brought them back to reality.

"Jesus!" exclaimed Alex as he gave the side to the car.

Laura was about to say something when Alex took a swift turn and spoke.

"We are here," he said, coming closer to the entrance.

Before them was a small gate. It was open as if somebody had already been there before them. Alex and Laura went inside and parked the car.

Laura got out of the car in a hurry and ran back toward the gate as if to confirm something.

Alex saw her reaching the gate in a hurry, her body came to rest and he could see her just staring at something from a distance.

Alex quickly followed her.

As he came closer, Laura was panting.

"Take a look at this," she said, reaching to take a breath at the same time.

RUDOLPH CLARK

CHAPTER 41

Alex and Laura stood there for a while looking at each other wondering what the hell was going on. Alex was the first one to break the silence.

"This is impossible!" he exclaimed unable to share his shock.

"Does this mean, he was the one who called you and told you about the locker?" Laura said in a softer tone, looking at him.

"Yes, but how can this be? He is working with Cody," he said, thinking something.

"Alex, I think we should go inside. That's the only way to know what's going on here," she said looking at him and simultaneously looking toward the front door of the house.

"I think you are right, let's go inside," Alex said, slowly walking ahead followed by Laura.

As they came closer to the house, Laura noticed that it was really quiet and there seemed to be no movement. Alex too noticed the same. He also noticed that the lights in the upper bedroom of the bungalow seemed to be bright. It was weird since there was no sound coming from anywhere.

As they came closer, Laura moved a little further toward Alex, grabbing his hand.

"Alex, I think something is wrong. I don't think we should go inside," she said almost whispering.

"I'm not going anywhere until I get some answers," Alex said, telling her about his need to move ahead.

"What if it's a trap?" Laura said, trying to stop him.

"Even if it is, it doesn't matter anymore because we are already here," Alex said as he kept moving.

As he came a few steps away from the door he stood still to notice if there were any movements at all, a sound, maybe. But there were none.

"All right, the coast is clear. I think we can move ahead," Alex said, looking back toward Laura who was still holding his hand.

It didn't take Alex much time to reach for the door.

To his surprise, it was already open.

"What's this?" Alex said as he pushed open the door.

Laura too was a little taken aback which did not make any difference for her as she was already scared.

As Alex and Laura moved inside they saw that the place was in jeopardy. Things were half broken; there were holes in the wall.

Alex was quick to understand what had happened.

CHAPTER 41

"These are bullet holes. Somebody was already here before us," he said, thinking something and looking at the wall.

Laura could smell chlorine in the air coming from somewhere at the top of the house.

"Alex, the smell, there has been some kind of blast," she said looking at him.

"Damn, we have to find this guy as fast as possible," Alex said as he quickly took the stairs to reach up.

As he did, it was only to find a huge hole in the wall. Laura was right, it was a blast.

Alex somehow reached the bedroom door dodging a part of a still-burning wall. It was only to find a bedroom half destroyed and in the middle of the room lay a body.

It was Rudolph.

Alex came closer and checked to see whether there was any chance that he was still alive. The bullets in his chest and the explosion had left no scope for survival.

It was not late before Laura came up to see Alex next to the body.

"Is this—" she began to ask when Alex interrupted her.

"Yes, it's him. Somebody killed him before we could reach here and I think that person is none other than Cody," Alex said, thinking something trying to understand the situation. "Cody's men might have figured out that Rudy was helping us and decided to kill him," Alex said in a heavy voice.

"But what about the locker and the letters written by David? How would he know about them?" Laura said, reminding Alex about the locker and the letters.

"I think Rudy had them for a long time, he might have found them through the Professor. I think somehow, he was trying to save them from Cody's men. You remember Uncle Jack said that a long time back Rudy, my father and Professor were friends?" Alex said, beginning to remember what Uncle Jack had told them.

"But that still does not explain why Rudy didn't tell you about all this earlier," Laura said in confusion.

"How could he, Laura? We were always running, besides I think he had a change of heart and wanted to help us," Alex said, still thinking.

"I don't know, Alex. It all sounds a bit confusing," Laura said.

"Don't you remember when we were at Mr. Shaw's house? I got a call and told everyone that we were in danger and all of us left in hurry," Alex said, trying to tell Laura something.

"Yeah," Laura said looking at him.

"It was him, Laura. He called me to tell me that Cody's men were coming for us," Alex said, telling Laura the incident that took place at Mr. Shaw's house.

"So, he was trying to help us out all this while and we all thought that he was trying to kill us," she said, now understanding what Alex was saying.

"The question right now is why he called us here today," Alex said, his mind going everywhere. He was now studying the place and trying to imagine what went in where.

CHAPTER 41

"Only Cody's men could answer that one," Laura said, looking at the body.

"There are bullet holes down in the main hall," he said instantly as if talking to himself. "He came running up the stairs into this room," Alex continued to imagine when suddenly Laura spoke.

"Wait, why this room? There are three rooms here, why did he choose to come into this one?" she said looking at Alex, getting up and looking around.

"You are right, you are right!" Alex said, his voice becoming louder.

Suddenly his eyes stopped at something. It was something about the door.

"Laura, take a look at this," Alex said, calling her over.

"This is just not wood. There is a double coating, more like hard steel," Laura said, holding the door and noticing the heaviness.

"But then how come the bullets on his chest?" Laura asked, looking back at the dead body.

"Yeah," Alex said getting confused.

However, he soon realized where the bullets hit him from.

"The bullets came through the window, see the holes," Alex said, showing them to Laura who in turn came closer to the windowpane.

They both noticed there were bullet holes in the window. Alex observed what looked like a button situated in its bottom-left corner, almost hidden from the naked eye.

When Alex pressed the button a wall of glass came trembling down from the upper edge of the window. From what it looked and felt like, both were sure it was bulletproof.

"Poor guy, before he could press the button the bullets got to him," Alex said in disappointment.

"You are still missing the point, Alex," Laura said, looking at him.

"Yes, the room, of course," he said, turning his attention back to the body.

"Don't you think we should inform the police about this?" Laura said looking at the body of Rudolph lying there in the middle of the room.

"No, it will make things even more complicated. Besides, the police are still looking for you, we can't tell anyone anything. Not until we find what we are looking for," Alex said, taking a look at a few things and trying to find something. "There is definitely something in this room or else he wouldn't be guarding it for nothing, think about it," continued Alex moving around the place.

"I agree, Alex. I think I should have told Uncle Jack and Ben to come along, maybe they could help," Laura said, thinking something.

"There is no point discussing that now, is it? I still don't understand why you didn't tell them about the locker and the letters," Alex said, blabbering.

"Now that we are here, I think we have to tell them about Rudolph," Laura said, still moving around on one side of the room.

CHAPTER 41

"You bet we will, however this time, you will tell them the whole story. I'm not up for it," Alex said, now coming toward Laura.

Laura took out her cell and gave a ring to Ben. She wanted to tell Ben the whole story and the reason why she couldn't tell him about the old incidents earlier but there was no response.

She tried a couple of times but there was no response.

"Alex, I have been trying to reach Ben, but he is not picking up the cell," she said, sounding a bit worried.

"Try calling Mr. Shaw or Uncle Jack. Maybe he has forgotten his cell somewhere, you never know," Alex said, not bothering much as he continued to search the room.

Laura left the room to move outside to get range in her cell. After a while she came back again, this time sounding really worried.

"Alex, I have tried everyone. No one is picking up, I think we should hurry back to them," Laura said, holding the cell in her hand, and walking toward Alex.

"Are you sure?" Alex said, this time taking notice.

"Yeah," Laura said confirming.

It was then his cell began to ring again. As he was walking down with Laura behind her, he took out the cell from his pocket. He felt relieved and turned behind to show it to Laura. It was Ben. Alex answered the call.

"Yeah, Ben, we were about to call you," Alex said putting the cell over his ear.

"I am afraid Ben is not doing so great, Alex," said the voice from the other end.

Alex immediately stopped.

"Who is this?" questioned Alex, a little disturbed by the voice on the other end.

"As you may have seen by your own eyes, Rudolph is no more," said the man, this time giving a clue to Alex whom he was talking to.

"Cody!" exclaimed Alex as he looked back at Laura.

Laura, in turn, felt her heart sank as she heard Alex say that name out loud.

"I knew there was something wrong," she said, looking at Alex.

"Nothing is wrong, my dear. In fact, everything has become right, just according to the plan," Cody said overhearing Laura's voice.

"If anything happens to Uncle Jack and Ben, you consider yourself dead," Alex said in rage.

"Now, now, calm down, little Alex. You see, I had no intention of harming anyone from the beginning. But as history would like to put it, things have never gone my way, until just now," Cody said in a cynical tone.

"What do you mean?" asked Alex.

"I mean, my boys have come back with a work half done. I want you to complete it, Rudolph was given a file and it was given by John. The clues that John left behind lead to the ultimate constant and that file can lead me to it," continued Cody.

CHAPTER 41

"What is in that file?" questioned Alex yet again.

"That file consists of the research David collected. It might reveal what some call the 'Theory of Everything'," Cody said.

"You and your lady friend must find that file and bring it to me," continued Cody, stating his objectives.

"And what if we don't?" Alex said in a provoking tone.

"Don't be a fool, Alex. You know the consequences, call me when you have the file," replied Cody and ended the call.

"Damn!" exclaimed Alex as he disconnected the call.

"What is it?" Laura said, noticing that there was something terribly wrong.

Alex told her about the conversation. He told Laura that Uncle Jack and Ben were now hostages of Cody and he also told her about the file. Now, finding the file was inevitable.

"Come, let's go back to the room," Alex said as they made their way back to the body of Rudolph.

They searched and searched, but there was nothing that they found that could help them get to the file. Later, Laura decided to search the entire house. Alex too decided to help her as there was nothing more left to do. They turned the whole place upside down, the hall, the kitchen, the rooms, even the garden, but it was useless.

"This can't be, it's not here," Alex said, looking at Laura.

They both led themselves down on the couch dead-tired and motionless, still trying to think.

NUMERICAL ENIGMA

"Where is it?" Laura said in a way, talking to herself.

"I think we should at least move the body, it has started to smell," Alex said, noticing the foul smell.

Suddenly Laura stood up.

"Of course," she said, looking at Alex.

"What? What is it?" Alex said, realizing Laura might have found the file.

She quickly ran upstairs and Alex followed her rapid footsteps. As she entered the room, she stood next to the body,

"What Laura? What is it?" Alex said, breathing heavily.

"It's the body, Alex, it's the body."

CHAPTER 42

Alex looked at her trying to understand what she meant.

"Will you try to explain?" he said, looking at her in disapproval.

"I didn't notice it before but there was something weird about this floor. It's like every time I walked over it, it made this hollow sound," she said, telling Alex what she had in mind.

"You are right, besides we have looked everywhere except beneath his body," Alex said, tapping on the floor a few times and noticing the sound Laura had told him.

"Wait, do you hear that?" she said looking at him with a faded smile.

"Yeah," he said with an immediate response.

"Let's get this body away from here," Alex said, moving toward Laura and the body.

As Alex tried to lift it, he realized that it was heavy.

"Do you mind helping me out here?" Alex said in a way amused by Laura who was just standing there looking at him.

Actually, she was feeling a bit gross touching a dead body like that. The foul smell wasn't a big turn-on either. Nonetheless, she had no choice.

"All right," she said as she moved to give Alex a hand.

It was a while before they were able to shift the body of Rudy to check if there was something there.

Laura looked at Alex as they kept the body on one side of the room.

Half of the room was already a wreck that was another reason both Alex and Laura had not thought about the body or the floor.

"I think there is definitely something beneath this floor," Alex said, simultaneously looking at Laura and the wooden floor.

"I just told you that," Laura said, taking the credit for the idea.

"No, I mean if we look back at the way he was laying there, it was as if he was trying to open something," Alex said telling Laura what he was thinking about.

Laura felt a little restless. She wanted to see what was down there. Alex too was eager now.

"All right, let's see what we have here," Alex said, moving to where they had moved the body from.

"There should be a handle or something in here," Laura said, trying to search for the opening.

"I don't see anything here," Alex said as he tried to find a handle. He thought it must be small that is why it was not visible. However,

CHAPTER 42

after looking at the edges on all sides of the wooden plank on the floor, they couldn't find any knob or a handle.

It was then that Laura noticed something. There was a gap between the planks where Alex was sitting.

"Alex, get up I think I have found something," she said moving closer to him.

"What? What is it?" Alex said as he moved his eyes to where Laura was standing and found the gap.

It was thin, barely visible.

"Why didn't I see that?" Alex said, looking at the gap.

"Cause you were sitting on it and I wasn't," Laura said as she tried to put her fingers between the planks.

"What are you doing?" asked Alex, beginning to ask her if she needed a hand.

"I'm trying to pull it up," she said applying force to her fingers.

Alex saw that there was some movement.

"Here, let me help you out," he said pushing his fingers inside the gap.

He soon realized that his fingers were touching something.

"What is this?" he said, looking at Laura.

"What?" Laura said a little taken aback.

"It seems like a hook of some sort. Wait," Alex said trying to pull it with his fingers.

It was not late when Laura heard the sound of a click. She looked at Alex.

"I think it has opened," Alex said, looking at her.

Laura saw Alex eagerly pick up the plank. Her eyes slowly became wider.

When Alex removed a few planks, Laura saw something emerging in front of her eyes. It was some kind of a safe.

"I think we have found it," Alex said, looking at Laura.

"I think we have, now the question is how do we open it?" she said as she saw that it was a combination lock.

"We did come this far, didn't we? I think we'll be able to figure this one out too," Alex said, sounding a lot more confident now.

"I think it's a three-digit combination," Laura said, looking at the chest.

"Yeah, I see you are right. It's made of titanium and I think the wrong combination will blow the whole place up," Alex said, noticing a few more things about the chest.

As Laura looked further inside, she saw what Alex was pointing at.

Below, she could see that there were wires connecting to what looked like a bomb.

"Is that a—" she said catching her breath when Alex interrupted her.

CHAPTER 42

"Yes, that would be correct. It's a bomb," he said, giving a cautious look to Laura.

"What should we do?" Laura said, asking him in desperation.

"I don't think we have a choice, Laura. I have to open this thing," Alex said, losing options.

"We have to think of the correct combination," Laura said, looking at him.

They knew there was no other way out of this. They had to get the file.

"What was the combination of the locker in which we found the note of my father in London?" Alex asked, thinking something.

"It had something to do with some constant," Laura said, trying to remember.

"Yes, I remember now, it was the fine structure constant," Alex said, remembering.

"Of course, that was a three-digit combination lock as well," Laura said, getting the same idea as Alex.

"I think I should try that combination," Alex said, looking at Laura confirming before moving his hands over the chest.

"I don't know," Laura said, sounding really scared.

Deep inside, she was more scared for him than she was for herself.

"The bomb will blow only if I enter all three digits. If it accepts the first two, then I'm confident that we are on the right track," Alex said, getting the idea.

"What if it does not accept it?" Laura said, almost holding Alex back.

"Relax, Laura. If that happens we will have to just think of some other number, the bomb will not explode until all the three digits we enter are wrong," Alex said, calming her down.

"All right, be careful, Alex," she said as she gave him her approval.

Alex quickly entered the first two digits of the fine structure constant.

To his delight, nothing happened.

This made him confident and he was now positive that the combination was the same as the one in the locker where they had found his father's note.

Still, as Alex entered the last digit, his hands were shaking.

The chest opened automatically.

"Thank god!" Alex exclaimed. Alex had been right about the fine structure constant.

Just as they saw they were safe now, they burst out by giving each other a tight hug.

It was impulsive and moments later as they wrapped arms around each other which pulled their bodies together, they both knew it wasn't just a friendly hug.

Laura blushed, at the same time Alex felt a comforting peace, he had been longing for this.

CHAPTER 42

But there was no time to waste. Both got hold of their feelings and Alex was first to break her out of his arms.

"The file," he said, taking a red color file from the chest.

"Yeah," Laura said, looking at him with a smile.

"Open it, let's see what's inside," Laura said looking at him.

As Alex opened the file, he saw that each clue that the Professor had left behind was linked to a scientific idea and they were the same ideas that they had discovered along their quest for the truth.

There was a piece written by David.

It had all his research and letters that he handed over to the Professor.

Alex looked over to the letters and the research.

1. *"John, there are at present four important constants; c (speed of light), G (constant of gravitation, h (Planck's constant, the constant of action) and e (electric charge). It is now believed that the future of cosmology might reveal a few more, but there exists one ultimate constant. This constant would only be found by intimately combining all the Universal constants as I mentioned. There would be a few others that could be found later in the future. I, though, seldom agree that this combination would possibly point toward the string being the ultimate constant.*

   As for what I think it would be something more than physical.

2. *"However, by my study of the ultimate constant, I believe that this uniform string theory will not lead to the UFT because it would lack the knack for proportionality, as I had told you before in my previous letters. John, I have found that the function of the ultimate constant has to stand for all of the universes if there exist any other than the one that we are in, for the same reason that it (the ultimate constant) has to be pure. It has to be beyond the realms of human measure. Just like in the case of a fine structure*

constant, which is a pure value formed by the combination of other universal constants h, c and e. This following letter almost proves what I have been searching for, Einstein was searching for that pure constant but couldn't find it, however I still have to work on the details of the subject.

I would soon be sending you this letter. It is concluded in two parts.

"With the question of the universal constants, you have broached one of the most interesting questions that may be asked at all. There are two kinds of constants: apparent and real ones. The apparent ones are simply the outcome of the introduction of arbitrary units, but are eliminable. The real [true] ones are genuine numbers which God had to choose arbitrarily, as it were, when He deigned to create this world. In my opinion now is – stated briefly – that constants of the second type do not exist and their apparent existence is caused by the fact that we have not penetrated deeply enough. I therefore believe that such numbers can only be of a basic type, as for instance π or e."

Rosenthal-Schneider replies and mentions the ideas of Planck, with whom she studied as a student, about the three special constants that he used to create his 'natural' units:

'However, I am still worrying and that is why I pester you again with my questions about what the universal constants are as Planck used to enumerate them: gravitational constant, the velocity of light, the quantum of action, which are not dependent on external conditions like pressure or temperature, and which therefore are pleasantly distinct from the constants of irreversible processes? If all these were entirely non-existent, the consequences would be catastrophic. If I understood Planck correctly he regarded such universal constants as "absolute quantities." If now you were to state that they are all non-existent, what at all would be left for us in the natural sciences? It is much more worrying for an ordinary mortal than you can imagine.

Einstein sensing that he has misled his correspondent, responds in greater detail on 13 October 1945 with a complete analysis of the situation.

CHAPTER 42

"I see from your letter that you did not grasp my hint about the universal constants of physics. I will therefore try to make the matter clearer.

1. Basic numbers. These are those which, in the logical development of mathematics, appear by a certain necessity as unique individual formations.

e.g., $e = 1 + 1 + 1/2! + 1/3! + \ldots$

It is the same with π, which is closely connected with e. In contrast to such basic numbers are the remaining numbers which are not derived from 1 by means of a perspicuous construction. It would seem to lie in the nature of things that such basic numbers do not differ from the number 1 in respect of the order of magnitude, at least as long as consideration is confined to "simple" or, as the case may be, "natural" formations. This proposition, however, is not fundamental and not sharply definable."

The illuminating exchange of letters With Rosenthal-Schneider on constants ends on 24 March 1950

Alex moved on to see the important aspects of his father's research briefly, the ones he came across with Laura, Uncle Jack and Ben.

"C" ←→ STRING THEORY

|

V

[SUPERPOSITION] → "QUANTUM INTERPRETATION OF MANY WORLDS": THE ORIGINAL RELATIVE STATE FORMULATION IS DUE TO HUGH EVERETT IN 1957.]

"Many-worlds is a deterministic theory, since the wave function obeys a deterministic wave equation at all times. All possible outcomes of a measurement or interaction are embedded within the universal wave function although each observer, split by each observation, is only aware of single outcomes due to the linearity of the wave equation. The world appears in-deterministic, with the usual probabilistic collapse of the wave function, but at the objective level, which includes all outcomes, determinism is restored."

|
V

[CHAOS THEORY & "QUANTUM INTERPRETATION OF MANY WORLDS"→ DETERMINISTIC THEORIES]

|
V

[DYNAMICAL SYSTEMS]

|
V

[MATRIX MECHANICS → ϕ]

|
V

[MAX BORN → RICHARD FEYNMAN → PROGRAMS → PATTERNS OF ELECTRONS]

|

CHAPTER 42

V

[φ + SIGNAL PROCESSING]

|

V

[SIGNAL PROCESSING +LOGIC GATE□ =D-]

|

V

[=D- + COMPUTERS]

|

V

[STRANGE EQUATIONS]

[EDDINGTON'S → $666 + 6 + 6 + 6 = (6 - 6/6)^{(6+6+6)/6} + 6^{(6+6+6)/6} + (6+6/6)^{(6+6+6)/6}$]

[EDDINGTON'S → $10^{80}, 10^{40}, 10^{20}$]

After reading the following file, Alex proclaims, "Laura, my father was a genius! There is definitely more to Eddington than what meets the eye."

CHAPTER 43

"What is it?" Laura asked, looking at Alex and the file in his hands with great curiosity.

"Well, to be honest, I don't know. I mean, I don't see the complete picture yet," Alex said, still going through the pages of the file.

"Show it to me," Laura said leaning her head more towards his shoulders so she could see the contents clearly.

It was not long before she took the file from him and looked at it. Alex looked at her as she turned the pages while he gave it a deep thought as well.

"These are references to the clues that we have found," Laura said momentarily turning her eyes from the file toward Alex.

"Yeah, I saw that, Laura. I think the file the Professor burned before his death was a copy of this," asked Alex looking at Laura distantly.

"Yes, that can really be the same one, now that you mentioned it," Laura said looking at Alex who was now lost in his thought.

"Follow me," Alex said suddenly making his way outside the room.

CHAPTER 43

"Where are you going?" Laura asked, following him in a hurry.

"I need to look into something," Alex said, entering another room.

There was positively no damage there, Laura saw that Alex was relieved by this as he turned his eyes around one of the corners of the room.

The computer, that was what Alex was looking for, she thought as Alex made himself comfortable on the chair and switched it on.

"Pray that it connects," Alex said, looking at Laura.

"Why are you going on the net? What are you searching for?" Laura said as she brought a chair and sat next to him.

As the computer connected to the internet, Alex smiled and turned to Laura to tell her what was on his mind.

"There was something about quantum mechanics and many worlds that we didn't look into before, and I am just going to do that," Alex said as he proceeded to open a page on the net.

Laura watched as Alex opened a page that spoke about the history of quantum mechanics.

"There was something in the file about matrix mechanics which grabbed my attention," Alex said as soon as the page opened. "OK, I think there is something here," Alex said as his eyes begin to read the wiki page.

Laura saw that Alex was still struggling to find what he was looking for.

"Wait, let's just go back and revise all the clues that the Professor left for us, maybe that will make it easier," she said, trying to help Alex.

"Yeah, that might help," Alex said, thinking of it as a good idea.

"OK, first, there was this letter which spoke about the ultimate constants," Laura said going back and remembering the letter.

"Yes, that led us to the second clue which was the article on the special theory of relativity, focusing on how important the constant of the speed of light was," Alex said, telling Laura about the connection.

"So, the first clue was the constant of the speed of light," Laura said, looking at him.

"Yeah, the next thing we did was to fuse it with the string theory. I think that was an important step," Alex said, remembering the incidents at Einstein's residence.

"Why was that important again?" Laura asked, trying to reconnect.

"That led us to the discovery that everything and everyone in this universe has their own time, simply put, time becomes personal, it is not absolute anymore," Alex said, reminding her.

"I am sorry, I'm forgetting the theory," she said, acting a little anxious.

"Don't you remember what Dexter told us about time being different for heavenly bodies, the moon and the planets?" Alex said, trying to clear her memory.

"Yes, but that was over vast distances," Laura said, still not able to remember.

CHAPTER 43

"Yes, but when the constant of the speed of light is taken into account within the dimensions of the string theory we see that its influence is seen even within the smallest of distances. Don't you remember anything Dexter told us about how the constant of the speed of light depends on distance and how the string theory influences the distance, the folding of space and its multiple dimensions? How can you forget that?" Alex said, unable to understand how Laura could overlook such important things.

"Yes, yes, I do remember now. That's when he told us about theoretical equations in the string theory and how it happens," Laura said, immediately remembering everything.

"All right, what came next?" Alex asked, thinking for a moment.

"I think the idea of individual time even over the smallest of distances led us to the idea of super position and parallel universes which in turn led us to the *Quantum Interpretation of Many Worlds*," Laura said, this time, she being the one to remind Alex.

"Of course, it was because superposition was an essential part of quantum mechanics as well as the *Quantum Interpretation of Many Worlds* theory and after that came the Chaos theory," Alex said moving further on.

"What was the connection between the Chaos theory and the *Quantum Interpretation of Many Worlds*, again?" asked Laura, yet again unable to remember.

"They were both deterministic theories, otherwise dynamical in nature, remembering the book in the Professor's library and the name of Richard Feynman written on one of its pages," Alex said, taking it easy this time long, and reminding Laura with patience.

"Yeah, how can I forget that? That's what led us to the most important—the first symbol in the letter that my father left us," Laura said, wondering while looking at Alex.

"That's right, the Probability Density Function," Alex said, suddenly turning his attention back to the page display in front of him.

"Look, even this page talks about it," Laura said, noticing the symbol on the page.

"Yeah, I know that's the reason I'm here. Look, this brief history of quantum mechanics here states that in 1926, Max Born with his fellow assistant Pascal Jordan found a new kind of mathematics with the help of matrices, this was essential to the study of quantum mechanics," Alex said, reading the page.

"Look here, it also says that this discovery came into being as another student of Born, Werner Heisenberg, came to him with a paper that spoke about transitional probabilities of quantum jumps by the electrons, using the initial and final state of the electron," Laura said, without understanding much of it. "What does he mean by transitional probabilities of quantum jumps?" Laura asked, turning to Alex.

"It refers to the different state of electrons, what Born did along with his assistant Pascal was to help understand these transitional probabilities or different states of the electron with the help of the systematic language of matrices. This language of mathematics, however, became famous as matrix mechanics," Alex said, slowly understanding where this was going.

"Moreover, the Probability Density Function is the outcome of this matrix mechanics," Alex said, understanding the history a little more.

CHAPTER 43

"What does this mean?" exclaimed Laura, looking toward the page.

"The Probability Density Function shows the state of the electron with the highest probability," Alex said, speaking and reading at the same time.

"What exactly are you saying?" asked Laura as she saw him thinking something intensely.

"To simply put it, Probability Density Function shows us what state is the electron in," Alex said, turning away from the page now.

"What is it? What are you thinking?" asked Laura, looking at Alex as he seemed lost in his own thoughts.

"I am just thinking if these states of the electron have something to do with the signal processing and the logic gates that Bruno Rosie and Walter Bothe developed individually," muttered Alex, trying to think of a connection between the two.

Maybe this was one of the ways in which the two symbols were connected to each other in the letter the Professor gave Laura.

"Anyway, we will get back to this later. Show me the file," Alex said taking his attention away from the computer and to the file Laura was holding.

"Let's see, now, after we found out about the Probability Density Function we found that *Quantum Interpretation of Many Worlds* like Chaos can have a pattern, eventually referring to everything is predictable. What was important was to find what force was driving this predictability," Alex said, going back to his conversations with Uncle Jack.

"Yes, I remember, you said that if we could find the force that was driving this pattern it could lead us to the ultimate constant and would prove the theory of *Quantum Interpretation of Many Worlds*, correct?" Laura said letting him know that she too remembered the conversation.

"That's when we begin analyzing the second symbol on the letter," Alex said, getting up and thinking hard now with a file in his hands.

"Now, we know that it started with Walter Bothe and Compton Effect," continued Alex.

"Yes, we know this 'cause he shared the Nobel with Max Born in 1954," Laura said, confirming that they were on the right track.

"Later, his experiments were succeeded by Bruno Rosie who successfully created the first electronic circuit," Alex said.

"That was the first logic gate, the 'AND' gate," Laura said, looking at Alex for confirmation.

"You are right, but that is where the story ends," Alex said in disappointment.

"What do you mean the story ends?" Laura said, moving closer to Alex.

"I mean, I don't know where to go from here, the 'AND' gate is our last clue," Alex said, looking at her and feeling exhausted.

"No, this file is our *last* clue," Laura said taking the file away from his hands.

CHAPTER 43

"Come here and look into this, this is the file Cody wants. If we can find out what he is looking for in this file before he does, we might just beat him at his own game," Laura said, correcting Alex.

"I already have, there is something about Probability Density Function and signal processing, not to mention some equations of Eddington. But it's all in the language I can't understand, it's too complicated," Alex said, coming closer to Laura and rubbing his forehead.

"What do you mean it's too complicated?" Laura said as if she never expected Alex to say something like this.

"I mean, it's too deep, too technical, probably something beyond anyone's grasp," Alex said, raising his hand which explained how helpless he was.

"That's your father you are talking about," Laura said looking at him furiously.

"I know, I know, all right. I'm just happy it wasn't him, otherwise, he would have been dead just like Rudy," Alex said, rubbing his hands over his face.

"I know, I'm sorry. But I really hope there was something we could do," responded Laura.

Just then the phone in one of his pockets began to ring. It was not long before Alex and Laura knew who was calling.

Alex picked up the call after a few rings.

"What is it?" questioned Alex, hiding the anxiety unsuccessfully as he spoke.

"You know what I'm looking for, have you found it?" said the voice from the other end.

"No, we are still looking for it, I don't think it's here," Alex said, pausing for a moment as he looked at Laura.

"Don't you play games with me, you little boy. You will be in for a lot of pain if you do," Cody said, his voice sounding as wicked as ever.

"You know I don't have much patience, find it quick and bring it to me if you want to see your precious friend and Uncle Jack alive," continued Cody.

"Look, I am trying, alright? Just give me some time," Alex said, trying to buy some time on his hands.

He knew he had to think of a plan.

Before he could say anything else, Cody disconnected the call.

"He is getting impatient," Alex said looking at Laura.

"I know but we must think of something before it's too late," Laura said, encouraging Alex not to give up. "I know you are worried, Alex. But don't you have a plan or something?" Laura asked, thinking Alex always had something going on in his mind to get out of trouble.

"Not this time, Laura. He has my best friend not to mention Uncle Jack," Alex said, putting himself down back on the chair.

"That's exactly my point. What did he say on the phone?" asked Laura curiously.

"He wants the file," Alex said looking at Laura.

CHAPTER 43

"But if we give it to him, how do we know that he will release Uncle Jack and Ben?" Laura said, thinking worriedly.

"I know we can't trust him, but I don't think we have much of a choice," Alex said reading the situation they were in.

"So, what should we do?" asked Laura not knowing what she should be doing.

"We will wait for him to call and I'll try to convince him that the file is not here. I think that should probably give us enough time to think of something," Alex said, trying to come up with a plan.

"Seems like a good idea," Laura said, hoping things would work out.

After a few minutes, Alex's cell began to ring.

"You better speak the truth. I'm almost on a verge of shooting your friend here. Do you have the file or not?" Cody said, his voice reaching the peak of insanity.

"Look, please, you have to believe me. There is no file here," Alex said, trying his best to get Cody's attention.

"Alex, you and me both know Rudy didn't guard that room for nothing with all that bulletproof glass and steel door," Cody said, making Alex uncomfortable.

"What do you mean?" Alex said catching his breath.

"The file is in that room. You better find it before it's too late. My men had been following Rudy long since they had been following you. I'll give you half an hour to find the file, after that consider your friend and Uncle Jack dead," Cody said, almost wildly.

"No, please, I'll bring the file to you in half an hour. Please don't hurt Ben and Uncle Jack," Alex said, feeling helpless.

"Now, hurry," Cody said, making sure that Alex heard him.

"Yes, yes, of course. We will bring the file to you in half an hour," Alex said, looking at Laura momentarily.

Laura could see that Alex was scared now.

"Find it, Alex, find the file. You have half an hour, I'll message you the address in a few minutes to the place we are meeting," Cody said with his last words.

Alex looked at Laura as he disconnected the phone. One look was enough for Laura to know that they had no choice now. They had to give the file to Cody.

"He knows about the bulletproof window and the door of that room, we have to go," Alex said coming over to Laura.

"It's OK, Alex. It's OK," Laura said, caressing his face.

As they made their way outside for the car Alex opened the file one more time to take a last look.

Suddenly, Alex stopped and looked at Laura.

By now Laura was well aware of Alex's reactions and his facial expressions. She knew he had found something.

"Tell me," Laura said, coming over.

"I found the link between the two symbols in the letter the Professor gave you before he died."

CHAPTER 44

Just as Alex was about to tell Laura about the pattern he was thinking about, he saw a white car moving toward them.

They entered the providence slowly as if deliberately trying to hide their movements.

"It's them, isn't it?" Laura asked, looking at Alex for confirmation.

"I think you are right. He must have sent them to take us in," Alex said, agreeing.

"I thought as much. He would leave no stone unturned in order to avoid our escape. Quickly, this way," Laura said, taking Alex's hand and moving across with him, trying to hide.

"What if they read what's on the computer?" Alex said, remembering that he had forgotten to switch off the computer.

"It's OK, I switched it off before I came following you," Laura said, telling him to relax.

"That's good, we will wait for them to get inside. Then we'll make our move to the car," Alex said, letting Laura know beforehand what they'll do.

They waited patiently for them to pass by.

Just as the men entered the residence, Alex and Laura made their way back to their car.

"I know why they are here. Cody must have sent them to get the file from us and get rid of us at the same time," said Alex, swiftly getting inside the car along with Laura.

Alex was careful to let Laura enter first in order to keep her safe.

"What? You mean they are here to…" Laura said, hesitating at first.

"Yes, they are here to kill us," Alex said, whispering.

"Let's get the hell out of here," Laura said, looking at him.

Just then, the cell Alex had kept in his pocket started to make a beeping sound.

It was a message from Cody.

There it was, staring at Alex, the meeting point Cody mentioned earlier in his last phone conversation.

"We have to get to this address," Alex said, looking at his cell.

"How far it is from here?" asked Laura, looking at Alex sounding a little worried.

"It's far, but I think we'll make it, but first we have to get out of here," Alex said, leaning toward Laura.

"So, what are you waiting for? Start the car," Laura said, in confusion.

CHAPTER 44

"Wait, we have to do this at the right time," Alex said, thinking of a plan.

"What are you saying? We have to get out of here as soon as possible," Laura said, wanting to shout but somehow keeping her voice in control.

"Shut up, Laura. I'm trying to think here," Alex said, trying to get her to keep quiet.

"What are you thinking?" she asked, frustratingly looking at him.

"If I start the car they will hear us and would come to follow us. So, I am waiting for them to reach the upper room, after that we will have time to get out of here," Alex said, explaining to her.

"OK, why you didn't say that to me before?" Laura said, calming down.

"I would if you let me," Alex said to Laura, sounding a little annoyed.

They waited for a few moments more until they heard voices coming from the upper room.

Alex turned the keys and the moment there was ignition, he moved his foot right on the accelerator and they swiftly made their way outside the gates.

It was not long before Laura noticed that they were being followed.

There was considerable distance between their cars, but Alex was still nervous.

"Alex, what are you doing? Drive faster," Laura said, as she saw the cars approaching.

"Would you keep your mouth shut and let me drive?" Alex said, trying to concentrate on his driving.

The car in their pursuit was slowly starting to get closer. Alex saw the distance closing in the rearview mirror. He pushed his foot completely on the accelerator. The car in chase too started to follow their trail again aggressively.

Knowing that it would be difficult for them to pursue, the men in the car started to shoot. The bullets started to hit the car and Alex shouted in panic.

"Laura, keep your head down," shouted Alex, keeping his hand over Laura's head, pushing her down. Bending his head down on his seat, Alex was trying to protect Laura from the bullets.

As Alex looked back in the rear mirror, his mind was in tension. There was not just one car that was following them, but two.

Suddenly an idea plunged into his head. He made his car lose speed. Alex had seen that there was a cliff ahead; he thought maybe he could get rid of the cars if he held his calm.

Driving through the zigzag roads, he kept his feet on the break, allowing the car behind to come head-to-head with him.

As the car behind him started to come close he looked for the opportunity before glancing out a little.

Alex was trying to push the car off the cliff. He waited for the opportunity to derail the car off the road.

As he glanced outside from his side of the window, while still bending his back to keep low, he noticed that the firing had stopped for some reason. Now glancing outside a little more he could see in the car a man with a gun pointing toward him.

CHAPTER 44

He gave an evil look to Alex as the other car started to come dangerously close to his.

This was when Alex swiftly turned his steering towards the other side, allowing his car to bang into theirs giving the other car a hard push from the road. The driver of the other car lost control and it started to move towards the edge of the cliff.

"Fuck you," exclaimed Alex as he saw the other car fall off the cliff.

Looking at the car falling off the cliff the other car that was still behind, started to fire again but they decided to stay behind and not try to overtake. Alex knew they would not try to share the same fate as that of their friends.

It was a hard race. The only thing Alex was hoping was somehow to get enough lead so as to make an escape.

"Alex, there is still one more car behind us," Laura said, in a way warning him.

"I know, just stay put," Alex said, trying to make her feel a little comfortable whatsoever.

"What are we going to do?" Laura said, looking at him for an answer.

Just then Alex saw a truck ahead and thought of overtaking it; maybe he could give him a sign.

As Alex came head-to-head with the truck, the truck driver could see that Alex was riding the car bending in his seat. Alex gave him a sign with his hand, a gesture pointing back toward a car that was following him. The truck driver understood.

As Alex made his way ahead and the car behind tried to follow him, the truck driver turned the truck so as to avoid the car behind him to overtake. The car again tried to overtake them from the other side but again failed to do the same.

By now Alex had a good lead. The car tried to overtake the truck again and again but failed to do so whatsoever.

Alex looked back and then turned to Laura.

"It's safe now, you can get up," he said, looking at her gently, moving his hand gently over her head and face.

"What happened?" she asked wondering where the car behind them had disappeared all of a sudden.

"Didn't you see I made a gesture with my hands to that truck driver behind us and he decided to help us out?" Alex said, telling what had happened.

"I was too scared to look at anything, I was just keeping my head down there," she said softly, still looking behind making sure that they were not followed anymore.

"It's OK, I understand. I was scared too," Alex said, looking at Laura.

Laura responded with a faded smile.

"What are we going to do now? Do you have a plan?" Laura asked, looking at him.

"As a matter of fact, I do. I think we are going to make a stop," he said thinking something.

CHAPTER 44

"Stop, but where?" asked Laura, wanting to know what was on his mind.

"I'm going to inform the police about the situation," Alex said looking at her.

"Police? But you just told me some time back it's a little risky considering that the police are still looking for us," Laura said, reminding him that the police were still looking for them with respect to the Professor's murder.

"I don't think we have much of a choice here. These guys are trying to kill us and now I have come to think of it as our last chance," Alex said, looking at Laura. "Don't worry, it will be all right. You just hold on to that file," Alex said, with confidence.

This made her a little relaxed.

The cell kept next to Alex and Laura began to ring again.

As soon as Alex picked up, he heard, "I know you have the file now. I hope you are bringing it to me. My fingers have already started itching and with the gun in my hand I don't think your uncle has much time," Cody said in a devilish voice.

"No, don't do it. We have the address, I am coming to you now," Alex said, pleading to him on the phone.

"Alex, please hurry," Alex heard the voice of Uncle Jack in the background.

"Uncle Jack, don't worry. We are coming for you," Alex said almost shouting desperately.

"Make it quick," Cody said before disconnecting the call.

"Everything will be all right," said Laura as Alex threw the phone on the back seat of the car. She was trying her best to calm him down.

"We have to hurry. We have to find a police station somewhere around here, before it's too late," Alex said, looking ahead and driving faster again.

They drove only for a few miles after which Laura told him to make a stop.

They had finally found a police station.

Alex and Laura quickly made their way inside and told the officer in charge everything that they had gone through in the last couple of days. They told him about the Professor, his death, the clues, what the Professor had left them and finally about the file.

After hearing their story, the inspector decided to capture Cody at the same address he had given to Alex.

"We will be following you closely, don't you worry. When the time is right, we'll capture him. Until then, you must do as he says," said the inspector telling them about the plan.

Laura and Alex nodded their heads in confirmation.

"But inspector, what if he gets to know that you are following and helping us?" Laura asked, still a little unsure of the plan.

"Don't you worry, girl. We will maintain a safe distance, now you both don't waste any more time. Go on now," continued the officer telling them not to worry and move fast.

"All right, let's go," Alex said, taking Laura's hand and making his way back to the car.

CHAPTER 44

Soon he was driving toward the address, hoping for everything to go just according to the plan.

It was not long before he reached the place. It was a rather old, abandoned warehouse.

He saw a man walking around and he looked like someone who worked there a long time back. Alex could guess, because he looked old.

Cody must be waiting for me and Laura inside the warehouse. If I could find another way inside the place it, could really help to capture Cody. Perhaps this old man would know another way in, thought Alex as he made his way up to him, getting out of the car and telling Laura to come along.

"Hey, old man. Do you know another way inside this place?" Alex asked, coming closer to the old man.

The old man gave him a strong, steady look before replying, "Sure, just follow me."

The old man started to walk in another direction. Alex looked at Laura in a way asking her for confirmation.

Soon they started to follow the guide. He was rather old, so his steps were slow and weak.

It took some time for them to get inside but Alex was happy that things were working out. "Thank you, you can leave now. We will find our way from here," Alex said turning towards the old man, giving him farewell.

"It is strange that both father and son would have to die by my hands," said the old man, pointing a gun toward them.

NUMERICAL ENIGMA

That was when Alex realized it was him. He had disguised himself as a worker so that no one would recognize him.

"What are you looking at? I am Cody..."

CHAPTER 45

"Hand the file over to me," Cody said, looking toward Laura with his stony eyes.

"Where are Ben and Uncle Jack? We want to see that they are safe," Alex said, looking at Cody in compulsion.

"Bring them," Cody said loudly making sure that his men heard him.

They must have been hiding waiting for his orders, thought Alex as he looked around to see if there was anyone else.

In a few moments, a few men started to arrive from every side. Alex was right. All his men were waiting for his command.

Suddenly Laura got sight of Ben and Uncle Jack.

"Alex, look, they are here," Laura said, bringing his attention to the direction in which she was pointing a finger.

"Ben, are you all right?" she said trying to make her way toward him but she was immediately stopped by Cody.

"Stay where you are, not a single movement," Cody said, looking at Laura. "Now, the file please," Cody said looking at Laura cautiously.

"Please don't give the file to him, Laura," Ben said suddenly in a loud voice making sure that she heard him loud and clear.

"Wait," Alex said looking at Cody and Uncle Jack.

"What is it now?" Cody said, looking at him impatiently.

For some time now Uncle Jack had not spoken and Alex wanted to know if everything was all right with him or not.

"Uncle Jack, are you all right?" asked Alex, raising his voice.

Uncle Jack just nodded his head vaguely giving him confirmation.

"I hope that matches your expectations," Cody said, giving Alex a cold look.

Laura too gave Uncle Jack a good look.

"Now, without any further delay pass the file to me, young lady. That is, if you all want to get out of here alive," Cody said in his same cynical tone, pointing the gun at Laura.

"How do we know that if I gave you the file, you will let us go?" Laura said, looking at Alex and Cody at the same time reluctantly.

"I don't think you have much of a choice here," Cody said, telling her she doesn't have many options.

Laura looked at Alex one final time.

"Do it, it's OK," Alex said, giving her approval.

CHAPTER 45

As Laura forwarded the file to Cody, he grabbed it instantly.

"I have been waiting for this moment for a long time," Cody said as he opened it to view the contents.

"If you are assured now, we did just as you told us. Let Ben and Uncle Jack go," Alex said, looking at Cody hoping to get a positive answer.

"Not so soon, let's see what we have here," Cody said, beginning to read the file. "Yes, *Quantum Interpretation of Many Worlds*, this is how it all began," Cody said going through the initial bits of the file.

As he began to read further, the smile on his face begin to disappear.

"What is it?" asked one of his men.

"His research is incomplete. There is something I am still confused about. I understand the connections your father was trying to find," Cody said, looking at Alex.

"You mean the connection between the theories of chaos and *Quantum Interpretation of Many Worlds*," Alex said with a smile.

"Yes, I know both these are deterministic. If you should know long back during the days of Caltech, when I and your father were working on our Ph.D., I was also working on the same theory that he was. It was because of me your father had to leave Caltech. It is obvious for me to know a thing or two about your father's research not to mention my men have been following you around, noticing your every move," Cody said, bringing clarity to how he knew about the deterministic link between the two theories.

"Cody, now that you have the file, should we get rid of our friends here?" said one of the men pointing the gun toward Laura and Alex, eager to pull the trigger.

"Not so soon, wait a minute, there is something troubling me here, Alex and I bet you can help me solve this little problem," Cody said, looking at Alex with desperation. "Do you mind enlightening me about what patterns David is pointing toward in his research?" Cody asked, knowing that Alex would definitely have the answer to his question.

"Only on one condition, if you promise to let Ben and Uncle Jack leave from here unharmed," Alex said, looking at Uncle Jack and Ben at the same time.

"You don't seem to be in a situation to bargain, little boy," Cody said, pointing the gun toward Laura.

"Fine, suit yourself. Kill all of us, you'll never get what you are looking for," Alex said, taking a risk on their life.

Cody stood there standing, Laura and Alex looking into his eyes. He was staring at them with ice-cold eyes.

"Fine, we'll have it your way," he said looking at all of them one by one. "Let go of Jack and that other boy there," Cody said looking at his men who were still holding Uncle Jack and Ben tightly by their shoulders. "However, if you are trying to play any games, let me warn you, none of you will ever leave this place alive," continued Cody, looking at Alex making sure he got his point.

"I understand," Alex said, nodding his head.

"Now hurry up and tell me what you know about the patterns," Cody said, waiting for Alex to answer.

CHAPTER 45

"Mr. Cody, patterns my father was referring to in *Quantum Interpretation of Many Worlds* are the transitional probabilities for quantum jumps, otherwise known as the states of the electron," Alex said, explaining while looking at Laura.

"Yes, but what that's got to do with the ultimate constant?" Cody asked, listening to him.

"I don't know," Alex said, looking at Cody's face.

"Stop giving me the half-truth. Tell me the whole thing or I'll kill her," Cody said, raising his voice and pointing the gun toward Laura.

"Hey, come on, I know Max Born found the Probability Density Function in quantum mechanics to exclusively predict the state of the electron. He was able to invent this before he supported Warner Heisenberg and Pascal Jordan to create a new kind of mathematics to understand quantum mechanics. It was this new mathematics that involved matrices which later became famous as matrix mechanics," Alex said in a spur of panic.

"Stop giving me history lessons. I know all that, he did that in 1926," Cody said, trying to make sense of all that Alex was saying.

"Did you know how he did that?" Alex said looking at Cody, raising his eyebrows.

"How?" asked Cody in curiosity.

"He did that by avoiding the rule that electron moved in orbits, instead, he used the initial and final state of the electron to predict its next state," Alex said looking at Laura, Ben and Uncle Jack. He was trying to analyze and bring together the broken pieces of David's research.

"I still don't understand what this has to do with the ultimate constant. You are all bunch of useless fools, you don't know anything," Cody said, becoming violent.

"Listen to me, man. Whatever that you are looking for is in these changing states of the electron, your ultimate constant is there," Alex said.

"Now, wait a minute. Are you saying that the changing states of the electron have a pattern to them?" Cody said, finally getting his hunch and lowering his gun.

"Yes, that could be. No wait, that is absolutely right. There is a pattern to the changing states of the electron," Alex said, agreeing with Cody.

There was a moment of pause. Everybody stood silent as if to grasp where all this was leading.

Cody was yet again disappointed as his mind still refused to comprehend anything.

"OK, so the states of the electron adhere to a pattern. What's next? You have clues you are keeping hidden from me," Cody said, looking at Alex.

"Listen to me, I told you what I had on me. I don't have anything else, you must believe me," Alex said helplessly.

"Then you better get ready to die and say your goodbyes to your friends," Cody said, raising his gun again.

"But I won't kill you first, I'll kill your girlfriend. That should be more fun to watch," Cody said, pointing the gun toward Laura, changing his direction.

CHAPTER 45

"No, please, wait," Uncle Jack said suddenly letting his voice heard after a long gap. "Alex, try. You are the only one who can get this whole thing together," Uncle Jack said, encouraging him.

"Shut up, you old man," said the guy who was still holding him.

"Ha-ha! For once, you are right, Jack. I'll give you a little time if you want to see your friends alive. You must give me the complete truth about your father's research," exclaimed Cody with a sinister look in his eyes.

Alex paused, trying to think hard. There was something that occurred to him before they left Rudy's residence. He had found a connection between the two symbols in the letter given to Laura by the Professor.

His mind now was trying to connect all those little clues together that they encountered from the beginning of their journey. The letter, the symbols and the importance of patterns and proportions... He remembered telling Ben that all constants are nothing but proportions.

Slowly his own words started to come back to him.

"The proportions are nothing but patterns and where there is a pattern there will be predictability."

"The ultimate constant is not just the pure number without any dimensions of length, density, or temperature, it is a physical force."

"Only the ultimate constant will reveal the ultimate force."

"The ultimate constant will have its influence over all universes, not just ours. That is what makes it ultimate."

NUMERICAL ENIGMA

"The ultimate constant like all other discoveries in science will help in making reality more accessible and easier."

Soon, all these clues that he had encountered with Laura from the beginning began to appear in his mind.

First was a letter by Albert Einstein.

Then the two symbols that the Professor wrote in the letter.

Exploring the constants, leading them to believe how important the constants are and finally the discovery of the second clue.

The second clue which they found at Einstein's residence, the article on special relativity which brought their attention to the constant of the speed of light.

The third breakthrough by combining the constant of the speed of light with the string theory.

The hint of superposition, leading them to believe that the whole story was somehow linked to the connection between the chaos theory and *Quantum Interpretation of Many Worlds*.

The fourth finding in the library at the Professor's residence in the form of the Chaos book which brought the connection between the chaos theory and *Quantum Interpretation of Many Worlds* to life with the help of Richard Feynman's Path Integral Formula or otherwise known as Born's Probability Density Function or the Born Rule.

Every constant has a function, even the ultimate constant will have one, his words again started to whisper in his head.

Yes, the first symbol in the letter meant the Probability Density Function – they had found the function they were looking for.

CHAPTER 45

The second symbol "=D-" stated there was a logic gate.

The history of the second symbol…

It all started with Walter Bothe. Walter Bothe and Max Born shared a Nobel in 1954.

The thoughts Alex was having now shifted to the findings related to the second symbol. This was because, he was trying to make a connection between "=D-" and the "ϕ".

Walter Bothe and his experiment…

The Compton Effect…,

Walter Bothe was succeeded by Bruno Rosie. Bruno Rosie and the first electronic circuit.

A few minutes had passed by since Cody had told Alex to think hard and find the truth about David's research. As Cody saw Alex mumbling something, he got a hint that Alex was definitely onto something.

He walked closer to him.

"What, what is it? What are you saying?" asked Cody, looking into his eyes.

"Nothing, nothing. Just give me some time, I am trying to concentrate here," Alex said, looking at him and trying to buy time.

Alex was mumbling to himself. "What is this second symbol "=D-"? How does it relate to the Probability Density Function or otherwise the first symbol in the letter? "=D-" Circuit and signal processing."

Just then an idea hit Alex like a hammer on his head.

"=D-" Circuit and signal processing," muttered Alex to himself.

Laura looked at Alex, trying to know what was going on in his mind. The glow on his face told Laura that Alex was hiding something.

Even after getting the answer, Alex was trying to buy as much time as he could. He knew the police could come here any moment now.

"Look I don't think I can wait anymore, so, just get on with it," Cody said, finally losing his patience.

"The patterns in the states of the electron represented by the matrices in matrix mechanics are connected to signal processing. A connection such as this can bring about a revolution in the field of signal processing. It could bring about new development in the fields of electronics," uttered Alex heavily, telling the truth about knowing that he could not make Cody wait any longer.

Cody responded a little late but this time with his eyes becoming wide. "Yes, of course, the "=D-" circuit, a technology beyond imagination," he said, coming up to a conclusion.

Just then, a voice startled everyone, "Everybody, stay where you are. Drop your weapons!"

CHAPTER 46

The police officers were there to arrest Cody and his men.

"Game over, Cody," Alex said, looking at Cody with contentment.

Ben looked at Alex and smiled. "Hell yeah! I knew you had a plan," exclaimed Ben, jumping in joy.

"You are right, Cody," Alex said, pointing toward what Cody had on his mind. "The 'AND' logic gate is the result of the state of the electrons and therefore a pattern in states of the electron would lead to a new scientific invention," continued Alex.

"So, wait, what are you saying?" Ben asked, looking at Alex.

"Ben, calm down for god's sake! There are men with guns around you," Laura said, in a way telling him to shut up.

"Yeah, right," Ben said, suddenly taking back his words, realizing his situation.

Laura had managed to calm him down but looked at Alex in interest.

"Alex, are you saying your father was going to invent something?" asked Laura, looking at him.

The highly intense conversation between Alex, Cody and others had shifted the attention of the police officers.

"I believe so," Alex said, looking at Laura with certainty.

"Well, what was it that he was trying to invent?" asked Laura yet again, this time sounding a little more desperate.

"I don't know, but I bet it has something to do with the signal processing and the logic gates," Alex said, turning towards Cody.

"What about the Theory of Everything or the Unified Field Theory, predicting the reality, the idea about all of us having a different time or the ultimate constant?" asked Laura, remembering the conversation that they had earlier back at Uncle Jack's place. She paused for a moment looking at Uncle Jack.

"You think we were wrong about all that?" questioned Laura.

"No, in fact, I think it all makes sense, this new technology or this device my dad was trying to invent, maybe it could help us in achieving the Theory of Everything or maybe help us predict reality," Alex said with confidence, coming to an understanding.

"A device that would predict the future, are you guys even listening to yourselves?" Ben said, suddenly jumping into the conversation.

"It's not impossible," Cody said, speaking up after a decent silence.

"You know what my father was trying to make?" Alex said, looking at Cody.

"If I knew, I would have already made it. The truth is, I don't have the slightest of an idea," Cody said in rage and frustration.

CHAPTER 46

"Then why did you say it's not impossible?" Laura asked, looking at them.

"'Cause nothing is impossible in quantum physics. There are things which are still far beyond the imagination of many when you start talking about quantum theory. Of course, much mystery lies in the heart of quantum theory and it's not surprising that David could have found an answer to one such mystery," Alex said.

"All right, this is enough, all of you. I want all of you to drop your weapons on the ground," said one of the police officers.

The officer had been keeping shut listening to their conversation but he had decided to take control now.

"I think he is lying, I bet he knows what your father was up to," Ben said, looking at Alex, encouraging him to pursue Cody to tell the truth.

"I think Ben is right. This is your last chance, Cody. Tell us what my father was making," Alex said, coming closer to Cody, holding his callers in frenzy, and pushing him back.

"I said, I don't know. I am as clueless as you are," Cody said, looking at Alex.

By the look in his eyes, Alex knew that he was telling the truth.

"I said, nobody moves," said the officer yet again, warning everyone.

Alex turned after hearing the officer.

"What the hell is going on here? What does he mean by that, 'technology beyond imagination'," asked the officer, sounding confused about what Alex and Cody were talking to each other.

"Please arrest this man, officer. He killed my father," Alex said mercilessly.

In the spur of the moment, a new idea crawled up into Cody's mind.

"They are making a fool of you, officer. This boy here and this young lady, the police in California are looking for them," Cody said, trying to divert the attention of the officer. "If you don't believe me, call the officer there and you will know the truth," continued Cody, pointing toward Alex and Laura.

Laura and Alex tried to tell the truth to the officer by reminding him of everything they had told the officer earlier.

"Officers, don't listen to him. Look at all the men around holding weapons. They are all his men, and he has been trying to kill us from the beginning," Alex said.

Noticing an opening, Cody quickly got hold of Laura and pulled the gun closer to her head.

"Nobody makes a move, or you gonna see a bullet passing through her head," Cody said, grabbing Laura and moving away from Alex.

"Don't move!" said the officer pointing the gun toward Cody now.

"Too late, officer," Cody said with a sinister smile.

"Now you'll carefully answer my entire questions one by one, Alex. Make sure you speak nothing but the truth," Cody said with busting rage.

"Don't push it, Cody. This is the end," Alex said, looking straight into his eyes.

CHAPTER 46

"What do you want to know?" asked Alex, taking a moment to look at Laura.

The look on her face this time was a little different she was not scared or afraid of anything. She had a strong and steady look on her face as if she was waiting for something.

"That guy you met, a few days back, the one who told you about chaos theory," Cody said, reminding him of Russel.

"I don't know what you are talking about," replied Alex, pretending to be clueless.

"Don't fuck around, Alex. Your friend Russel, what did he tell you?" asked Cody, pushing the gun harder on Laura.

"How do you know about Russel?" asked Alex in confusion, not sure what Cody was trying to ask him.

"Don't forget my men have been following you around, boy," Cody said, with a wicked smile.

"We met him in order to know more about the Chaos theory. He helped us to understand what you already know. I still don't understand what you are looking for," Alex said, looking at him in frustration.

"Tell me from the beginning what he told you," Cody questioned, still pursuing Alex.

"He just told us that both Chaos theory and *Quantum Interpretation of Many Worlds* were deterministic theories but you already know that," Alex said, raising his hand, telling Cody to back off.

"From the beginning, Alex," Cody said with bitterness, his eyes sparkling with aggression.

Alex looked around to find that Cody's men had restrained their position. All of them were holding guns again and this time even the officers were helpless. The situation was back to where it started.

"He told me that there is a way to randomness, there is order in disorder, patterns which can be found and then predicted within the system," Alex said, telling Cody of all the discussion he had earlier with Russel.

"Stock market," uttered Cody, paying attention to him.

"Yes, systems that elaborate the fact of simplicity within surface complexity," Alex said, looking around and turning toward Cody.

"What did he tell you about the nature of dynamical systems?" Cody continued to delve deeper into the topic.

"No details, just the specifics," Alex said shaking his head.

"What?" Cody asked, making sure Alex heard him.

"Non-linear equations, yes, he told me that they are the theoretical backbone to such dynamic and deterministic theories, Chaos and *Quantum Interpretation of Many Worlds* being one of them," replied Alex, becoming hyper.

"And what did he tell you about the Probability Density Function?" Cody asked, wanting to know more.

"The function plays an important role in predicting and determining the valid results out of the random outputs projected by the non-linear graphs," Alex said confidently.

"What more did he tell you about the function?" Cody continued to question his mind.

CHAPTER 46

"Feynman's Path Integral Formula that is famously known as the Sum Over Histories which some believe is a better representation of the Probability Density Function, however, he told me the Probability Density Function was still the tradition of choice for many," Alex was about to say further when Cody stopped him.

"Just tell me already, stop beating around the bush," Cody said, stressing on his point. "I know David and John must have left something that made you go through your friend Russel," continued Cody.

Alex was now sure that Cody had been watching every step. Also, it reminded him of the book that they had found in the library at the Professor's residence.

"Chaos was part of it. What we were really discussing was the stock market and the element of predictability in it, like you already know it is a dynamical system and we were trying to find a connection between Chaos and *Quantum Interpretation Of Many Worlds*," Alex began to make things clearer for Cody. "He told me about the Chaos Cable," Alex said, now focusing on the conversation he had with Russel.

"Geometry of Time Series," reciprocated Cody, his mind going through all of his life's work.

"Yes, an idea of Chaos that helps predict the flow of money is the stock market," continued Alex, thinking himself.

"I have heard about that pertaining to a notion that suggests how the flow of money in the stock market resembles the flow of water and fluid mechanics. Controlling the flow of water at certain time intervals at different points reveals patterns," Cody said, as if reading what Alex had on his mind.

"Turbulence, a phenomenon that led some to believe there were patterns to be found in statistics of the stock market, that money could be made predicting the rise and fall of certain stocks," Alex said restlessly.

"And Geometry of Time Series (Chaos Cable) is used to help predict this," Cody said this time. "Further, Geometry of Time Series which is nothing but non-linear statistics (graphs) similar to ones found in the theory of *Quantum Interpretation of Many Worlds*," continued Cody, looking at Alex.

"We know this because it is through these graphs that we come to know the valid position of a certain electron out of all the possible results which the theory of *Quantum Interpretation of Many Worlds suggests*," answered Alex, looking straight at Cody.

"Yes, the Probability Density Function that helps validate the correct result from the rest," Cody said, looking back at him.

"Something same happens in the stock market, only instead of Probability Density Function, a generic algorithm otherwise known as a program, is used to predict and determine the rise and fall of certain stocks," Alex said, telling Cody everything he knew.

"But what led you to this discovery in the first place?" asked Cody curiously.

"The Professor left a book related to the stock market for us in his library. Inside it was the clue that linked Richard Feynman and Probability Density Function to Chaos theory and the stock market. After that, all we had to do was to find the connection," answered Alex, looking at Ben and Laura who looked at him with dim eyes.

"And you did well to find it," Cody said with a faded smile. "The story is not all over. The Probability Density Function reveals

CHAPTER 46

patterns in *Quantum Interpretation Of Many Worlds* just as the computer program does for the stock market, also I know that theory of signal processing relies a lot on the Probability Density Function and position of the particle it predicts. Now, all I want to know is how does the patterns of states of the electron revealed by the Probability Density Function influence signal processing," Cody said coming up with the final question.

"You should know that would mean a theoretical design for technology unlike any other," Alex said, moving closer to Cody.

"And you are going to give me that technology because you have lost everyone close to you, your dad, your mother, the Professor and now I'm sure you don't want to see her die, do you?" Cody continued to mentally torture Alex.

"NO, Alex, don't. Don't tell him, our lives are not worth this," uttered Laura, still bound in the strong grip of Cody's arms, with the gun held next to her face. Ben and Alex were surprised to see Laura being so calm and composed and yet strong and steady at the same time.

Cody and others had so much attention on Alex that nobody noticed that one officer had achieved to pick up his gun. Slowly he started to take steps closer to Alex, so that he could get his attention.

It was not late when Alex saw the officer moving closer to him, but he didn't want Cody to see what was happening. Everyone was too engrossed in looking at Cody and Alex that they failed to see the sign the officer was giving to Alex.

Alex saw from the corner of his eyes that the officer was thinking of swinging his gun at him.

"No, I can find the answer for you, you just have to let her go," Alex said, still acting helpless, trying to divert the attention of Cody and the rest of the gang.

"How will you find the answers, Alex? How?" Cody questioned with the curiosity of the devil glittering in his eyes.

The officer was ready to throw the gun, and Alex nodded.

"All answers you need to know are in that file, let me have a look at it," Alex said, allowing Cody to shift his attention toward the file.

Just as Cody looked at the file, the officer threw the gun. Alex snatched the file from Cody's hand and the gun landed in the eager hands of Alex but it was too late. There was a gunshot. The officer was on the ground. Alex looked in the direction from where the sound came.

He stood there staring, unable to believe what he was looking at. Everyone was stunned.

The man holding the gun finally spoke. "I am sorry, Alex," Uncle Jack said.

CHAPTER 47

"Uncle Jack, you?" whispered Alex. That's all he could do, for the real don had revealed himself.

"Sorry to disappoint you, Alex, but an old man like me doesn't have much time to do something the world can remember me by," Uncle Jack said in a rough voice. "Let me tell you something, I never liked your father from the beginning, from the time he stepped into John's life," Uncle Jack said, beginning to say something.

"What do you mean?" questioned Alex in confusion.

"I and John were such best friends, we used to hang out discussing ideas and then your father came and pushed everyone aside in the scientific circle," Uncle Jack began talking about his days in Caltech.

"What do you mean, you didn't like my father from back during the Caltech days?" uttered Alex, trying to confirm his belief.

"Of course, I didn't. No one did, it was like he had a stick stuck up his ass, defying everyone, disapproving other's ideas, like everyone was an ass," Uncle Jack said, suddenly becoming restless. "He had a cool prodigy image about him, like he would be the next guy to make something happen. I don't blame him, 'cause he did, but at the expense of making others feel stupid about themselves," Jack said with despise.

"Never, my father is not what you are portraying him to be," Alex said, pointing his gun toward Uncle Jack.

"You don't know anything, boy. You were never there to witness the embarrassment I and others faced at the hands of your father," exclaimed Uncle Jack in jealousy.

"You were saying that because you couldn't do what he could, and you never were able to achieve what he did alongside the Professor," Alex said, putting his point across. "My father trusted you, the Professor trusted you, but you betrayed their lives. You are a disgrace to be called a friend," continued Alex.

"The Professor put himself in trouble when he decided to be friends with your father. He knew how much others hated David, still, he spent his time discussing ideas, going for games with him, hell he knew someday David would make him fall into trouble and yet he persisted," Uncle Jack continued to reveal the poison he had carried in him for David and the Professor.

"Admit it, Uncle Jack. You were jealous, jealous that the Professor considered my father to be a better friend than you," Alex said, trying to show Jack the truth. "You hated the fact that the Professor never took your ideas into consideration, the way he took my father's," continued Alex.

"Well, that I would give the credit to him. If it was not for him, we would not have come so far," Uncle Jack said with an evil smile.

"It is still beyond you and it always will be, you will always be a loser," Laura said, now it was time for her to speak up.

CHAPTER 47

"Should I kill her now?" Cody said, struggling with Laura as she was trying to get out of his grasp.

"Not now, they deserve to know the complete truth," Jack said looking at Laura and back toward Alex.

"My father considered you like a part of the family and this is how you decided to repay him for his kindness," Laura said.

"I was out of his life the day David came into his life. If I remember correctly he even stopped answering my calls," Uncle Jack, said remembering the days from his past when he was still a student at Caltech. "It was all because of your father," continued Jack, now looking towards Alex.

"Who do you think you are? People get busy, it's not like the Professor ever thought of you as a stranger, he always treated you like his younger brother," Alex said, remembering how Professor used to talk about Uncle Jack when he was young.

"If he would have, he would have told me that David was still alive," Uncle Jack said with vengeance.

"What do you mean?"

"Back in the time that David was still writing to John, I found one of his letters, it was not like John told me himself, it was luck," Jack said, looking at Alex furiously. "It was one of those days and John was sitting and discussing Cody and his attack," Uncle Jack said looking at Alex.

"That means..."

"I'm afraid you are right. It wasn't just Cody who was planning attacks on John, it was both of us," Jack said, now bringing the whole picture to Alex's attention.

"So you planned an attack on yourself," Alex said in disbelief.

"Yes, I did, but the objective was really to get rid of John. But it was not possible then," Jack said in disappointment.

"But if this is the truth that would mean Rudy…" said Laura looking at Alex.

"Laura, I thought you'll never ask. I thought you wouldn't miss that. Rudy was never working with Cody, never to really start with," Jack said, giving a malicious smile yet again.

"So, you…" Alex said suddenly realizing the horrific truth.

"Yes, it wasn't Rudy or Cody who killed your father, Alex. It was me who killed David," Jack said and began laughing.

Cody joined him, laughing cynically while Alex and Laura looked at each other with overwhelming emotions.

"Don't you think it's time you tell her too?" Cody said beginning to tell Jack to now say everything that he had been keeping a secret.

"Rudy was always trying to help Professor and David, he always tried to warn your father," Jack said, looking At Laura.

"But you always diverted my father toward thinking that Rudy was the enemy and *you* were his friend," uttered Laura, looking into Jack's eyes.

"That was the plan, my dear. We couldn't ever let your father know that I was involved with Cody," Jack said, softly coming toward Laura.

"You bastard," Laura said, in rage.

CHAPTER 47

"There is no need for you to get hyper, soon you both will join your family," Cody said, speaking up.

"Rudy had the papers that were connected to David's research, papers he sent to the Professor anonymously," Cody continued to tell them.

"I swear when this is all over, I'll send you to hell. That's where you belong," Alex said wildly.

"Gladly, but I don't see that happening, Alex," Uncle Jack said, bringing his attention to the surroundings.

Uncle Jack's security that had been helping Alex and others had now turned against them. Alex noticed among the men was the guy who took a shot for him back when they were running from Cody's men.

"So, it was all part of your plan," Alex said, now leaving his mind in no doubt.

"Of course it was, the next thing on the list was to get my hands on the papers that Rudy had, that happened to be my only drawback until very recently," Jack said, looking at Laura.

"No, it was you, it was you who killed my father," Laura said in pain.

"I am sorry, child, that crime also had to be done by these hands," Jack said devilishly. "I couldn't bare the pain of killing my old friend but he asked for it. He refused to give me the papers, and he had to pay the price," continued Jack, thinking back to that moment. "That's when he threw the papers in the fire. I thought at that moment that the research was gone forever but thanks to your father he decided to leave clues to you both," continued Jack.

"So, that is how Cody always knew where we were going. That is how he had been following our trail," Ben said, it had been too long that he was keeping quiet, listening to all that Jack was saying.

Jack looked at Ben before replying.

"So, you do have a mind. I was beginning to think you were useless after all," Jack said, turning towards Ben.

"You won't get far with this, Uncle Jack," Ben said.

"Oh, I will, Ben. I know I will, really. But don't you worry, you and your friends here would not be there to see it," replied Jack, showing his true colors.

"You kept informing Cody of our whereabouts. Those men at the Professor's residence, they were yours," Alex said, now suddenly understanding.

"Right again, I'm beginning to feel overexposed here," Jack said, looking at him.

"That is how you reached us at Rudy's place, but you were there even before us and you got rid of him too," said Laura, thinking over the recent events.

"I had to, there was no other choice. I wouldn't take the risk. You see, in all these years I had been able to keep my identity and my motives hidden. However, in the last few years, I had a feeling that somebody had been stalking me and I couldn't help but think that it was Rudy," Uncle Jack began to clarify why he had to kill Rudy.

"What made you so sure?" Alex asked in retaliation.

"There were two reasons. One, that no matter how much I tried I would never get my hands on him and second, I had reasons to

CHAPTER 47

believe that David had come to know the truth about me, but he couldn't tell John about me because I killed him soon after also. David's research that is in that file was not with the Professor. That left only one person that would have it," Uncle Jack was about to say something when Alex interrupted.

"Rudy..."

"My men failed to find the file but thanks to you and Laura, we have it in our hands now."

"But how did you find Rudy?" Laura said, thinking something.

"When you took off from Robert's house, my men were following you understanding your route. You were heading toward an area with a few residences, I did an internet search and that narrowed down to only one house with its history connected to Rudolph Clark. Cody had his men scattered all over the city so we got to Rudolph before you did," Jack said, uncovering his part of the story. "From then whatsoever, you know the story," Jack said, looking at Ben and the others.

"And then you made up a plan of getting yourself and Ben captured to make us believe that your life was in trouble. If we failed to find the file you could bribe us," Alex said, understanding Jack's evil plan.

"Bingo and you fell for it. I knew you would do anything to save your Uncle Jack, wouldn't you?" Jack said stepping forward momentarily.

"Not you Jack, for Ben," Laura said, looking at Jack.

"Well, it doesn't matter. I was successful in fooling John to believe Rudy was working against him and I was successful in fooling you kids into thinking I was working with you. All in all, it's one and the same thing," Uncle Jack said coming over to Laura and simultaneously looking at Alex and Ben.

"You don't know anything about me," Laura said disgustingly.

"Cody was in Sacramento when I and John were there. He and I planned an attack which later I was able to blame on Rudy. Your father was so blind by my friendship that he failed to see the truth," explained Jack.

"You are a murderer, Jack. Nothing but a cold-blooded murderer," yelled Laura as she heard Jack tell stories of deception again and again.

"Yes, I am, but for such technology to my credit and my name carved upon the history, it will be all worth it," Jack said, with bloody eyes.

"A history written in the blood taken from innocent lives is not a history, it's a massacre," Alex proclaimed.

"May well be, but I wouldn't be forgotten," Uncle Jack said.

"You are not human, you betrayed and murdered families of your friends and that is how people will remember you, Jack, a monster," Alex said pointing the gun toward Jack.

"And now, don't you be stupid, Alex. You see Laura here and your friend, you don't want to see them die, do you?" Jack said playing with Alex's emotions.

"Now open the file, read and come to the conclusion. How do the patterns of states of the electron in *Quantum Interpretation of Many Worlds* there influence signal processing?" Jack asked coldly.

Alex opened the file slowly, looking at Laura and Ben.

CHAPTER 47

"Don't do it, Alex. Don't tell him," shouted Ben, staring at Alex.

"Now Alex, you are running out of time," Jack said, looking at Cody, who was ready to pull the trigger any moment.

Alex opened the file. As he went over the contents everything he had encountered and everything his friends told him started to come back.

"You can do it, Alex, you are his son."

"Out of all the people you should know, he was your father."

"Every constant has a function, even the ultimate constant does."

The image of the letter flashed across his memory. There were many things that were going through his mind.

I can't do it, thought Alex to himself.

"Come on, Alex. Stop testing my patience," Jack said, looking at Alex, feeling helpless.

As everybody was looking at Alex feeling clueless nobody looked at Laura, who did something peculiar with her necklace. It was as if she pressed a jewel on it and it began to glow.

As she did that, she looked toward Jack.

"There is still one thing you have to know," she said, looking at Uncle Jack.

Jack looked at her in confusion, unable to understand what she meant.

"My father didn't tell you everything," Laura said that and she quickly held her grip hard on Cody's palms and twisted it back, snatching the gun from him and moving toward his back.

She pointed the gun into Cody's neck, showing a batch to Jack.

It read, F. B. I AGENT: LAURA GABLE

"I was just waiting for you to blow your cover, you JACK-ASS!!!"

CHAPTER 48

"You were right about one thing, Jack," Laura said, looking at Alex and Jack. "It ain't over, until it's over!" continued Laura with a smile.

Alex was now pointing the gun toward Cody.

"Tell your men to lay their guns back on the ground, or else you both will be dead before you know it," Laura said furiously.

"Put your guns down," Jack said, knowing his biggest fear had come alive, he wouldn't do anything anymore.

"Laura, you were from the FBI?" muttered Jack, looking at her.

"Since the very beginning. You were right, my father did choose me and Alex for a reason," Laura said, it was her turn to tell the truth.

"I underestimated John, I never knew," Jack said, noticing the tables have turned against him.

"You are damn right, you underestimated him," Laura said. "My father knew about Rudy and he knew about you. I had a hunch that you were behind all this, but I needed to be sure," continued Laura strongly, still marveling both Cody and Jack.

"So, that is why you played your part till the very end," Jack said, still astonished by the turn of events.

"Yes, it was because I had to be sure, I needed proof to confirm my beliefs and now I don't need anymore," answered Laura, still looking into the murderous eyes of the killer.

"Laura, you should have told me," Alex said looking at her.

"Believe me, I wanted to tell you but I didn't want to spoil my cover. I wouldn't take that kind of a risk," Laura said, looking at Alex.

"I so want to kill them all," Alex said with killing instinct as he moved to pull the trigger.

"Please, don't. I didn't kill your father, he did," Cody said in fear.

"Don't, Alex. It's your Uncle Jack, Cody is the one who did all this. It is he who should be blamed for all this. He killed David back in 1985," Uncle Jack said reluctantly, staring at his eventual death before his eyes.

"Don't you dare, you cynical, good-for-nothing, old fuck," Alex said, looking at him in fury.

"It is he who killed your families, he deserves death more than anyone else," said Cody, pointing his finger toward Jack.

"Don't, Alex. You don't have to take the law into your own hands," Laura said, trying to calm Alex down.

"So, back in the hotel when Cody's men were following us, and you manage to escape, that time," Ben began to question Laura.

CHAPTER 48

"Yes, you did see me, Ben. I was with another agent and we were discussing what to do next," answered Laura, looking at Ben and agreeing with him.

Laura already knew what Ben was thinking.

"So what were you telling him, back then?" questioned Ben yet again.

"I was telling him about the men that were chasing us. Back then I had decided to tell Alex the truth about my identity," Laura continued to answer Ben.

"And then?" asked Ben curiously.

"I couldn't. The agent told me to hold on a little longer till we knew my belief about Uncle Jack was right or not," Laura said, looking at Alex and Uncle Jack simultaneously and glaring at her surroundings.

"I knew it, I told you, Alex, didn't I?" Ben said, enthusiastically looking at Alex.

"Yes, you did, my friend. You sure did," Alex said, looking at Laura with a smile.

"So, you knew about Uncle Jack since when?" Alex asked.

"I knew when we first met him," Laura said, looking at Alex.

"How did you find out?" This time it was Alex who questioned her.

"It was imperative for him to know everything, even about the letters that David send my father. That is when I began doubting him," replied Laura, answering Alex.

"When he was telling us about his time with the Professor back in the years of 1970s and 1980s," Alex said noticing Laura's point.

"Exactly, if my father trusted him he should have told him about the letters but he didn't, that made me suspicious of his intentions," Laura said, continuing to bring more light to the subject.

"That is why you told me not to tell him or Ben about the locker and the letters we found, that explains it," Alex said, understanding why Laura had been keeping secrets.

It was something that had been bothering Alex for quite a while.

"Yes, that is right," Laura agreed, nodding her head.

"Wait, what letters?" suddenly Jack questioned curiously at the mention of the letters.

"Yeah, what letters?" Ben said with equal curiosity.

"The letters my father kept safely in the locker which only he and Rudy knew about, the letters that belonged to David," Laura said, looking simultaneously toward Cody and Jack.

"You found them," Cody said in amazement.

"We have been trying to get our hands on them for so long," Jack said looking at Cody.

"What was in there?" questioned Jack.

"None of your concern, it was meant for only me and Alex to be found. You were wrong, my father knew about Rudy. David's file which me and Alex found was not given to Rudy by David, it was passed onto Rudy by my father," Laura said, bringing Cody and

CHAPTER 48

Jack to finally face the truth. "Anyway, it is nothing that should concern you any longer," continued Laura, looking at everyone.

"Please, you have to tell us what was in that file," Jack said, begging Laura to tell him.

"I should kill you right here, you should be just happy that you are alive," Laura said, trying to stop herself from pulling the trigger.

"Laura, when is the FBI arriving here?" questioned Alex.

"They are already here, behind you," Laura said, giving a sign with her eyes.

As Alex turned back, the agents were already taking care of the situation.

"Please don't do this, I'm your Uncle Jack, Laura. I know you since you were a baby. Your Uncle Jack," Jack kept mumbling as the FBI agents took him into custody.

Resisting his arrest, Jack became more and more furious.

"I'll kill you, I'll kill you both, like I killed your families. I swear I'll kill you," those were his last words.

Cody, on the other hand, just followed him silently.

"Finally, it's over," Ben said, feeling relieved as the menace that they were involved in disappeared.

"So, what's next?" Ben asked, looking at Laura and Alex.

"I don't know," Alex said looking at both of them.

"What if he does come out and tries to kill us again?" Ben said, feeling a little uneasy.

"I don't think he will live to come out," Laura said.

"What do you mean?" asked Ben in confusion, waiting for Laura's response.

"She means he is 70," Alex said, turning toward Laura with a smile.

"Right, adding he got his due in the end," Ben said with a smile spread across his face as well.

"I think you should take a look at that file once again," Laura said, looking at Alex.

"I think we all should," Alex said as he opened it again.

"What are we looking for?" Ben asked as he saw Laura and Alex observing the contents of the file deeply.

"The connection," Alex said, still looking at the file.

"Right, when you mentioned about the patterns of states of the electron by the Probability Density Function you mentioned the 'AND' Gate," Ben said, trying to remind Alex of something.

"Ben is right, what was that all about?" questioned Laura.

"What I was thinking back then was related to Bruno Rosie, he used the position of electrons to predict the first electronic circuit."

"That's right, you told us about it, it was also called the coincidence circuit," Laura said, getting a hunch.

CHAPTER 48

"Correct, what I was getting back was if states (positions) of the electron projected by the Probability Density Function could help in the construction of the 'AND' gate then," Alex was interrupted by Laura.

"Then the patterns of states of the electron would be related to a construction of something same as the 'AND' gate," she said with a glimmer of hope. "Alex, I think we are close," she said, now looking at them.

"You are right, that was what I thought too. In fact, it will not be surprising if that crossed Jack's mind as well," Alex said with confidence. "The question is what construction it is pointing at," continued Alex.

"Wait, look here, there is something here," Ben said, noticing something in the file.

Both Laura and Alex looked at the file to see what Ben was pointing at. Below them was an arrow diagram which connected certain headings.

[MATRIX MECHANICS $\rightarrow$ ϕ $\rightarrow$ SIGNAL PROCESSING $\rightarrow$ LOGIC GATES (=D-) $\rightarrow$ COMPUTERS]

"This is obvious 'AND'. Are the first logic gate and the logic gates related to computers?" Alex said frustratingly.

"Relax, Alex. Maybe your father found something within the logic gates that were related to computers," Laura said.

"I think we have to research this a little more," Ben said, not knowing what they were getting at.

"Hey, but Walter Bothe did not invent the first electronic logic gate. Why are we forgetting this?" Alex said, suddenly remembering something.

"That was Bruno Rosie," Ben said remembering.

"Yes, but Walter Bothe is the guy who shared the Nobel with Max Born in 1954," Laura said, thinking of the connection between Bruno Rosie and Max Born.

"Max Born found the function in 1926," Alex said, thinking hard now.

"Guys, I think we are missing something very important here. We need to focus," Alex said, in a way getting Laura and Ben to think hard.

"Whatever it is, it is definitely related to Bruno Rosie and Max Born," continued Laura.

"More than that, I think it is related to their works," added Alex. "Max Born invented the Probability Density Function to reveal the states of the electron," Alex said, focusing.

"Bruno Rosie made use of those states of the electron to invent the first electronic circuit," added Laura.

"The circuit that forms the basis of all the electronic gadgets," Ben joined in.

"The computer has been one of the most resourceful invention," Alex said, going over the data that they had in their hand. "Bruno Rosie, Max Born, Walter Bothe," Alex started muttering to himself.

Suddenly an agent came up to Laura.

CHAPTER 48

"Agent Gable, although I'm really sorry for your loss, I am here to congratulate you for cracking this case successfully, your father would have been proud of you," said the man, who appeared to be her boss.

"Thank you, sir," she said, looking toward him.

"Your father was a great man and from what I have heard here, the same goes for you, young man," said the man, looking toward Alex.

"Alex, he is Mr. Daniel, he is my superior," Laura said, introducing Mr. Daniel to Alex.

"You are a brave young man with a sharp mind and I hope you crack your father's research. It will be something we all are looking forward to," said Mr. Daniel patting both Alex and Ben's backs.

"I think I should send a message to the authorities. That should keep you all out of trouble," said Mr. Daniel taking out his iPad.

Laura saw that Mr. Daniel was struggling with something.

"What is it, Mr. Daniel?" she asked with concern.

"Damn! The network here, it's so slow. It will take some time for my message to get through, but it will be OK. You guys can go home," said Mr. Daniel.

"Thank you, Mr. Daniel," Ben said.

That's when Alex found it, it was a brainwave.

"What is it?" Laura and Ben asked suddenly, they knew with the smile on Alex's face that he finally knew what they were looking for.

"The patterns in the states of the electron projected by the Probability Density Function can help design logic gates unlike any other. One that can be used to build a distinct computer. That was what my father was trying to build. He was trying to build a Quantum Computer."

CHAPTER 49

"Alex, what's gotten into you? What are you talking about?" Laura asked, overwhelmed by his sudden outburst.

"The computer, the probability function, so this is what it's been all about. Why didn't I think of it before?" exclaimed Alex, wondering in amazement.

"Will you stop being an ass and tell me what is this all about?" Ben said in amusement.

"The letter by Einstein and the symbols "=D-" and "ϕ" were given to tell us the direct connection that the Probability Density Function has with the computers," Alex said, beginning to explain.

"What connection?" Ben asked.

"The computer works on two states of the electron. Quantum Computer, on the other hand, needs to work on multiple states of the electron," Alex said, trying to connect the dots.

"So?" asked Laura, looking at Alex in disbelief.

"Don't you see it? The patterns that Probability Density Function reveals within the random states of the electron are the theoretical design for the logic gates used for the Quantum Computer," Alex said in excitement.

"You mean to say, it's like a blueprint for the construction of Quantum Computer," said Laura, sharing his excitement.

"Hey, but I don't get it. What does this Quantum Computer do?" asked Ben, still unable to understand the gravity of the situation.

"The invention of a practical Quantum Computer will be like the first time airplanes became a reality, or when computers, cell phones and the internet came into reality. If we think about how and the ways in which these inventions have changed our world, it's nothing compared to the possibilities of a Quantum Computer, its applications are far-reaching and to some beyond imagination," Alex said, trying to make Ben understand.

"What do you mean?" asked Ben, demanding certain examples.

"Physicians and scientists all over the world believe that a Quantum Computer can make time travel possible and teleportation, and can explain many mysteries related to our universe, mysteries that still remain unsolved," Alex said, giving them a few examples of things that Quantum Computer can do.

"Does that involve predicting the future?" asked Laura, thinking something.

"It might, Quantum Computer can offer numerous possibilities," Alex said, answering Laura's question.

"Does that mean it would be able to reveal the ultimate constant that your father was trying to reveal to the scientific community?" Laura said, grabbing the attention of Alex.

Alex paused for a moment and moved toward Laura.

CHAPTER 49

"Of course, that makes perfect sense. That is what my father was trying to do, he was trying to find the ultimate constant through the Quantum Computer," explained Alex.

"And here we have it," Ben said, pointing towards the file.

"This is the design, we have it in our hands," Alex said, looking at Laura.

"Right, the patterns in the states of the electron but how did you find out?" asked Laura, inquisitively.

Mr. Daniel was listening to their conversation silently.

"It was when Mr. Daniel here said the network was very slow. That is when it struck me that a normal computer is very slow," Alex was interrupted by Ben.

"Because of just two states of the electron they work on," Ben said, looking at Alex.

"Right, that is when I thought that if this is about the computer, it might be in some way related to the speed of the computer as well," Alex said.

"That is when you thought about the Probability Density Function and the connection it might have with your finding, isn't it?" Laura said with a smile.

"Yes, that is when it did, when I thought about the speed of the computer and how it depends upon the states of the electron," Alex said, replying to Laura with a smile.

"And you could relate to the fact that if somehow you could add more states to the computer, it will result in a more advanced machine," added Ben, getting the point Alex was making.

"That led me to believe that the patterns of states of the electron which the Probability Density Function produces might be the answer to increase the present states of the electron," Alex said, talking about his conclusion.

"Right," Laura said, nodding her head.

"However, that's just the general idea," Alex said, thinking much deeper now.

"What is on your mind now?" Laura said, looking into his eyes, which seemed as if they were lost somewhere.

"Think about it, what makes the computer work on the two states of the electron which we call binary?" asked Alex, simultaneously looking toward Ben and Laura.

They both looked at each other, thinking for an answer to the question that Alex had asked them. They then turned toward Alex with a blank faces.

"The 'AND' gate, my dear friends," Alex said, bringing them to light.

"The first electronic circuit," Laura said, now looking up to Alex and Ben.

"The 'AND' gate is used in almost all electronic devices. It computes the two states of the electron," Alex said, walking a little further from Ben and Laura.

"But—" Ben was about to interrupt when Alex spoke again.

"Wait, there is more, the 'AND' gate is the component that drives the gadgets of today. But imagine a logic gate that could produce more states, such a logic gate would then help in the construction

CHAPTER 49

of a Quantum Computer," Alex said, telling Ben and Laura what was on his mind.

"So, what you are trying to say is that this blueprint, these patterns in the states of the electron that we now know can help build a logic gate that would produce multiple states of the electron," replied Laura.

"Exactly, more precisely, the state that comprises of the binary that is 0 or 1 and an additional state which is both 0 and 1 at the same time," Alex said, trying to bring more clarity to Laura and Ben.

"So that is the reason why the Professor wrote the two symbols "=D-" and "ϕ", that was the connection that he was trying to make between the Probability Density Function and the logic gates," Ben said, understanding the point that Alex was making.

"Now you get it," Alex said.

"Your father was a genius," Ben said, looking at Laura. "And you're too," continued Ben, this time looking at Alex and giving him a smile.

"So, all the clues that we have been encountering were leading us to this," Laura said, looking at Alex.

"Well, I don't think there can be any other explanation," Alex said, questioning the situation with his facial expressions.

"I mean, think about the two symbols on the letter," continued Alex as he stood there, looking at Ben and Laura.

"The constants, the link of the speed of light to the string theory and later to *Quantum Interpretation of Many Worlds*," added Ben.

"Yes, the chaos and *Quantum Interpretation of Many World* connection," Laura joined in.

"Not to mention the patterns in the chaos theory of the stock market and its connection which we found in the patterns in the states of the electron," Ben said again.

"The two theories were dynamical in nature, chaos and theory of *Quantum Interpretation of Many Worlds*," this time it was Laura's turn to speak up.

"And finally, the signal processing. Yes, all of it does make sense now," Alex said with a conclusion that they had finally found his father's full theory.

"So, the Professor wrote those symbols so that we would find the blueprint for the design of a Quantum Computer," Ben said, thinking back on their journey.

It has been one hell of a roller coaster ride.

"Whatever it is, the clues that the Professor left for you were very specific, getting our attention toward the importance of the constants of nature with that letter," Ben said, complementing Laura's father.

"Yes, the papers from Einstein's residence which confirmed our belief in the importance of the constants," Laura said, remembering taking the risk of entering the study and going through the papers at Einstein's desk.

"Also, the link between the constant of the speed of light and the string," Alex said, now the memories coming back to him as well.

"Yeah, what was that all about?" asked Ben, losing the track of their quest.

CHAPTER 49

"Superposition, Ben," Laura and Alex said together.

"Yeah, I always forget that," Ben said, touching his forehead, facing down, and raising his eyebrows in amusement.

"That's what led us to *Quantum Interpretation of Many Worlds* and then towards chaos, and the concept of superposition. I must say I was not much sure about it until I saw the connection in Einstein's paper," Alex said, remembering his nervousness.

"Man, we were really up to our necks trying to find the next clue relating to chaos, weren't we?" Ben said, thinking about the conversation with Russel. "Thanks to you, Alex, we found the book in the library," continued Ben. "I must say you were really perturbed when it came to entering your house, with those men standing outside your house."

"Relax, Ben. That was all a part of my cover," Laura said with a grin on her face.

"What are you talking about? You were not scared?" asked Alex, raising his eyebrows.

"No, Alex. I was never really scared from the beginning. I just had to act that way 'cause I didn't want to expose myself to you. But yes, I was emotionally broken by this whole case, he had no right to kill my father," Laura said, thinking something.

"I understand," Alex said, looking at her.

"Yeah, me too," Ben said, looking at Laura.

"But I remember, after we got to know that chaos was a dynamical system and we're trying to find the link between the chaos and the quantum, why did Uncle Jack help us understand so many notions about *Quantum Interpretation of Many Worlds?*" asked Ben, opening his heart about the confusion that was on his mind.

"He wanted to get to the bottom of this just as bad as you did," Alex said, looking at Ben. "His motives were always selfish. He wanted to publish the research in his name and take the credit," explained Alex. "And he sure did fool us," Alex said, thinking how he made a fool out of himself by trusting Jack.

"We all were in dark, Alex. He fooled all of us," Laura said in a way trying to ease him.

"Yes, that was when we found *Quantum Interpretation of Many Worlds* and Chaos were dynamical systems," Alex said.

"I think it was then that we found the meaning of the first symbol "ϕ"," Ben said, remembering that part perfectly. "So, we shifted our attention towards the second symbol "=D-"," Ben said, taking out the letter.

All of them looked at it.

"This is what led me to have a history lesson about the working of computers by Russel," Ben said, remembering how bored he was when he listened to him.

"Next, we came across the famous names attached to it, people like William Bothe and Bruno Rosie," Alex said, understanding what they had gone through.

"Who knew then that all of this would end up changing the views that we had about signal processing system?" Laura said.

"Not just us, soon the research will change the way people look at signal processing, if it becomes successful in the making of the Quantum Computer," Alex said, looking at Laura confidently.

CHAPTER 49

"I am sure it will Alex, I am sure it will," Laura said, letting herself fall into his arms.

"OK, I think it's high time before we should head home," Ben said, feeling exhausted and tired from the events of the last few days.

Actually, it was not just him. Alex and Laura too were worn out, both emotionally and physically.

"I think you are right, Ben," Alex said, suddenly noticing Mr. Daniel had already left their company.

The three of them had been so involved in their conversation that they didn't notice his absence.

"All right, let's go," Ben said walking forward, Alex and Laura walking behind him. "Aren't you coming along?" asked Ben, turning back and looking at Alex.

"I think I'll take a day or two off from football and physics, maybe spend some time at the Professor's home," replied Alex, turning towards Laura.

"Whatever you wish, I'll give you a call later," Ben said as he took off with a few officials in their car.

The FBI had arranged for them to reach their destination.

Alex and Laura did the same.

As Alex was about to enter the house, Laura noticed that he had been engrossed in a deep thought.

"What is it, Alex? What are you thinking now?" she asked abruptly, hoping everything was all right.

"Nothing I was just thinking about the ultimate constant," Alex said, looking at Laura.

"You said yourself that Quantum Computer would help in finding it. Let the scientists and the physicists do their work. Alex, you need to relax, it's all over now," Laura said, trying to stop him from thinking too much.

"It's not just that, something else has been bothering me," Alex said with a worried look on his face.

"What?" Laura asked, perturbed by the way Alex was suddenly reacting.

"You remember the Eddington numbers we found in the locker?" Alex said, reminding her of the letters that they both had found in the locker.

"Yeah, what about them?" asked Laura now feeling a little restless herself.

"I still don't understand. What they were trying to say, I mean, why they were there in the first place is a mystery itself," Alex said, raising the question that had been crossing his mind over and over again.

Although Laura too was curious about how Alex felt, she decided to pass the question.

"Calm down, Alex. You just need some rest," she said, making him comfortable on a chair, as they entered the residence.

It was then that Laura's cell started to beep.

"Who is it?" asked Alex as he saw Laura picking up the cell.

CHAPTER 49

"It's Mr. Mauldin," she answered in an enigma.

"Pick it up," Alex said swiftly.

And she did. She heard the voice of Mr. Mauldin from the other end.

"Tell Alex to come and see me at once, there is an important piece of information regarding Sir Arthur Eddington he must know if—"

"What is it, Mr. Mauldin ?" asked Laura as she looked at Alex, who was looking at her eagerly.

"A piece of information that his father left which I forgot to share with him."

As Laura kept the receiver, she looked at Alex.

"Alex, I think you are right, there is something strange about Eddington and his numbers."

CHAPTER 50

Soon after getting the call from Mr. Mauldin, Alex and Laura got the first flight to Oakland.

Deep within, Alex knew that there was something important that was waiting to be discovered. However, sitting in the fight there was something more important at that spur of the moment that he had to do.

He had to tell Laura about his feelings. It had been too long that he had held the truth in his heart. Now it was time.

"Laura, I need to tell you something," Alex said, turning toward her. He could see her eyes slowly opening and then closing back again.

"What is it?" she said, softly, her lips barely moving.

"The past few days that I spend with you and all these things that happened with us, if your life was ever to fall into danger, I would have happened to sacrifice myself to save you. The truth is I have always loved you, since the very beginning, you are my first love," Alex said, letting all of his feelings out.

He paused for a moment to see Laura's response.

CHAPTER 50

Laura didn't say anything, she just smiled and moved her lips closer to his face and kissed him gently on his lips.

With her eyes closed, Laura said, "I love you too." She made herself lean on his shoulder, before kissing him once again on his face.

It was not until a few hours had passed that they realized that they had reached their destination. Soon they were making their way to Mr. Mitch.

Upon reaching him, they were eager to know, why Mr. Mauldin had called them. Laura had not told Alex about what Mr. Mauldin had told her earlier on phone.

"Alex, I'm sorry. It completely slipped my mind earlier, but these are some papers your father wanted you to have. I apologize that it didn't occur to me earlier," Mr. Mauldin said handing over the papers to Alex.

As Alex read the papers, he noticed that they looked very familiar.

"These are the same as the letters we found in the locker that belonged to the Professor," Alex said, looking at Laura.

"There must be some reason your father must have left them for you," Laura said, encouraging him to think of an explanation.

Alex kept staring at first, it had the same equation Mr. Mauldin had shown him earlier. Only this time, there was something written about coincidence circuit, signal processing and matrix mechanics with a matrix drawn under it.

$$[666 + 6 + 6 + 6 = (6 - 6/6)^{(6+6+6)/6} + 6^{(6+6+6)/6} + (6+6/6)^{(6+6+6)/6}]$$

PROBABILITY

NUMERICAL ENIGMA

THE MAIN IDEA OF 'COINCIDENCE DETECTION' IN SIGNAL PROCESSING IS THAT IF A DETECTOR DETECTS A SIGNAL PULSE IN THE MIDST OF RANDOM NOISE PULSES INHERENT IN THE DETECTOR, THERE IS A CERTAIN PROBABILITY, p, THAT THE DETECTED PULSE IS ACTUALLY A NOISE PULSE. BUT IF TWO DETECTORS DETECT THE SIGNAL PULSE SIMULTANEOUSLY, THE PROBABILITY THAT IT IS A NOISE PULSE IN THE DETECTORS IS. p^2 SUPPOSE. $p = 0.1$ THEN $p^2 = 0.01$ THUS THE CHANCE OF A FALSE DETECTION IS REDUCED BY THE USE OF COINCIDENCE DETECTION.

In 1925, Born and Werner Heisenberg formulated the matrix mechanics representation of quantum mechanics. On 9 July, Heisenberg gave Born a paper to review and submit for publication.[15] In the paper, Heisenberg formulated quantum theory avoiding the concrete but unobservable representations of electron orbits by using parameters such as transition probabilities for quantum jumps, which necessitated using two indexes corresponding to the initial and final states. When Born read the paper, he recognized the formulation as one which could be transcribed and extended to the systematic language of matrices, which he had learned from his study under Jakob Rosanes at Breslau University.

$$\sqrt{2}X(0) = \sqrt{\frac{h}{2\pi}} \begin{bmatrix} 0 & \sqrt{1} & 0 & 0 & 0 & \cdots \\ \sqrt{1} & 0 & \sqrt{2} & 0 & 0 & \cdots \\ 0 & \sqrt{2} & 0 & \sqrt{3} & 0 & \cdots \\ 0 & 0 & \sqrt{3} & 0 & \sqrt{4} & \cdots \\ \vdots & \vdots & \vdots & \vdots & \vdots & \ddots \end{bmatrix}$$

They were the same lines he had read earlier on the wiki page. Why did his father leave such a thing? Alex sat there staring at the paper, thinking hard, and then it finally came to him.

"This is unreal," he said looking at Laura and smiling. "Laura, listen to me very carefully. In mathematics, we often come across

CHAPTER 50

certain numbers, or otherwise equations we cannot explain. Their existence is an enigma. An example of such an equation is like the one I have in my hand $[666 + 6 + 6 + 6 = (6 - 6/6)^{(6+6+6)/6} + 6^{(6+6+6)/6} + (6+6/6)^{(6+6+6)/6}]$), an example of such numbers is found in the form of basic numbers like phi. (ϕ Golden ratio = 1.618) or π (Pi = 3.14). People have been trying to justify their existence for centuries. None have succeeded. The reason for this is that their existence exceeds the limitation of mathematics. In life, too, there are certain notions you cannot explain, you just have to accept them," Alex said, talking slowly so that Laura understands everything. "The connection that my father was trying to show us between the Probability Density Function and the 'AND' logic gate was not just for the purpose of creating a Quantum Computer but what he was really trying to do was to show us a deeper truth between the states of the electron and the logic gates, a truth I failed to see earlier," continued Alex looking into her eyes.

"What truth?" Laura questioned him, breathing heavily.

"Think about it, why do people all over the world experience coincidences? The 'AND' gate produces a signal when the states of two electrons are the same which is a coincidence but logically it is not possible. How can two electrons have the same state? The formulation of matrix mechanics by Max Born and Werner Heisenberg suggests the transitional probabilities for quantum jumps, using two indexes, the initial and final states of an electron. How can two electrons have the same initial or final states? Logically "coincidence" is not possible until and unless…" Alex said, raising his eyebrows, remembering the page from the wiki.

"Oh my god, it's like when you spoke about the Quantum Computer having multiple states of the electron, like both 0 and 1 at the same time. Does that mean…" explained Laura finally getting what conclusion was Alex getting at.

"These coincidences, whether in life, in mathematics or any other part of our reality, represent events that are common to…" paused Alex.

"Common to what? Say it, Alex!" Laura said with a smile.

"The fact of two electrons sharing the same state means a simple truth, that there are parallel or multiple universes, an alternate reality. So now, *Quantum Interpretation of Many Worlds* has practical evidence. Hence the theory stands true, there are other universes and the coincidences happening around us, there is a mirrored result showing the average events common to parallel or otherwise multiple universes. Events that coincide with each other, time to time, like a shadow falling on a shadow. The force which co-incites these events is what we call Coincidence," Alex said, overwhelmingly.

"So, you are saying that like gravity and electromagnetism having a constant, so does coincidence?" Laura said with wide eyes.

"Deep within the matrices of matrix mechanics lies the constant which Einstein was searching for, the one referred to by him in his letter he wrote in 1945."

Laura looked at the letter once again. She had taken the letter from Ben when they had departed last and had decided to bring it with her when Mr. Mauldin called them. Laura looked at the letter one more time to confirm the point Alex was making. It all made sense.

"With the question of the universal constants, you have broached one of the most interesting questions that may be asked at all. There are two kinds of constants: apparent and real ones. The apparent ones are simply the outcome of the introduction of arbitrary units, but are eliminable. The real [true] ones are genuine numbers which God had to choose arbitrarily, as it were, when He designed to create this world. In my opinion now is

CHAPTER 50

– stated briefly – that constants of the second type do not exist and their apparent existence is caused by the fact that we have not penetrated deeply enough. I therefore believe that such numbers can only be of a basic type, as for instance π or e."

"Found within matrix mechanics concluded by the Probability Density Function are the pure (real) dimensionless numbers - arbitrary units representing the states of the electron, these pure states of electrons are radicals, they are ever-changing, and their value depends upon observation. Within these pure numbers is where the ultimate constant lies, it is that which gives rise to the idea of coincidence hence, the invention of coincidence circuit," Alex said, not believing that he had finally found it. "But most importantly, because coincidence is not a phenomenon it is a force, a force that makes things happen."

Epilogue

A few weeks later, Alex and Laura were walking out of Caltech, with Alex submitting his father's research into the right hands.

Walking alongside Alex, Laura looked at him and asked, "Do you really believe that there are multiple or parallel universes? I mean there is another me and there is another you."

"As a matter of fact, I do. Do you remember when I told you about coincidence?" reciprocated Alex with a question.

"Yeah, you said that is not a phenomenon, it's a force," Laura said, remembering.

"Why?" she questioned curiously.

"Well, I have been thinking, what do you think drives that force? On second thoughts *who* do you think drives that force?" Alex said with a faded smile.

"Wow! Are you saying there is a god? I thought you were an atheist," Laura said, mocking him with a wide smile.

EPILOGUE

"I don't think I am anymore," Alex said, looking at Laura, wondering what the future had in store for him.

"You know, something? I didn't notice it before, but don't you think it's a strange coincidence that the symbol for Probability Density Function and the Golden Ratio is the same, even though the two were discovered years apart from each other?" Laura said, wondering something.

Walking alongside each other Alex looked at her and after a brief pause said, "Laura, for people who believe there are no coincidences."

www.ingramcontent.com/pod-product-compliance
Lightning Source LLC
LaVergne TN
LVHW091526060526
838200LV00036B/505